DOWN TO EARTH LANDLORDING

An Investor's Guide to Successful Property Management

by

Donald Beck

Return Service Requested

Do not Forward

DOWN TO EARTH LANDLORDING

An Investor's Guide to Successful Property Management

by

Donald Beck

Illustrations by
Bob Patterson

Cover by
Angela Werner

Book Design by
Michael Höhne

Published by
Multi-Media Productions

DOWN TO EARTH LANDLORDING
An Investors Guide to Successful Property Management
by Donald Beck
Published by: Multi-Media Productions
Post Office Box 3053 Dept. B
Maple Glen, PA. 19002 USA
First Edition - 1984
Second Edition (Completely Revised) - 1993
Third Edition (Completely Revised) - 2002
ISBN - 0-9633163-0-3
Printed in the United States of America

DEDICATION

This book is dedicated to my parents for always being there with an understanding word and a helping hand. It is also dedicated to the Landlady of my life, my wife Debbie, who has helped me clean more toilets and ovens than we both care to remember, answered endless phone calls, shown units, ran credit checks, calmed me down on those bad days, and did the hardest job of all—edited this book.

ACKNOWLEDGMENTS

I also would like to acknowledge two people who have had a major influence in my life and in the writing of this book.

William Marshall — Friends thought I was crazy leaving a tenured teaching position at age 34 to make it on my own in Real Estate/Property Management with our first child due in less than six months. Bill was the catalyst who not only said go for it, but backed his conviction by offering me a job in his Financial Planning firm if the positive cash flow would not support us. I never had to accept his offer, but his confidence and constant encouragement that I could make it on my own helped me decide to take the self-employment plunge. I have not for one minute regretted the decision.

Richard Solo — Debbie and I bought our first investment property from Dick in 1978. Our friendship has grown ever since. Dick became my mentor when my real estate knowledge was non-existent. He used his 25 years as a real estate broker to help me close deals I would never have dreamed possible. He has become a second father to me, teaching me how to look at a problem from all perspectives before making a decision. This has not only helped in my real estate investing but in my life, for which I will be always grateful.

TABLE OF CONTENTS

BECK'S LAWS OF LANDLORDING .... *X*

INTRODUCTION .... *XI*

1. ORIGINS OF LANDLORDING *1*

2. TREAT LANDLORDING AS A BUSINESS *5*
Landlords Must Wear Many Different Hats •• The Landlording
Team •• Slumlords Are Out •• Why Tenants Rent

3. THE BETTER IT LOOKS, THE FASTER IT RENTS *9*
Give Exterior "Curb Appeal" •• Interior Looks •• Painting ••
Carpets, Hardwood Floors •• Creepy Crawlers •• Ceiling Fans ••
Who Makes the Final Decision?

4. COMMON REPAIRS *15*
Save Time and Money by Standardizing •• Appliances ••
Preventative Maintenance •• The Repair Call •• Plumbing ••
Electrical •• Heating •• Air Conditioning •• The Tool Box ••
Repairing Damaged Walls •• Repairing Broken Windows and
Screens •• More Knowledge = Better Cash Flow

5. HELPFUL MAINTENANCE TIPS *23*
Maintenance Tips •• Remove Stubborn Stains •• Water
Consumption •• Lead Paint •• Working with Contractors

6. KNOW THE LAW – DON'T DISCRIMINATE *27*
Fair Housing Guidelines for Landlords •• Fair Housing Credit
Reporting Act •• Avoid Rental Discrimination •• Things Testers
Look For •• Exemptions to the Fair Housing Act •• Fair Housing
Quiz •• Answers to Fair Housing Quiz •• Occupancy Qualifying
Criteria •• Rental Standards for Tenant Selection •• Protect
Yourself with Documentation •• How to Answer Prospective
Tenants' Tough Questions •• Criminal History of Prospective
Tenants •• What Can You Ask About a Disability? •• 12 Ways
Landlords Discriminate Against Prospective Tenants

7. DECISIONS BEFORE ADVERTISING *35*
Characteristics Of The Average Tenant •• Know the Fair Market
Rent for your Area •• How Much Security Deposit to Charge ••
Utilities •• Pets Versus No Pets •• Smokers Versus Non-Smokers

8. ADVERTISING *41*
Ways To Advertise •• Writing an Ad •• Additional Advertising
Techniques •• Renting to the handicapped

9. QUALIFYING THE PROSPECTIVE TENANT *45*
Start Screening from the Initial Phone Call •• Screen Calls with
Tape Machine •• Scheduling Appointments •• Prospective
Tenants' Questions, and a Landlord's Response •• Prospective
Tenant Checklist •• Credit Reports and What They Mean •• Red
Flags with Prospective Tenants

10. *SHOWING THE APARTMENT* 55

    Scheduling Appointments with Present Tenants •• Continue
    Screening when Showing the Apartment •• Showing Occupied
    Units •• Showing Vacant Units •• Showing Units That Don't
    Show Well •• Make Repairs Before Showing Vacant Units •• The
    Professional Tenant •• Your "Gut" Feeling •• Protect Yourself
    when Showing Units

11. *RENTAL APPLICATION* 59

    Processing the Application •• Credit Checks •• Pets •• Why mov-
    ing? •• Calls from Fellow Landlords •• Financial and
    Employment Verification •• Visit the Prospective Tenants'
    Home •• Rental Deposit to Hold Unit •• Acceptance Letter ••
    Denial of Request for Tenancy •• Tenant Move-In Checklist ••
    after They Are Approved •• Legal Reasons To Refuse To Rent ••
    Traits of Fraudulent Applications •• You're Not in the
    Subsidized Housing Business

12. *LEASE AGREEMENTS* 73

    What Is A Lease? •• Make Your Lease a Valid Contract •• Four
    Types of Leasehold Estates: •• Plain Language Lease •• 1. Names
    of Landlord & Tenant(s) •• 2. Leased Property •• 3. Starting /
    Ending Dates of Lease •• 4. Money Owed at Move-In •• 5. Rent
    •• 6. Additional Rent Charges •• 7. Number of Occupants •• 8.
    Utility Services •• 9. Inspection •• 10. Changes to the Leased
    Property •• 11. Insurance •• 12. Landlord Not Responsible for
    Tenant's Property and Tenant's Guest Injury •• 13. Bad Checks
    •• 14. Additional Signers to the Lease •• 15. Illegal Activity •• 16.
    Care and Use of the Leased Property •• 17. Tenant's
    Responsibilities •• 18. Landlord's Responsibilities •• 19.
    Landlord's Right To Enter Leased Property •• 20. Damage to
    Leased Property •• 21. Lost Keys •• 22. Repairs •• 23. Tenant May
    Not Transfer or Sublease •• 24. Waterbeds •• 25. Smoke
    Detectors •• 26. Vehicles •• 27. Lead Based Paint Notice •• 28.
    Pets Not Allowed •• 29. Together and Individual Liability •• 30.
    Taking by the Government •• 31. Binding Arbitration •• 32. No
    Jury Trial •• 33. Landlords Right To Mortgage the Property •• 34.
    Sale of the Property •• 35. Truthful Application •• 36. Lawn Care
    and Snow Removal •• 37. Notices •• 38. Phone •• 39. Cable •• 40.
    Death During Lease •• 41. Landlord Does Not Give Up Rights ••
    42. Survival •• 43. Changing Terms and Conditions of Lease ••
    44. Renewing Lease •• 45. Tenant Breaks Lease •• 46. Tenant
    Moves Before End of the Lease •• 47. What Tenant Owes
    Landlord if Tenant Breaks Lease •• 48. Landlord's Rights if
    Tenant Breaks Lease •• 49. Notice to End Lease •• 50. Notice to
    Leave the Leased Property (Notice To Quit) •• 51. Reporting of
    Past Due Rent Owed •• 52. Security Deposits •• 53. Return of
    Security Deposit •• 54. Additional Conditions Between Landlord
    and Tenant •• Additional Rules •• Antennas and Satellite Dishes
    •• Appliances •• Appliance Insurance •• Insurance •• Billing for
    Utilities that Remain in Landlord's Name •• Discount for

Prompt Payments •• Discount for Repairs by Tenant •• Military
Release from Lease •• Pets Allowed •• Painting •• Repairs ••
Tenant Fails to Move In after Giving a Deposit •• Transfer and
Lease to Another Person •• Transfer of Lease to New Owner ••
Basement / Crawl Space Water Damage •• Storage Area ••
Signatures •• Common Illegal Clauses Found in Leases ••
Divorce and Separation

13. *RENTS* 97

Rent Increase Schedule •• Raising Rents •• $1 Rent Increase =
$100 in Increased Property Value •• Make Repairs Before
Sending Rent Increase Notices •• Notice to Change Terms of
Tenancy •• Excuses Why Rent Will Be Late •• Ways of Collecting
Rents •• Additional Rent Collecting Techniques •• Bounced
Checks •• Types of Rent Payments •• Ways of Collecting Late
Rents •• Notice of Lease Termination

14. *SECTION 8 HOUSING - RENT CONTROL*
WARRANTY OF HABITABILITY 105

Section 8 Housing •• Reasons to Accept Section 8 Tenants ••
Reasons Not to Accept Section 8 Tenants •• Rent Controls ••
Tenants Can Escrow Rent under Warrant of Habitability

15. *ALTERNATIVE RENTALS* 109

Student Housing •• Resort Rentals •• Furnished Rentals for
Corporations •• Furnished Rentals - Fire Insurance Claims ••
Assisted Living Facility

16. *SOURCES OF ADDITIONAL INCOME* 113

Insufficient Funds •• Late Fees •• Coin Operated Laundry
Machines •• Ways To Cut Heating Costs •• Storage Bins ••
Parking •• Ways To Cut Electric Costs •• Ways To Cut Water and
Sewer Bills •• Develop a Marketing Plan for Your Rentals ••
Rental Price Range vs Exact Rent •• Longer the Stay the More
Reward Options Available

17. *GOOD WILL PAYS DIVIDENDS* 119

Treat Tenants the Way You Would Want To Be Treated ••
Important Numbers and Helpful Hints •• Stay In Control of
Your Emotions

18. *EVICTIONS* 123

Reasons for Eviction •• Promise To Pay or Vacate •• Five Day
Notice To Pay or Vacate •• Promissory Note •• Notice To
Perform or Quit •• Filing for Eviction •• File Judgment and Lien
Tenants' Bank Account •• Request for Payment of Judgment ••
File the Judgment with the Court and Notify the IRS of "Debt
Forgiveness" •• Pay Tenant To Vacate •• Ways To Collect Rent
After Tenant Has Vacated •• Tenant Files Bankruptcy •• Be
Prepared when Going to Court •• Don't Feel Guilty about
Evictions

19. TENANTS AND DRUGS 133
   Drug Sniffing Dogs

20. RENTING TO COUPLES, RELATIVES, AND FRIENDS 135
   Don't Rent to Relatives or Friends

21. A CONTROL SYSTEM FOR PROPERTY MANAGERS
   AND ON-SITE MANAGERS 137
   Questions To Ask During Interview of Property Manager •• Contract for
   Contractors •• Qualities Needed for On-Site Managers •• Forms of Payment
   for On-Site Managers •• The Horror Stories •• Sign a Management Contract
   •• Bond Managers •• Commandments for Handling Service Repairs ••
   Employee vs. Independent Contractor - The IRS's "20 Questions"

22. INSURANCE, FIRE SAFETY, AND SECURITY 147
   Insurance •• Renters Insurance •• Reducing the Risk of Slip and Falls •• Fire
   Safety •• Security •• Death of a Tenant •• Ten Safety Showing Tips ••
   Checklist to Prove Abandonment •• Tenant in Jail or Hospital

23. RECORD KEEPING 155
   Tenant Move-In Checklist •• Tenant Listing •• Bookkeeping •• Rental Income
   and Expense Record •• Rental Income •• Work Order •• Service Request ••
   Profit and Loss Statement •• Organize Regular Monthly Bills ••
   Repair/Service Record •• Notice To Vacating Tenant •• Distribution of
   Security Deposit

24. TEN BIGGEST MISTAKES MADE BY LANDLORDS 161
   1. Failing To Verify Income/Lease Records and Leases Before Buying ••
   2. Using Poor Techniques for Screening Prospective Tenants •• 3. Failing To
   Use a Lease or Using a Lease Improperly •• 4. Failing To Know Your State's
   Landlord/Tenant Act •• 5. Failing To Collect Enough Security Deposit ••
   6. Failing To Raise Rents Enough or at the Right Time •• 7. Using Poor Rent
   Collection Techniques and Late Fee Enforcement •• 8. Failing To Have a
   Control System in Place for Managers •• 9. Failing To File for Eviction Soon
   Enough •• 10. Failing To Run Real Estate Investments as a Business

25. A FINAL WORD 169
   Make Them Accountable •• Get Involved Politically or Lose Your Rights as a
   Landlord •• Choose To Control Your Financial Destiny •• I Give Myself
   Permission to Succeed.

GLOSSARY 173

THE PROPERTY MANAGEMENT FORMS 177

DOWN TO EARTH LANDLORDING
   HOME STUDY COURSE 180

PROPERTY MANAGEMENT FORMS

Acceptance Letter	Chapter 11	Page 65
Advertising Report	Chapter 8	Page 42
Checklist to Prove Abandonment	Chapter 22	Page 153
Co-Signer Agreement	Chapter 12	Page 81
Denial of Request for Tenancy	Chapter 11	Page 67
Distribution of Security Deposit	Chapter 12, 23	Page 91, 160
Employment Verification	Chapter 11	Page 61
Five Day Notice to Pay or Vacate	Chapter 18	Page 125
Happy Thanksgiving Letter	Chapter 17	Page 120
Important Numbers and Helpful Hints	Chapter 17	Page 121
Independent Contractor Agreement	Chapter 21	Page 140
Inspection Sheet	Chapter 12	Page 79
Insurance Records	Chapter 22	Page 148
Landlord Verification	Chapter 11	Page 62
Lease Cancellation Agreement	Chapter 12	Page 89
Management Contract (On-Site)	Chapter 21	Page 139
Manager's Monthly Report	Chapter 21	Page 141
Notice of Debt Forgiveness	Chapter 18	Page 129
Notice of Insufficient Funds	Chapter 16	Page 113
Notice of Late Fee Charge	Chapter 16	Page 114
Notice of Late Rent	Chapter 13	Page 100
Notice of Lease Termination	Chapter 13	Page 103
Notice to Change Terms of Tenancy	Chapter 13	Page 99
Notice to Perform or Quit	Chapter 18	Page 127
Notice to Vacating Tenant	Chapter 13	Page 104
Pet Agreement	Chapter 12	Page 86
Pet Violation Letter	Chapter 12	Page 87
Phone Screening	Chapter 9	Page 46
Profit and Loss Statement	Chapter 23	Page 159
Promise to Pay or Vacate	Chapter 18	Page 124
Promissory Note	Chapter 18	Page 126
Prospective Tenant Checklist	Chapter 9	Page 51
Rental Application	Chapter 11	Page 59
Rental Deposit to Hold Unit	Chapter 11	Page 66
Rental Income and Expense Record	Chapter 23	Page 157
Rental Standards for Tenant Selection	Chapter 6	Page 31
Rent Increase Schedule	Chapter 13	Page 98
Repair/Service Record (10 forms)	Chapter 21, 23	Page 142, 158
Request for Payment of Judgement	Chapter 18	Page 128
Service Request	Chapter 23	Page 158
Tenant Listing	Chapter 23	Page 156
Tenant Move-In Checklist	Chapter 11	Page 68
Waterbed Agreement	Chapter 12	Page 84
Work Order	Chapter 23	Page 159

PREFACE

One day, while standing on a corner waiting for the light to change, I saw a man put on a burst of speed trying to catch the bus. Unfortunately, the bus pulled away before he made it to the intersection. Thinking of something to say to console him, I joked, "Gee if you had run a little faster, you might have caught that bus." To this day I will never forget the expression on his face and the profound answer, when he replied, "Sir, it was not a case of running a little faster but of starting a little sooner."

That is exactly what all landlords need to do. They need to get started now, to learn all they can about this business called landlording.

Think of buying an investment property as a wagon and landlording skills as the horse. Many first time investors learn techniques to buy the wagon (with little of their own money) and then fail to learn how to manage the horse. Remember the horse, (landlording skills), is what pulls the wagon, (investment property) not the other way around. What good is a nothing-down deal if the tenants don't pay their rent, or worse yet, suppose you have no tenants? In either case you won't have the money you need to pay the mortgage.

This book is dedicated to keeping landlords from making the mistake of putting the cart before the horse. I decided to write it because I felt that my experiences were like everyone else's.

I bought my first investment property and then went looking for books on how to manage it. I had a high negative cash flow, and I didn't need the added problem of vacancies because I didn't know what I was doing.

For weeks I bought books and diligently read them from cover to cover. I soon discovered that unless I owned a 50 to 100 unit complex, half the information was worthless. I didn't need to know about on-site managers, three-part service request forms, or finding the best landscaping maintenance contracts. I needed to learn how to find good tenants, how to keep them, and what to do if I had a bad one. Unable to find out what I was doing wrong, many of those first days, as a landlord, were spent in trial and error.

It is amazing how negative cash flow, with no tenants, makes one sink or swim very quickly. Too many landlords sink and must sell their properties for the price they paid or even take a loss. If they had done more research, or read a book like this, they might not be speaking negatively about real estate.

If my wife and I could work full time jobs, and still find time to own and manage over 80 rental units, valued in excess of three million dollars, in our "spare time," you can too. Learn from our mistakes and follow the suggestions outlined in the book. Do a first rate job of property management and watch your equity grow faster than you ever imagined.

BECK'S LAWS of LANDLORDING

Tenants lock themselves out of their apartments only after dark.

Tenant's friends and relatives seem to die or become deathly ill between the first and tenth of each month.

When a tenant calls and says "How are you"—sit down, because something major just broke.

If there is a stray cat or dog in the neighborhood, they will find your rental.

Tenant's ability to see dirt and damage decreases proportionately with the length of time they occupy the unit.

Whatever can fit in a toilet bowl will attempt to be flushed down.

If it is 10 degrees and you pay the heat, you can be sure that windows are open in more than one unit.

At least one rent check will be "lost in the mail" each month.

The trash can for chewing gum is the carpet.

Sinks have a tendency to fall off the wall when tenants brush their teeth.

The ashtray for cigarettes is the carpet.

Your best tenants seemed to get transferred in the middle of winter or in the slowest rental market in history.

Heating and plumbing problems always occur between 5:00 PM on Friday and 8:00 AM Monday morning.

If a tenant decides to replace a washer in a faucet be prepared to repair the plumbing in the house.

Things break 200 times faster in your rental properties than your own home.

Female tenants are the only people on the face of the earth that can reproduce children in less than nine months.

Tenants' dogs have been known to change breed and gain 50 pounds in less than one week.

If you have a question about anything, your tenant will have an answer.

The hardware store always closes five minutes before you arrive.

If the dumpster looks half full, tenants will place their trash along the side of the dumpster so the animals will have something to eat.

Tenants will swear under oath that whatever is broken now was that way when they moved in.

INTRODUCTION

As a landlord, I love it when interest rates rise to double digits. I have found that when interest rates are at 14%, I accept 3 out of 4 applicants. When interest rates are at 6%, I reject 3 out of 4, and here's why. As interest rates go up, more people are forced to rent because they can't afford to buy. Their credit is good—they just can't afford the high mortgage payments. Hence, I get a quality tenant. On the other hand, when interest rates are low, people applying for my rentals are very different. They can now afford mortgage payments, but other obstacles hold them back. The two main reasons seem to be no savings for the down payment because they live paycheck-to-paycheck and bad credit so they can't get that mortgage. They must live somewhere, so they come applying to rent. If they have no down money for a house, they won't have the security deposit for my rental. If the banks rejected them because of bad credit, why would I accept them?

When interest rates drop, many more people can afford to buy, which means fewer will rent and vacancies will dramatically increase. I used to think that, too, but after being a landlord for over two decades where I have seen interest rates fall as low as 6% and shoot up as high as 18%, I realize it just doesn't happen. As long as there are people on the face of this earth, there will people who just can't get it together to buy.

When interest rates hit the 6% mark in 1999, 34% of Americans were still renting and 28% of those did so by choice. As we begin a new millennium, people want to be more flexible in their lifestyles. They want freedom to move and want to be able to do it quickly, with little stress. As workers change jobs, not having a house to unload is a major issue. It also gives them the flexibility to take advantage of emerging opportunities anywhere in the world. As people look for better ways to manage their personal, family, and learning time, convenience is paramount.

I had a couple apply for a large two-bedroom townhouse who told me they were selling their house. When I asked why, the husband said he was tired of cutting the grass and fixing plumbing problems. They wanted more personal freedom and to have someone else take care of these time-consuming and stressful maintenance items. I was happy to fill their need!

The demand for rental units will fluctuate up and down with interest rates but the demand will always be there. Now it becomes imperative to find the best possible tenant to rent your apartment, and that is where I am going to help.

To survive in landlording does take lots of work and patience. Developing basic principles and practices of management helps to insure your investment dollar. After all, we are in this business to make money as painlessly as possible. Let me share with you over two decades of landlording skills that I have learned from being in the trenches. I have made many mistakes on my journey, learned from each one, and want to share with you the solutions that work. GO FOR IT!

CHAPTER 1

ORIGINS OF LANDLORDING

We will do today what others won't so that we can live tomorrow like others can't.

Some people dream worthy accomplishments while others stay awake and do them.

You cannot change the people around you...
but you can change the people you are around.

Landlording can be traced back to the feudal system where neither private ownership or the free transfer of title to real property was possible. The king had supreme control of the land and had sole determination of its transfer. The land was divided by the king among the lords who redistributed it to individuals called serfs. Rights to the land flowed downward while services and obligations moved upward.

The lords assumed control of an area and controlled the local economy as well as legal jurisdiction. Hence the land was controlled by the lords. There were no standard procedures among the lords, and much chaos ensued.

Slowly, a system of royal courts was established with circuit judges presiding. As the number of decisions from actual trials grew, "common laws" became more established.

At the beginning of the thirteenth century, the practice of private ownership of land began. It was called the allodial system. This system survived for more than 400 years. With the allodial system full ownership of property was given to the title holder. Under English common law this meant the landlord owned the land and all that was built upon it.

During the very early colonial days in America only Barons and Lords were allowed to have the privilege of receiving a land grant. These nobles rented the land out to "tenants" who controlled the land for a set number of years. This became the equivalent of today's lease. Since each man's word was sufficient to make a contract, no written agreements were used. The tenant's only responsibility was to make payment in the form of crops, crafts, artistry, or military service. A typical year's lease would require the tenant to give to the "landlord" 15 bushels of wheat, four fat fowls, and one day's service with horse and wagon.

Money was very rarely used as payment. The landlord was not required to make any improvements or to change the use for the benefit of the tenant and was not liable for any injuries occurring on the property. If a fire destroyed the tenant's dwelling, the landlord was not obligated to rebuild and the tenant was still required to make full rent payment. If the payment was not received, the landlord could seize all the tenant's crops, animals and property on the land, then terminate the tenant's lease. The Barons and Lords commonly used their own militia when it became necessary to "evict" a non-paying tenant. If the tenant objected for any reason the courts would consistently rule in the landlord's favor. It would not be until the late 1800s that tenants would gain any legal footing in the judicial system.

As America began to grow, English nobility continued to own the land but often sold large portions to individuals. William Penn is a good example of how this worked. King Charles II owed William Penn's father an unpaid debt that totaled $80,000. Penn, a Quaker, asked the king if the debt could be repaid with wilderness land in America. They agreed, and Penn told King Charles II he wanted the land named "sylvania" meaning woods. The King added Penn to the suggested name to become Pennsylvania or Penn's Woods. Penn carefully laid out the City of Philadelphia between the Delaware and Schuylkill Rivers with streets laid out in a gridiron effect. Deeds for individual ownership were created which resulted in few land disputes.

In 1774, the King issued the Quebec Act, which declared that only the Crown could grant land in the western territories. This enraged the colonists.

When the Declaration of Independence was drawn up, a clear message was sent to the King of England. The development of the country was being stifled by imposing unreasonable conditions on acquiring new land.

After the American Revolution, representatives from all the states met in Philadelphia to plan a government. The newly created Constitution clearly bolstered the rights of private property owners. When it denotes "life, liberty, and property" it is generally agreed that the term "property" means the rights to hold title to, make legal use of, pledge, mortgage, sell, or transfer. This allodial system of ownership is the distinguishing feature of real estate ownership in the United States. Private ownership of land is free and absolute, subject only to governmental and voluntary private restrictions.

It wasn't until the early 1900s that landlording took on the characteristics by which we know it today. It started with the construction of multi-family dwellings by rich people who traveled frequently and needed someone to manage their investments at home. With the invention of the elevator, even more high rise buildings and apartments were built and more and more landlords were needed to manage them.

The landlording profession expanded dramatically during the mid 1900s, to all socio-economic levels. Problems developed because most landlords had the same mentality as their "land-lord" ancestors and often went too far when dealing with tenants. Over the last few decades laws have been passed which have given tenants more rights. By the 1980s, the trend had swung the other direction and tenants now had more rights than the landlords.

It took three centuries for the tides to do an about face. Three hundred years ago a tenant would immediately be evicted for being lazy (failure to pay rent) while today the laws will not allow landlords to ask even basic questions such as a prospective tenant's birth date and marital status. The laws need to become more equitable for both sides.

CHAPTER 2

TREAT LANDLORDING AS A BUSINESS

To dream anything that you want to dream. That is the beauty of the human mind. To do anything that you want to do. That is the strength of the human will. To trust yourself to test your limits. That is the courage.

— Bernard Edmunds

The people who are successful in real estate are the ones who have good property management skills and decision making skills. This fact applies to the small time investor, as well as to the owner of a large apartment complex.

Landlording is a serious business and should be based on sound business principles. You cannot take college courses to learn this job. It is learned by doing it. Good old common sense will go far, as long as emotions and personal feelings can be kept under control. **Remember, if you fail to prepare, be prepared to fail.**

A landlord must be patient, organized, honest, authoritative, and enthusiastic. A good landlord, like a parent, also must have a fair set of rules backed by strong enforcement. I know it feels good when someone likes and loves you, but it is far better when you have their respect.

Gaining that respect is a tough job because it means not always being perceived as the "nice guy." Every person's situation is different, and understanding and compassion are certainly important. No circumstance is absolutely black or white. Flexibility is important, but remember you are always in charge. This is a business for you, not a hobby. There are plenty of good prospective tenants in the market place, so dealing with the bad ones is not necessary.

To survive in landlording does require work and patience. Development of basic property management skills will help you survive as a landlord as well as protect the financial investment you have made. After all, we are in this business to make money as painlessly as possible.

LANDLORDS MUST WEAR MANY DIFFERENT HATS

Landlording is a unique business that requires many different hats to be worn at different times. A landlord must have the skills of a:

Carpenter	Electrician	Bookkeeper
Locksmith	Realtor	Plumber
Mediator	Roofer	Banker
Lawyer	Painter	Diplomat
Psychologist	Bill Collector	Exterminator
Advertising Agent	Landscaper	Writer
Drywaller	Repairman	Accountant
Listener	Salesman	

Fortunately, one need not wear all these hats at the same time; but the more skills you master, the more money you will save. Knowing how to do minor repairs, such as changing a five cent washer in faucets, repairing a bent door jamb, and using a tester light to check a hot water element, will go a long way in reducing expenses. See Chapter 4, Common Repairs, for more detailed information.

THE LANDLORDING TEAM

Some times it will not be possible for you to wear the appropriate hat. You will have to call someone else to handle the situation. Compiling a list of people (your team) who know your goals and objectives, and who are trustworthy and reliable, can make all the difference in the world. Don't be afraid to change your team. Remove the ones who do not service you and add those who do. Here are suggestions for people to have on your team.

Accountant	Appliance Repair	Carpenter
Electrician	Exterminator	Handyman
Landscaper	Heating Company	Rental Agency
Lawyer	Plumber	Snow Remover
Realtor	Credit Bureau	Tree Surgeon
Painter	Carpet Contractor	
Newspaper Agency	Paving/Sealing contractor	

SLUMLORDS ARE OUT

"What do you mean I can only get $60,000 for this duplex?" shouts the Slimy Slumlord to the Realistic Realtor. "That's what I paid for it five years ago!" "I know sir, but what you have in this duplex is double

depreciation," replies the realtor. "O.K., I give up. What is double depreciation?" stutters the slumlord. The realtor quietly explains that the property has been depreciated for tax purposes, but it has also depreciated in real value because needed repairs were never made. The property looks awful. When routine maintenance goes by the wayside, property value does not keep up with inflation. It won't be long before the word "SLUMLORD" will be invisibly pinned on the owner's chest.

Too many people buy property just because the accountant shows all the tax advantages. He fails to mention the hours that will be needed to keep the property a good tax shelter and income producer. The smart investor will very quickly learn property management techniques and love his accountant. The naive investor, who fails Management I, finds that the headaches become constant. Ultimately, he sells the investment, and fires the accountant.

About 75% of all income properties are sold because the owner is tired of doing property management. They are tired because they did not treat the property and the tenants as if it were a business. It was not a top priority to fix the leaky roof or running faucets or remove the tree that blew over in the storm two months earlier. When the tenants see you don't care, they will stop caring. Create a positive image by showing you care and the tenants will work with you instead of against you.

The Disney organization implements the concept of creating a caring image better than anyone. They must have one person, for every twenty people in the park, picking up trash. This is why the place always looks clean—which psychologically makes us feel more at home. When we feel secure, we stay longer and spend more money.

During my last trip to Disney World, I was walking behind a man who threw a napkin on the ground. It stood out like a sore thumb. It was the only trash anywhere in sight. Before I knew what I was doing, the napkin was in my hand and, with just a few steps, it was in a trash can. All of a sudden it hit me what Disney had accomplished. They had conditioned me to WANT to keep the park clean. Do the same with your tenants by creating a caring image and meeting their needs promptly. Use the techniques outlined in the following chapters and demonstrate a strong desire to be a good landlord. No one will ever pin that "SLUMLORD" sign on you.

WHY TENANTS RENT

1. THEY CAN'T SAVE MONEY — Most tenants can't save money because most live from pay check to pay check. That is why only 5% of rental applications show a savings account. If they had a savings account they would buy a home for themselves. Don't be surprised when a tenant calls saying his rent will be late because he was hurt on the job and the Workmans' Compensation check won't be in for two weeks!

2. THEY ARE TRANSIENT — Be aware that part of landlording is tenant turnover. Tenants move, on average, every three to four years while home owners move every seven years. The type of jobs held by people who rent run the full gamut from accountant to zoo keeper. Depending on the price of your rental property, the reason people rent are many fold. Generally, the lower priced rentals will be occupied by tenants who have unskilled jobs or seasonal employment. They often are laid off and must move to be closer to their next job. The higher priced rentals could be middle management people or yuppies who stay in the area for a year or two and then move. They also might be the 2% that have a savings account but want to explore an area for a year before purchasing.

3. THEY FEAR OWNERSHIP — This group will always be renters because they fear the responsibilities that home ownership brings. They are the pessimists of the world that feel if anything can go wrong it will and if it's in the house they occupy, let the owner fix it. I had a tenant apply for one of my units who was selling his home because he "was tired of cutting the grass and making repairs."

Tenants like the idea that when something breaks, someone else is responsible for fixing it and paying the bill. I am glad to fill that need because I'm the optimist. I see the needed repair as a way of keeping the tenant happy, but also as a way of improving the value of the property. Now, when the tenant squawks at the rent increase, I point to the new carpet, kitchen floor, or new stove. If he doesn't like it, he can move and I will find a new tenant who will, in most cases, pay even more rent than he would have paid!

CHAPTER 3

THE BETTER IT LOOKS
THE FASTER IT RENTS

MANLEY'S FIRST LAW OF LANDLORDING — Good properties attract good and bad tenants. Bad properties only attract bad tenants.

Destiny is not a matter of chance, it's a matter of choice. You make your way, you choose your way, and you make it happen.

— William Jennings Bryan

I couldn't agree more with the title to this chapter. If the grass is long, bushes overgrown, gutters falling off, and paint chipping from the shutters, the good prospects will just drive by. The ones who do stop to see the unit probably live in something worse. When they say, "I like what I see" —BEWARE!

Keep in mind that good maintenance will justify higher rents, attract better quality tenants, and result in a steady increase in the property value. This maintenance comes in two forms: Exterior and Interior.

GIVE EXTERIOR "CURB APPEAL"

A beautifully landscaped property should reap 15% more in rent over an identical property without landscaping. This is called "curb appeal" and is definitely a psychological factor when prospects are deciding if they want to stop to keep the appointment. If they don't like what they see on the outside, there is no way to impress them with the inside.

Landscaping doesn't have to be elaborate. Simple, well-placed, low maintenance shrubbery and plants can do the trick. Evergreen trees work well because they are always green and need trimming but once a year. Low spreading rug junipers or cover bark are very nice for perennial patches and weedy areas. Sometimes the only curb appeal that is needed, especially in a good location, is a neatly manicured lawn.

Landscaping creates a feeling of comfort and relaxation while serving a functional purpose. It can be used to hide the backyard of a messy neighbor, provide a wind break or help with erosion. A study I read said that shade trees can reduce a properties heat gain by 80% and that strategically placed bushes were roughly the equivalent to increasing a property's insulation by 30%.

Don't forget the mailbox. Everyone seems to buy the standard black mailbox so don't do that. Buy a nice colorful mailbox and install it on a wooden post.

The other outside area that needs to be maintained is the exterior surface and trim of the building. If it needs painting, give it a fresh coat. Start with the side that faces the street and then move to the rest of the house. Remember the south and west sides of the house will need to be painted more frequently than the north and east sides because of the path of the sun.

Check around flashing, air conditioning units, and windows for areas that could be recaulked to keep water out or block unwanted air flows. See that all screens are in place, free from holes or cuts. Clear gutters and down spouts of debris and position the down spouts away from the house. Once, after a heavy rainstorm, I received a frantic phone call from a tenant saying there was six inches of water in her basement. The six inches turned out to be an exaggerated one inch and was caused by a section of down spout coming loose. The water from the roof was going directly in a cellar window instead of down the driveway to the street.

The bottom line with landscaping is that people want to rent in a community or on a street that is well maintained inside and out. If an apartment is sub-standard or overpriced, no amount of landscaping will help get that apartment rented. On the other hand, a landlords dedication to a green and pleasant environment outside sends a strong signal to prospective tenants that this landlord cares.

INTERIOR LOOKS

Some inside areas that should not be overlooked before showing and renting to a new tenant are plumbing lines. Turn on faucets and flush toilets. Any leaks or worn valves should be replaced now to prevent bigger problems in the future. All tile floors, ledges, shelves, and window sills should be cleaned. Nothing turns tenants off more than cobwebs hanging from the ceiling and dead insects covering the ledges. All light switches and fixtures should be cleaned and checked to see that they are working properly. Watch out for dead flies inside the globes!

The kitchen appliances should be immaculate and in working order. Be especially sure the oven is clean because that is the first place the woman will look when entering the kitchen. Make sure all drawers slide easily and that they are clean.

Bathrooms are very important too. The bathroom medicine chest always seems to have a few used razor blades and useless make-up containers with no lids. Get rid of partially used soap bars and half used toilet paper rolls. Check all areas that have caulk around them. When cheap caulk is used, it has a tendency to dry up and crack as well as turn undesirable colors. Replace any of these areas with silicone caulk. It is a little more expensive, but will last longer and acts as a bonding agent too.

Place air fresheners around the unit if it has been empty and closed up for any length of time. Odors build up in a closed house no matter how clean it is. Check to see that all smoke detectors have batteries and are in working condition. I supply each unit with an ABC fire extinguisher that is kept under the kitchen sink. If a tenant can put out a small fire quickly because that extinguisher is handy, a lot of damage to the unit and their belongings will be saved. Recharge or replace as needed.

PAINTING

Paint can transform the look of an apartment and needs to be high on the priority list before renting. Before painting make sure to prepare the surfaces to be painted. If the last tenant was a smoker the walls will need to be washed. Scrape off loose, flaking paint and "feather" the edges with sandpaper so there is a smooth transition for the new paint. Spackle holes left by nails. Put the spackle on the end of your finger and fill in the hole, wiping away any excess. When dry, a light sanding or wet sponge will remove any excess. Mask all surfaces you do not want painted such as windows, trim, doorknobs, hinges, etc.)

There are many different types of paint on the market so the question that needs to be asked is do you want to use a water based latex paint or an oil based paint? Oil paints are more durable and give a smoother coat but they are more difficult to work with and to clean up.

What makes the difference between a $30 gallon of paint and a $10 gallon of paint? It's the amount of titanium in the paint which gives more coverage. Cheaper paints contain little or no titanium and rely on clay. As a result, it may take three or four coats to cover the same area.

Another big difference is durability. The more expensive paints are more washable and offer greater scrub resistance. When trying to wash dirt off cheaper paint, you will probably wash off the paint itself. A higher quality paint will reduce the tendency of the paint to splatter because it contains an anti-splattering agent that produces less mess than inferior paints.

Paint comes in a variety of colors and finishes. Eggshell, Antique White, Pure White, and many others. Decide what colors fit your apartment the best and what type of finish you want on the walls? There is flat, satin, semi-gloss and high gloss. Flat paint is more forgiving and hides flaws well, but it doesn't stand up to scrubbing. High gloss paint is washable and easier to maintain, but it reveals surface imperfections and painting errors. Each has its own place in the house but the two that are used by landlords are either the satin or semi-gloss finish because of its washability. In bathrooms, flat paint absorbs moisture into the drywall and will cause mildew. Using a satin or semi-gloss the moisture will just run down the wall and not absorb into the drywall or plaster.

Look for sales and buy in quantity. Paint doesn't go bad and will always be needed as long as you stay in landlording. Buy the same lot batch when buying in quantity. This will make it much easier to re-paint small areas or just one wall and everything will still match. Painting is labor intense so saving a few dollars on cheaper paint does not make sense, especially if the unit needs to be repainted in five years but could have lasted eight years with a higher quality paint. Need drop cloths? Save old bed sheets or shower curtains.

Don't buy cheap brushes, rollers, or other equipment. Spending a little extra is worth it in time, effort and results. Use a natural bristle brush for oil-based paint and a synthetic bristle brush for latex paint.

CARPETS, HARDWOOD FLOORS

Carpets add warmth and make a unit more rentable. The color, quality, type of padding, price, and installation have to be considered. Let's look at each point, one at a time.

Neutral colors, blended in a tweed-like pattern, do well in the long run. Golds are bright and cheerful but show dirt and traffic patterns. Blue-greens hide the dirt better but are not as popular with tenants because many times it clashes with their furniture. The brownish tweeds with a slight pattern are the best for covering cigarette burns, stains, and traffic patterns.

Carpet quality varies greatly. Usually the denser the pile, the more expensive. Obviously, avoid buying the really cheap carpet with one strand every two inches, yet don't buy carpet that has pile so thick that your hand can't penetrate to the backing. The higher priced carpet will show wear patterns, stains, cigarette burns, and spills as easily as cheaper carpet. Buy a middle priced carpet and be happy to get six to eight years out of it. The carpet will definitely pay for itself in increased rent, and the cost can be written off over a shorter period.

The padding often is overlooked when selecting carpet. A medium priced carpet with a good padding will not only prolong the life of the carpet but also make it feel more expensive than it really is. Half-inch bonded pad is the best for the price. A carpet salesman might talk you into a polyurethane pad of the same thickness because it is cheaper but I have found that bonded wears better. Compare the two different paddings and see if you can tell the difference. If you can, so can your tenant.

Prices of carpet can vary widely from store to store. I have found that going to a carpet dealer and telling him that I am in property management, and have "X" amount of units with carpeting, will often help in getting a lower price. The bigger firms do not necessarily have the lowest prices. A small firm, knowing you can turn a lot of business their way, can make some pretty nice offers. Shopping around can be a lot of leg work, but it will pay off in good savings.

Don't forget remnants. Many times if I find just one room that needs replacing I will purchase a rubber backed remnant the size of the room. This type carpet doesn't need padding and if the floors are wood, a few nails around the perimeter will hold it in place. This will save you money whether you do the installation or not.

Installation is either included with the price of the carpet, or listed as a separate fee per square foot. Be sure everything is explained on the contract with the carpet dealer so there will be no misunderstandings later.

Make sure the installation address is the address of the rental property and not your home or business address. Clarify all instructions. Should the carpet people call the tenant to schedule the measuring and installation, or contact you? Do they have the names and numbers of you and the tenants and do they understand which is which? You might save

money if you know someone who does carpet installation. Get his price before visiting the carpet dealer so you can compare. He might be able to get a better price on the carpet if he purchases it for you from the dealer.

Before the installation, be sure to walk over the whole area. Listen for loose boards that squeak. Renail them or use screws to hold the sub-flooring tight. It is much easier, (and kinder to the ears), to take care of this common problem before the carpet is installed.

Before replacing the carpet, why not first try cleaning it? You'd be amazed how a good shampooing will rejuvenate a carpet. As a regular practice, always clean carpets before the new tenant moves in.

Use a rented steam cleaner. They are usually rented for 24 hours, so when you've finished the apartment, take it home and do your own carpets. Many times family members have borrowed it when I have finished. Sometimes three or four houses are cleaned for one rental price.

If you have many units, consider buying a steam cleaner. Let your tenants know they can use it at anytime. Get a $50 deposit to be sure it comes back in the same condition it left. It will pay for itself if you can get a few more years out of the carpet.

Another, costlier, option would be professional steam cleaning. The extra cost might be worth it, as it will do a thorough job with the greater powered suction motor.

If you are considering hardwood floors, consider these facts. Hardwood floors may look wonderful when properly maintained, but they can look terrible when they're not. Scratches and stains have to be sanded and refinished. This process takes away about 1/16 of an inch each time it is done. After three sandings, the floor nails will be exposed and then sanding will not be possible. Floor refinishing might need to be done every five years which makes the life span of the floor about 15 years. Replacing that floor will be costly.

CREEPY CRAWLERS

Cockroach comes from the Spanish word "cucharacha" meaning "crazy bug." They have been around for millions of years so are definitely survivors. There are over 1,600 known species but the ones most of us know are the West Coast or German Cockroaches (Blatella Germanica.) These critters do not practice safe sex. One pair of cockroaches can produce 400 offspring a year and each of those can do the same amount! Even with the average life span of a cockroach is only one year, the numbers can rise very quickly. They breed more quickly when

they are warm so summer is when they lay the most eggs. The females carry the eggs around in brown egg cases which protrude from the tail of their bodies until they are dropped. Each case holds about a dozen eggs and it takes 40–45 days to hatch. Cockroaches are nocturnal and have antennae that are very sensitive to movement and moisture. The little feelers on their tails sense air movement and air pressure which is why they can scatter so quickly when someone enters a room. It is not so much the light being turned on as our movement and the resulting change in air pressure that they sense.

Cockroaches will eat almost anything. They are attracted to starchy or sweetened matter and moisture. If they can't find decaying matter, they will eat brown paper bags, cardboard, glue, wood, and some clothing. They can go for three months without eating and a month without water.

Because they reproduce so frequently and reach maturity to breed so quickly, it is almost impossible to destroy them because they become immune to the chemicals being used to destroy them. For example, if an apartment is bombed or spayed with the same chemical once every two months, within six months there will be very little effect on them.

The best form of prevention is cleanliness. Do not leaving dirty dishes in the sink or dishwasher. Clean countertops and stove tops of grease and crumbs. Store shelf food in sealed plastic and clean the crumbs from the bottom of the toaster. All are potential feasting grounds.

Refrigerators and gas stoves are their all time favorite places. The refrigerator motor offers warmth and the water in the drip pan is a perfect watering hole. If the gas stove has a pilot constantly lit, this makes a nice nest for breeding. If the stove or oven are not used regularly it is a good idea to run the oven for a half hour every week to destroy any eggs, young, and to discourage the adults from nesting there. Pull out the stove and refrigerator on a regular basis to remove all liquid and food items that have fallen or rolled under them.

In multi-family buildings I have found they will stay close to the dirty tenant and their food source. Remove that tenant and they will scurry to find someone else to feed them. You will need to bomb the unit that they were in plus any units that have common walls and it should be done at the same time.

If you don't see cockroaches when you walk into an empty apartment it doesn't mean they are not there. The easiest way to tell if the last tenants had cockroaches is to look at the walls around nail holes where pictures were hung. Tiny raised brown areas are sure signs they had them.

If they are not exterminated before the new tenant moves in, crazy things might start to happen. For example, a newly married couple moved into my unit and couldn't stop talking about how they were going to decorate their apartment. Two days later the husband called to say his wife had seen a cockroach. That was one bug too many. She had retreated home to her mother's until the problem was resolved.

Another instance found me talking to a tenant who was "camped" in a phone booth. She had seen a cockroach and refused to go back into the apartment until he and his friends left permanently. I grabbed a can of ant and roach killer and headed directly to where I knew they would be hiding. I quickly located the little critters under the refrigerator and raided their hideout. I then emptied the rest of the can in every dark crevice and corner I could find before going to retrieve my timid tenant from the phone booth.

If a few cockroaches are seen, a can of over-the-counter spray will usually do the trick for a lot less money than an exterminator and control the problem before it spreads.

Another solution some landlords have found very effective is a mixture of condensed milk and boric acid. Mix the two together in equal amounts to make a paste. Add slightly more milk to make the solution thinner. Pour the mixture into a plastic squeeze bottle and apply under the sink, stove, behind cabinets, and along floor boards. Plug holes where pipes come up through the floor with fine steel wool.

Be sure to keep the product being used out of the reach of children and pets. Before using any product, check with an exterminator about the effects the chemical might have on pets or small children if touched or swallowed.

If you have a large building and the problem is constant, consider using a professional exterminator. This is the best way to control the problem. Exterminators will gladly place you on a yearly contract for sprayings.

Ants, depending on the type, might hang around longer before moving on. Ant traps or spray under cabinets and in corners will help this problem. Fleas will be in units where the tenants had a dog or cat. They lay their eggs in the carpet. The gestation period is a few weeks. The best thing to do is to set off some flea bombs that can be purchased over-the-counter. Shut all doors and windows, set off the bomb in the middle of a room or at the top of steps, and then visit a friend for a few hours. A real bad case might require two or three bombings. Wait a few days, to vacuum the rugs, so the chemical has a chance to penetrate and kill any larva.

CEILING FANS

If a unit does not have central air, seriously consider installing a few ceiling fans. A 52 inch ceiling fan, with light fixture, can be purchased for less than $50 and will add elegance and charm to the apartment. Look for ones called ceiling huggers that mount very close to the ceiling. Most tenants are impressed with them, and they are glad they "come with the unit." Smaller blade fans that are ceiling huggers can be purchased for half the cost and do a great job.

The first place to add a ceiling fan is in the kitchen. Next, place one in the bedroom and then finally the living room, if funds are available. There are many different styles, so there should be no problem finding one that will fit the motif of the home. The installation will take less than an hour per fan.

WHO MAKES THE FINAL DECISION?

In most cases the final decision will be made by the woman, so when scheduling appointments, make sure the woman will be coming on the visit. If she is not, try to reschedule so she can be there. Experts say there are ways to increase the "appeal" in the eyes of a woman. **Entry Impact**—it must be impressive. **Storage**—this could be large closets, a basement or attic storage. Garages and sheds are also pluses. **Natural light**—open blinds and curtains to get in as much natural light as possible. **Workable kitchen**—create as much counter space as possible. **Clean, Clean, Clean**—Clean everything from toilets, tubs, stoves, under kitchen sink, and last but not least windows and glass doors.

CHAPTER 4

COMMON REPAIRS

Efficiency is doing things right. Effectiveness is doing the right things efficiently.

— Zig Zigler

Things may come to those that wait . . . but only the things left by those who hustle.

— Abraham Lincoln

When problems develop or repairs are needed, it is a good habit to take care of them as soon as possible. When repairs are put off for weeks at a time, you are giving the impression that you don't care. The tenant then starts thinking, if the landlord doesn't care, why should I? A terrible cycle begins. If tenants are not reporting maintenance requests some time during the year, wake up and smell the damages!

React promptly, and many positive things can happen. The tenant realizes his requests, within reason, are being met. This shows you care about him and your building. Not only will he take better care of your apartment but the rent will paid on time.

I quickly learned in this business that we make the most money when units are occupied. We lose the most income when there is a tenant turnover. Everyday the unit sits vacant is lost income because of paying for advertising, heat if it's winter, plus painting, cleaning, and doing repairs. Every landlord's number one goal should be to keep tenants (your customers) happy so they don't move. I don't mean invite them over for dinner or waive late fees 6 out of 12 months, just treat them firmly but fairly. Take care of their needs. Whatever it is they want I will give some part of it. If the cost it is less than $50, they get it automatically. If they want new carpet throughout the whole house, the first floor might get done this year and the second floor the following year.

SAVE TIME AND MONEY BY STANDARDIZING

How many times have we made trips to the plumbing supply to fix that leaky faucet, the lock shop to get new keys, and the hardware store to match up a paint color? All of these take time. Much of that running around can be eliminated by standardizing material choices.

Use the same brand and model for faucets. Keep that brand faucet repair kit in your tool box so that repairs can be done in a matter of minutes. If you work with the same locksmith, have all keys set to use a master key. Buy the same brand and color of paint for easy touch ups. Vinyl commercial tile is heavy duty and made for rentals. When it is applied to a well prepared floor surface, it is very durable. If a tile or two is damaged, heat up an iron on the tile for a few seconds and it pops right out.

Another advantage of standardizing materials is taking advantage of sales on a specific product you are using. This is the time to stock up on items. Don't get sidetracked with close-out sales. Time is money and standardization will save you both.

APPLIANCES

The more appliances that are supplied the more repair calls there will be. The more appliances provided, the more rent should be charged to cover repairs and the convenience of having them available. The one appliance that additional rent won't cover if it dies, is the refrigerator. I stopped supplying refrigerators, didn't lower the rent, and saw no drop in applications. If they say I would like the unit but don't want to buy a refrigerator, I will offer to provide one for $15 a month in additional rent. I then purchase a scratch and dent refrigerator from an appliance dealer or find a used one in the newspaper that is no more than 3 years old. The average life of a refrigerator is 13–17 years so there should be ten or more years of useful life. The additional rent will pay off the refrigerator in less than two years and the remaining eight years is positive cash flow. As refrigerators get close to the end of their useful life I will not raise the rent but tell the tenants that the refrigerator is no longer part of the lease. They are welcome to continue to use it but if it needs to be repaired or replaced, it will be their responsibility. This also works well with washer and dryers. I explain another concept with refrigerators and other items in the Additional Income chapter.

Here is a list of life expectancy for the following items. It will vary according to quality of the product and installation, amount of use, level of maintenance, and local weather conditions.

Forced-air gas furnace	15 to 20 years
Water Heater	8 to 12 years
Garbage Disposal	5 to 10 years
Dishwasher	7 to 12 years
Ranges and Ovens	15 to 20 years
Built-in-Microwaves	5 to 10 years
Washer and Dryer	9 to 14 years
Galvanized Water Line	30 to 45 years
Refrigerator	13 to 17 years
Composition Single Roofing	16 to 20 years
(first roof)	

Copper water lines, PVC waste lines, and vinyl windows all have 50 year guarantees.

Property maintenance and improvements are critical in making a profit in the rental housing business. However, landlords have a tendency, especially in lower-to-middle income housing areas, to over-improve the property. Here is a listing of some of the more common over-improvements made by landlords.

1. Tearing out old but functional kitchen cabinets and installing new ones
2. Replacing old ceiling tiles with new when they could have been painted
3. Ripping up lightly worn carpet and installing new
4. Using a high grade carpet and padding
5. Replacing old paneling with new when the old could be painted over
6. Using paneling when drywall could have been used
7. Painting using multiple colors
8. Using wall paper rather than just painting
9. Removing wall paper rather than painting over
10. Using soft vinyl floors when tiles should be used

Your goal in getting a house ready to rent should be to provide an environment that is clean, safe, and functional. Clean is very important because people don't like other people's dirt. The two main areas they want to see clean are the kitchen and bathrooms. Safety and functionality are also important. If you see a potential "trip and fall" area, address it before it becomes a problem.

Strongly consider installing inexpensive items such as a ceiling fan/light, new outlet cover plates, or new knobs on kitchen cabinets.

PREVENTATIVE MAINTENANCE

Before discussing common repairs, let's talk about some preventative maintenance practices that may reduce overall requests.

The best time to do these preventive maintenance jobs would be when visiting the property to make other repairs. Check to see if faucets are dripping, listen to see if toilets are running, that caulk in the shower area is in good condition, and traps under sinks and tubs are not cracked or rusted. This is also a good time to let your eyes wander around the apartment. Do you see holes or crayon marks on the walls? Are there stain marks on the ceiling showing a leak from an upstairs bathroom, or holes in doors, or broken windows? Items you know were not this way when the tenant moved in should be pointed out to the tenant. They should be asked for an explanation.

Outside jobs to do include: cleaning gutters of dead leaves, nailing in loose gutter pins, pruning trees of dead branches, and patching cracked sidewalks.

Carry a service contract on the furnace. You pay for the contract and build this cost into the rent. This way you are sure the furnace is serviced each year. When something does malfunction, you and the tenant have someone to call for many of the common repair and service problems. Regular maintenance on a large ticket item such as a furnace is a very cost effective way to prolong the life of the system.

THE REPAIR CALL

Try to get as much information about the problem over the phone before going to see for yourself or calling a repair man. This will help you select the tools and materials needed for the repair if you are doing it yourself, or, it will allow you to give a better description to the repair man. Repair calls can often be handled over the phone by asking questions of the tenants and then describing what needs to be done. The refrigerator might not be working simply because a fuse has blown or the plug was pulled out. A water heater might need a new fuse or the circuit breaker reset.

PLUMBING

More cash flow is lost because of plumbing problems than any other. Seventy-percent of all maintenance problems and emergencies are plumbing related. When a tenant calls about a water related problem, take it seriously and act immediately.

After a unit becomes vacant, it's a good idea to turn off the water at the main shut off valve, whatever the season. You never know when a pipe can break, causing massive damage before it is discovered. I learned this lesson the hard way. A unit became vacant in January and the thermostat for the heat was set at 55 degrees. My mistake was in shutting a door to the laundry room that was exposed to an outside wall. The temperature never went above 10 degrees for the next five days.

On the sixth day the condominium association called to tell me they thought I might have a problem in the unit. When I asked why, they told me the neighborhood children were ice skating on my patio! Before I opened the door, I could hear the water gushing out of the hole in the laundry room pipe. It was at that moment I remembered the brand new carpet that had been installed two weeks earlier!

The pipe was fixed in 20 minutes. What took the time was renting a carpet vacuum to suck up three inches of water, lifting the carpet and padding to let it dry, and then have a carpet installer re-attach it to the floor.

Listed below are some of the common plumbing problems landlords will encounter. All can be handled with a few simple tools and some basic plumbing knowledge. Take a course at a local adult evening school or watch your plumber do the repair. When the charge is $40 to replace a five cent washer in a faucet and it only takes three minutes, you will learn quickly how to make that repair yourself!

Drippy Faucets

Drippy faucets can be stopped by replacing a washer on the bottom of the stem. The only tools needed are a Phillips head screwdriver to take off the cap, an adjustable wrench to take out the stem, and a flat head screwdriver to loosen the nut that holds the worn out washer in place. It's also a good idea to buy an assortment of different size washers to have available for any size job. Remember to turn off the water at the shut off before taking out the stem.

If the drip continues, rub your finger around the metal "seat" that screws into the hole where the washer is. If it is rough, this is what is causing the washer to wear out and it must be replaced. The tool to loosen this seat costs only a few dollars and will pay for itself the first time it is used. Take the old seat to the hardware store and they will find a replacement seat. There are many different size seats so one size does not fit all faucets.

The best way to avoid having to take each seat to the hardware store is to get in the habit of buying the same brand of faucet. I prefer single handle Delta faucets because they have one repair kit that covers almost all their faucets. There is also less wear and tear than a two handle faucet. Don't

skimp on the price of a faucet. The few extra bucks spent to get a brass faucet instead of a plastic one will pay for itself in less maintenance calls and longer life.

Toilets

Here are some of the more common problems associated with toilets and some simple repair procedures.

Tank is full of water but tank won't flush.

Check to see that the handle lift arm is not broken. If O.K. check to see if the chain is connected to the handle lift arm and also at the flapper.

Tank won't fill

Check to make sure the water is turned on at the supply line. If not the water, it may be a faulty ballcock valve or a stuck float assembly. Try to jiggle the float/arm. Corrosion may be causing it to stick just enough to prevent the ballcock water valve from opening.

Low water in the tank

The float must be reset. If there is an adjustment screw at the top, screw it down clockwise to move the arm up to get more water in the tank. The water level should be about an inch from the top of the tank. If there is no adjustable screw the float ball could be wedged against the wall of the toilet and not dropping to allow water in to refill.

Toilet runs constantly

Running toilets can double a water bill in three months. Since, in most areas, the sewer bill is based on water consumption, it too will double. Many toilet problems are associated with the parts located in the tank part of the toilet. Often it is a worn flap that no longer covers the hole in the upper tank.

These flaps wear out faster if the tenant has a toilet bowl cleaner jar in the tank. You know the one, it makes your toilet bowl sparkle and gives 10,000 flushes before it needs to be changed. Where does this water sit 99.9% of the time? Between flushes it is in the tank eating away the rubber gaskets. Before replacing the flapper, run steel wool or fine sandpaper over the hole opening to smooth any calcium buildup, so the flapper will seal tightly.

Another common problem is with the mechanism that controls the amount of water that enters the tank. If this floating ball or arm sticks, the toilet will continue to run into the overflow spout at the top. These items together can be purchased for less than $10. One such kit is Fluid Master, which is available in most hardware stores.

Poor flushing action

This problem is usually caused by not enough water in the tank. Try adjusting the float rod upward with either the adjusting screw on the ballcock assembly or by gently bending the float arm upward.

Flush tank leaks

Leaks at the ballcock connection need to have the nut inside and outside the tank tightened. This is where the water supply line enters the tank. Leaks at the two bolts on the bottom of the toilet can be stopped by holding a standard slot screwdriver on the nuts inside the tank while tightening the nuts under the tank with a wrench. Remember, porcelain cracks easily so be careful not to over tighten.

When replacing a toilet, always install a new wax ring over the hole in the floor where the toilet meets the floor. The wax ring is very cheap and will help seal the toilet to the floor.

If a toilet needs to be replaced, be aware that older toilets need approximately five gallons of water every time they are flushed. Newer models only require one and a half gallons per flush.

If you don't have individual shut off valves on each supply line, I strongly recommend that you install them. It can be most disconcerting to other tenants in the building if you have to turn off the water supply to the whole building each time you have a plumbing repair job. Look at every plumbing service call as an opportunity to, one by one, install these valves. In the long run you'll save time, money, and aggravation. Fellow tenants in the building will also appreciate it because their water isn't being shut off during each repair.

Broken J Traps

J traps are pipes that look just like the letter "J". They are part of the drain system and are under sinks. They are there to catch foreign materials before they clog up the drain farther below. Most have a hexagon type screw at the top and bottom of the J trap which can be removed to drain any water still in the pipe. This allows access to the bobby pins, clumps of hair, rings, and anything else small enough to fall in. Replacing a J trap can be done with an adjustable wrench by unscrewing both sides, removing, and installing the new one.

Clogged Drains and Toilets

When the J trap is removed and found to be clean it is usually a sign that the blockage is between the trap and the larger waste line to the street. If it is a grease or hair blockage, over-the-counter products will probably not work, but start with them anyway. Pour or sprinkle the drain opening product down the sink. If it is in crystal form, add some hot water to dilute and wait a few minutes. Run additional water and try using a plunger to free the blockage.

Another technique I have used consists of pouring a half a cup of baking soda and then a half a cup of vinegar down the drain. Wait a few minutes and pour boiling water slowly into the sink. If this doesn't work a metal snake should be used to dislodge the blockage. The snake is usually in a plastic holder that has a handle to turn the snake and clear the clog.

If this does not work, call a plumber, who will use an electric snake with a special cutting bit to remove the clog.

Help to prevent these clogs from occurring by installing a strainer in sinks and tubs to catch items before they get into the pipe. Many dozens of strainers can be bought for the cost of one plumber's visit.

Clogged toilets can often be unclogged with a plunger. If this doesn't work the next spot to check, before calling the plumber, is the bottom of the toilet where it meets the floor. Toys, tooth brushes, and apples are a few of the items I have found in this area. Fortunately, they become lodged at the base of the toilet and not down the waste line.

Start by turning off the water at the supply valve under the toilet. If there is no valve, the water must be turned off at the main valve. Use a small wrench to unscrew the water line attached to the toilet. Flush the toilet to remove the water in the upper tank. Use a plastic cup to remove as much water from the basin as possible. Next remove the two screws on either side of the tank that hold the toilet in place. Slowly pick up or tilt forward the whole toilet. This is easier with a helper so one can hold the toilet while the other checks the bottom for the obstruction. If the obstruction can not be seen, take the toilet outside and lay it on its side. Run a cord from the top to the bottom and tie a rag to the middle of the cord. Now you can pull the rag through the toilet, clearing any blockage. Since it is tied in the middle, you can go back and forth until everything is clear.

Replace with a new wax ring and set the toilet back down. Tighten the screws and re-attach the water line.

Shower Heads

Shower heads can be also a large drain on water consumption if the heads are old and do not restrict the water flow. Newer shower heads have a device built into the head that restricts the amount of water and this can save two gallons of water for every one minute the shower is on. For the average shower this means you will save 10 to 20 gallons of water.

Copper Piping

Copper piping can be replaced easily with a few tools and supplies. First turn off the water and drain the line. Use a pipe cutter to cut out the damaged section. A replacement piece with flanged ends will be needed to join the two pieces together. Before fitting the new piece, clean the ends with steel wool or emery paper. This helps the solder bond to the pipe. Flux should be placed on the joints to be soldered. For soldering, a small hand-held propane tank works well in most areas. After heating the pipe, apply the solder to the joint. If the solder doesn't melt right away, the pipe needs more heating. As soon as the solder starts to flow, remove the heat and move the solder around the joint, making sure all areas have been filled.

If one area is missed, it won't be discovered until there is water pressure in the line. At that point the line must be drained again, because solder won't adhere to copper if water is present in the pipe. If soldering a joint vertically, remember to heat the pipe above the joint. The solder will flow up into the joint.

Avoid soldering joints whenever possible by using compression fittings. The compression fitting is first placed over both ends of the pipe along with a smaller fitting on each end. Use two adjustable wrenches and screw them on tightly. Using Teflon tape on the threads, before tightening, is also a good idea. This can be done with water in the line and is easier than working with the solder.

Another piping material that is getting high praise is Polybutylene. It is flexible piping that cuts easily with a pocket knife or snips, and does not require flux or solder. Because it is flexible, fewer joints are needed to get around corners. The only drawback is that many staples are needed to keep it from sagging.

ELECTRICAL
Types of Outdoor Lighting

Electrical usage for common outdoor areas can be expensive. There are many different types of bulbs to consider.

Incandescent - The reflector or R type bulb will produce about twice as much light as a regular indoor bulb. If it has an aluminized reflector, or PAR type, the light output will be four times an indoor bulb. Both bulbs have a low initial cost, go on and off instantly, and provide a bright light for safety, security, and decoration. These bulbs last between 1,500 and 4,000 hours for the R type and 2,000 to 6,000 hours for the PAR type.

Quartz - An energy saving alternative to the incandescent bulbs because they are one and a half times more efficient. It produces a brighter light, lasts about 12,000 hours, fits a standard fixture, and goes on and off instantly.

Compact Florescent - Ideal for porch lights or lamp posts. This bulb is four times as energy efficient as an incandescent bulb. It has quick on/off capabilities with an average life of 10,000 hours. Be aware they may not fit every light fixture and they may not light up in very cold weather.

Metal Halide - Its bright white light makes it best for security lighting. They are five times as efficient as an incandescent bulb with an average life of 20,000 hours. The bulb does require six minutes to light up and will require a special fixture.

Pressure Mercury - Provides a very intense light with a golden hue that makes it a good light for security and showing off shrubbery. It is about three times as efficient as an incandescent bulb with an average life of 24,000 hours and will require five minutes to light up completely.

Pressure Sodium - Also provides a golden hue lighting that is seven times as energy efficient as a regular incandescent bulb. It requires three minutes to light up and will last 24,000 hours.

To increase the energy efficiency of all the bulbs mentioned, consider purchasing inexpensive automatic controls. Light sensitive photo cells turn lights on at dusk and off at sunrise. Motion sensors turn lights on whenever someone passes through the detector beam. A programmable timer, installed in the light switch, allows the light to go on and off many times a day.

The proper outdoor lighting can be an energy-efficient way to add to your tenant's feeling of safety, and increase the value of your investment.

Replacing Stove Elements

To replace electric stove elements, first turn off the electricity. Use a tester light to make sure the electricity is off; next, unscrew the two nuts to remove the burner. Some models will simply pull out. Check the wiring to each element while the lid to the stove is up. Look for any wires that are frayed, loose, or discolored. This is the perfect time to pick up new wire while replacing the element. Take the bad element, plus the make and model number of the stove to your local appliance parts store to order a replacement. If you're not sure what wire goes where or how to attach the element, have an electrician show you. Electricity, especially the 220V AC to a stove, is not something to work with if you don't know what you are doing.

Hot Water Heaters

Hot water heaters come in two basic styles, gas and electric. A gas fired water heater will have a flexible pipe coming into a box on the outside of the water heater, usually close to the bottom. This is the gas supply line and the gas control valve. Gas units also have a door at the bottom of the unit where you can look into the burner compartment and also light the pilot here. On top of the gas hot water heater will be a three and a half inch pipe that is the exhaust vent for the burned gasses created when the unit is on.

Electric hot water heaters do not have anything on the sides. Instead they have a wire coming into the top of the unit. This wire is enclosed in a metallic or vinyl sheet to keep it from becoming damaged. Electric water heaters are 220 volt appliances, so make sure electricity to the unit is turned off before doing any work. The water is heated by two elements that are inserted into the tank from the side. They are behind the two metal covers that are on the outside of the tank. When the covers are removed, you will see a small dial with numbers on it, wires attached to the dial and a large nut that goes over the threaded portion of the element. This treaded portion of the element is to hold it in place and seal the tank. The element on the bottom is rated for a higher wattage which means that it delivers more heat to the water when the thermostat calls for it. The element on the top is smaller and its job is to re-heat the water that has cooled down between usage in the house. Because there is no flame, electric water heaters do not need an exhaust vent.

Replacing Hot Water Tank Elements

Replacing heating elements in a hot water tank does take time. It is somewhat complicated but can be handled after reading a maintenance manual or watching a plumber do it once. In most cases the bottom element is the one that burns out first. This is because most areas of the country have a high degree of calcium in the water which solidifies over the years and falls to the bottom of the tank. As the calcium builds up, the element must work harder, causing it to burn out faster. Put a tester light on both elements before shutting off the electricity. The one that doesn't light up is the one that's burned out. If the heater is not on, because the water is up to temperature, shut off the electricity and use a continuity tester to check for the bad element. A burned out element will have no resistance and your tester light will not come on.

Next, shut off the water at the valve above the tank. Drain the water from the tank with a hose attached to the valve at the base of the heater. Opening the pressure relief valve on the side of the tank will help remove the water at a much faster pace. Turn off the electricity to the hot water tank and remove all wires attached to the element. Unscrew the four screws holding the element in place, or in some models, use a large socket wrench to unscrew the element.

Take the element to a hardware or appliance parts store with the make and model number of the tank to guarantee a match. Install the new element making sure the rubber gasket is snug against the opening before tightening. Attach the hot and neutral wires to the proper screws. Open the water valve and start filling the tank. DO NOT turn on the electricity until the tank is full of water. The element will burn out if not immersed in water.

Temperature and Pressure Relief Valve

Every hot water heater has one. They keep the water heater from exploding if the control valve or thermostat sticks in the "on" position. The drain for these valves must drain the water toward the floor and when possible drain it to the outside of the building.

HEATING

Nothing frustrates landlords more than to drive past their building during a cold winter and see half the tenants' windows open. Talk about watching your cash flow go out the window!

Always try to separate the heating expenses for each of the tenants in the building. This can be accomplished very easily if the heat is supplied by hot water baseboards. Install a flow meter and a circulator motor at the heater and add a thermostat in each apartment. The tenant can then be billed on a percentage basis based on the amount of hot water that passed through his flow meter. The tenants can include their heat payment with the rent.

Another alternative is a system that monitors the BTUs passing through the pipe to each apartment. Separate circulator motors and thermostats are not needed with this system. Usually the company installing the system will read the meters for you and bill the tenants directly.

If heating the building is unavoidably your responsibility, have the system serviced and maintained on a regular basis. Here are some other things you can do to cut expenses. There are systems on the market for hot air or water heat that allows the owner to control how high the tenant can turn his thermostat. A mercury ball is placed behind a locked thermostat box in each unit. All the tenant can do is turn the thermostat on or off. There is also a probe that monitors the outside temperature. If a tenant calls for heat and the temperature outside is warmer than inside, it will not turn on the heater.

I used this system on an old building that was not convertible and it cut my heating costs 40% the first year. I did have one ingenious tenant figure a way around the system though. I was using a mercury ball behind the locked thermostat box that was set for 70 degrees or under. This tenant liked a warmer unit so he built a small ledge out of a coat hanger above the locked thermostat. He placed ice cubes in a zip lock type bag and placed it on the wire ledge. This made the mercury in the thermostat think more heat was needed and it kept his unit nice and toasty—until I caught him.

AIR CONDITIONING

Preventative maintenance again is the key to the long life of air conditioners. Each spring the air filters must be cleaned to allow good circulation of air to the coils. If the air flow is blocked, the condenser will work harder and burn out sooner. Replacing the condenser is so expensive it might be a good idea to compare prices to replace the unit.

A common call from a tenant will be that the air conditioner is running but they're not getting cold. This could be from poor air circulation caused by an ice ring around the coil or the system could be low on freon. Both problems will require an air conditioning repairman. He will use special gauges to adjust the pressure and amount of freon your system requires.

THE TOOL BOX

A landlord's tool box is much different from a carpenter's tool box. A carpenter can build a house with a hammer, saw, tape measure, T-square, and nails. A landlord needs tools like a circuit tester, a hack saw, sink and toilet auger, a basin wrench, a pipe cutter, tub faucet socket set, caulking, and retractable Exacto knife. He further needs materials and supplies such as electrical tape, 3 in 1 oil, wood and metal screws, plumbing fittings, including a washer assortment, flux, solder, and caulk. A carpenter friend laughs every time he sees me with my converted fishing tackle box. He does admit that I have yet to be stumped for a tool when he helps me with repairs.

Unfortunately, not all repairs will be minor, and a repair man will have to be called. Use your landlording "team" list that should include an electrician, plumber, carpenter, appliance repair person, an exterminator, heating contractor, landscaper, snow removal person, handyman, trash and tree removal people to name a few. Word of mouth from satisfied customers is the best way to find the right person for each category. Pay these people promptly to encourage that the service will also be prompt.

REPAIRING DAMAGED WALLS

Depending on the age of the building the walls will be either plaster or drywall. Both are repaired using the same method. The older the building the more likely it is to have plaster walls. A way to determine whether a wall is plaster is to look at the area where a nail was driven to hang a picture. If it is chipped and has a repair area ten times larger than the nail, you have just discovered one of the disadvantages of plaster walls.

Small nails are fine for drywall, but whoever invented stickem wall hangers should be locked up for not putting a warning on the box: STICKEMS ARE HAZARDOUS WHEN USED ON SHEET ROCK WALLS. The departing tenant tries to pull one off and then stops because he quickly realizes the paper covering the sheet rock comes off with the sticker! The more he pulls off, the more will be deducted from his security deposit. He leaves the mess for you. What's worse, the tenant damaging your walls or you doing it yourself!

Stickems can be used on plaster walls. Nails are suitable for sheet rock and may be used in plaster walls if a small hole is first drilled to receive the nail.

When hanging anything over a few pounds, a stud should be found and used. Studs can be found by using a stud finder or by lightly tapping a hammer or your hand along the wall until the sound of the tapping changes. Try a small nail to test if you found one. Most drywall is either three eighths of an inch or half inch thick, so if after going in a half of an inch and if nothing solid is hit, move to a new spot and try again. Most studs are located 16 inches apart, so measuring from a doorway or a corner of a room should help locate a stud.

Holes under a quarter of an inch in diameter can be repaired by using spackle or joint compound. Spackle can be bought in cans as small as a few ounces or large as five gallon bucket.

Recently, I had a drywall job that I felt would need about a half a gallon of spackle. I decided to buy a gallon to cover myself. (Not literally.) While standing in line, I noticed the man in front of me had a five gallon bucket of spackle. He noticed my one gallon can and pointed to his price and then to my price. I almost dropped my gallon on his toe. The price was exactly the same. Needless to say I bought the five gallon bucket, and have used the free four gallons on many jobs since.

Remember to apply spackle in a thin coat, let it dry, lightly sand, and apply another coat. If put on too thick, it will crack in the drying process and look as bad as before starting the job.

If the repair area is smaller than two inches, apply a light coat of joint compound and then place drywall tape over the hole. Apply another light coat of compound and let dry. Sand with fine sandpaper and check for smoothness. If not smooth, repeat the step of applying a light coat and then sanding. Any hole larger than two inches should be cut out from stud to stud and replaced. A utility knife or a kiwi saw (drywall saw) will help open the area quickly and neatly. Be sure to cut to the middle of each stud because the new drywall will need to be nailed to the exposed portion of stud using drywall nails. Spackle around the edges and then place drywall tape over the top of the spackle. Using a putty knife, go over the tape to release any air pockets, and then place a layer of spackle over the tape. Let it dry for 24 hours and do a light sanding. Any uneven areas or exposed tape should be re-coated and allowed to dry.

REPAIRING BROKEN WINDOWS AND SCREENS

When replacing a glass window that is in an aluminum frame held together with screws, remove the screws on opposite corners. This will allow the frame to bend into two L-shaped pieces, which makes re-assembling easier when trying to align it with the new piece of glass. If the window that is to be replaced is in a door, window, storm door, or shower door, always replace it with Plexiglas or safety glass. Most states will hold you liable for injury sustained from broken glass if it can be proved that you replaced the glass with non-safety glass. It is a little more expensive, but not compared to a lawsuit. Furthermore, it is almost impossible to break, which will save the time and money in replacing it again. Plexiglas scratches easily, so make sure to use a mild dish detergent and a soft paper towel or cloth to clean.

Screens are much easier to replace once the proper technique is learned. Of all the property management books I have read, I don't remember any of them ever explaining how to replace a screen. I learned the hard way.

I would start by measuring the width of the screen needing replacement, and then I'd buy that width screening. After removing the old screen, I would place the new screening over the frame and start with a screw driver to force the rubber bead and new screen into the slots. As I pushed down, the opposite side of the screen would slide inside the slot area, which made it impossible to attach.

After struggling with many a screen this way, I mentioned my problem to my hardware friend. He said he had to repair one and invited me to watch. I didn't have very long to watch as he was done before I would have had the first side lined up. Here is the secret. Buy screening a few inches wider than what is needed. Lay it over the frame and push the rubber bead into the slot with a tool called a screen roller. It has one roller on either end about the size of a quarter, with a four inch piece of wood or plastic in the middle. The bead can literally be rolled into the slot. After all the sides are set with the bead, take a sharp utility knife and place it just outside the rubber bead and trim away the excess screen. This process will work on aluminum and fiberglass screening.

MORE KNOWLEDGE = BETTER CASH FLOW

I learned early, when negative cash flow was a common word in my vocabulary, that the more knowledge I could gain, the less money I needed to spend to hire a repair person. Repairmen enjoy talking about their area of expertise, and will gladly answer questions as long as they are not kept from completing the job.

There will not be many minor repairs you won't be able to do after observing them being done once. Some examples are: installing a garbage disposal, replacing a window pane, adding a new belt for a dryer, priming a heater that ran out of oil, grouting ceramic tiles, installing hot and cold water lines for a washer and dryer hookup.

The first time doing the repair will take longer to complete, but you will learn from your mistakes and will do the job faster the next time. Don't forget your friends with expertise in certain areas. If you must pay someone to do a job, it might as well be a friend. Help them with the job and thereby gain valuable hands on experience yourself.

Another excellent source for free advice for repairs is your local hardware store owner. He always seems to have some simple solution for what is often perceived to be a monumental problem.

CHAPTER 5

HELPFUL MAINTENANCE TIPS

A problem or emergency is not a problem if you're prepared for it!
— Nick Koon

If you can dream it - you can do it.
— Walt Disney

Ignoring maintenance is a good example of pay out now or pay out even more later.

At some point in this business you will find some of the following conditions in your rentals and maybe even your own home. Here are some common, over the counter supplies, to help with cleaning or removing stains.

MAINTENANCE TIPS

Wallpaper - Fill a spray bottle with hot water and ½ cup of fabric softener. Spray the walls and wait twenty minutes. Watch the wallpaper easily peel away.

Mildew - Spray one part bleach with two parts water in a small sprayer and spray all walls, grout between tub tiles, shower stall doors, and acoustical tiles. Wear protective gloves and goggles and leave immediately after spraying. Provide as much ventilation as possible. Leave on for one hour and wash off with a wet sponge.

Open Drains - Pour ½ cup of baking soda down the clogged drain and then ½ cup of vinegar. Wait a few minutes and slowly pour boiling water into the sink. If it starts to clear, try plunging and more hot water.

Grease Coated Oven Racks - Fill a tub with hot water and add crystal Drano. Let the dirty racks stand in the solution for at least a half hour. Rinse or wash in the dishwasher.

Vinyl Floors - Mix ⅓ cup of laundry detergent with ⅓ cup of crystal Drano with COLD water. Pour on the floor and spread around with a mop or a broom. Let it stand for at least 20 minutes and mop it up. It will remove wax build up, dirt, soap scum, and shoe scuffs.

Odors in Vacant Units - Place odor fresheners or containers of baking soda around the unit. The baking soda works well directly on carpet that has strong pet odors. Charcoal briquettes will also draw stale smells from units. To make sure the unit smells fresh before a prospective tenant arrives, place half a lemon in the stove and turn on low.

Odors from Refrigerators and Freezers When Electricity is Off - Instead of baking soda try used coffee grounds. Place in a tray and leave in refrigerator until all odors are gone. Another option is to wipe down the inside walls with diluted vanilla extract.

Food Streaked Dishwasher - Place Tang or another orange drink that has citric acid in the detergent cup. Run it through a complete cycle without dishes.

Chandeliers - Start by placing plastic on the floor or hang an old umbrella upside down from the chandelier. Mix 2 teaspoons of rubbing alcohol to one pint of water in a spray bottle and spray the chandelier.

Shower Heads - If they become clogged with mineral deposits put some hot vinegar in a small plastic bag and secure it around the shower head with a rubber band. Let the head soak for a half hour.

Skin Cleaner - Remove oil based stains, paint, and tar from your skin with vegetable oil. It leaves no irritation or smell and is environmentally friendly.

Garbage Disposal Odor - Pour in lemon juice.

Linoleum Floor Cleaner - Mop with a mixture of ½ cup vinegar in a bucket of warm water. The vinegar odor will go away shortly after the floor dries.

Door Flipper - Need to paint both sides of a door? Drive 3″ nails into the top and bottom of the door in the four corners. Place the door, resting on the nails, over two saw horses. When completed painting one side use the nails to turn over the door to paint the other side. Both sides get painted at the same time without runs.

23

Good-bye Groundhogs - Dump used kitty litter down the hole to their burrows. They will choose to move elsewhere.

Windows - mix two teaspoons of vinegar into a quart of water for sparkling windows.

Ceramic Tiles - mix ¼ cup vinegar, ⅓ cup ammonia, ½ cup baking soda and seven cups warm water. Store the solution in a spray bottle.

Bathtubs - For difficult bathroom stains, fill the tub with water and pour in pool chlorine and let sit. Some stains may be lifted with bleach. Put a paper towel over the stain and soak it with bleach. This will allow you to soak the stain, and let the bleach do its work.

Toilets - Efferdent™ tablets dropped in the toilet will help remove mineral deposits.

To clean out the tank of calcium deposits and rust, empty of water and fill with Coke or Pepsi. Another one is to turn off the water, drain the bowl and allow Lysol toilet bowl cleaner to remain in the bowl for at least two hours.

Decals - soak them in mineral spirits for a few minutes and then scrape off.

Pet Smells - Before replacing carpet that is not worn but just has pet smells, spray on OdorXit in the proper dosage. This product can be purchased by calling 1-800 ODORXIT or check out their web site at http://odorxit.com

Defrosted Freezer - After defrosting, spray it with a non-stick spray. That way the job will be easier to do the next time.

Carpet Dents - When furniture is removed the carpet is dented. Put an ice cube on each dent. The slowly released water will fill up and expand the carpet fibers without making a mess.

New Drywall - Use latex primers on newly finished drywall. Oil primers can't conceal the difference in texture between the joint compound and the drywall surface.

Light Bulbs - Before installing a light bulb put a light coat of petroleum jelly on the threads before screwing in. This will cut down on the risk of the bulb breaking in your hands.

Paint Brushes - Refurbish paint brushes that are stiff with old paint by soaking them in hot vinegar, then washing them in hot sudsy water. Use fabric softener in the final rinse water when finished painting. It will keep the bristles soft and pliable.

Painting windows - Paint will not stick to window glass that has been rubbed with a sliver of soap.

Burn Spots in Carpet - Small burn spots can be trimmed out if your carpet isn't woven. Use small sharp scissors to snip the fibers below the burn.

To hide larger burn areas trim fibers from an out-of-the-way spot, spread a thin layer of silicon adhesive down onto the backing and gently press the fibers into it. Let stand overnight and then fluff them up with your fingers. Trim them down to the same level as the surrounding carpet.

If you need to patch a damaged area, cut out a square of carpet from a remnant or an out-of-the-way area. When laying the patch in place make sure the fibers are running in the same direction as the existing carpet. Place the patch over the stains and cut around it with a very sharp knife. Pull up the carpet and anchor the patch with double-sided carpet tape. Slip the tape halfway under the existing carpet on all sides and press the patch in place. Set books over the patch for a while to make sure there is good contact.

REMOVE STUBBORN STAINS

Oil Stains from Concrete - Rub dishwasher soap on the oil stain. Let it soak in for a few minutes and hose off. If that doesn't work try an engine cleaner from an auto supply store. Let it sit for ten minutes and hose with water.

Oil Stains on Carpet - If the stain is fresh, it can sometimes be absorbed with flour. Sprinkle on the flour and let it sit. Brush and repeat again with fresh flour. It the flour doesn't work a cleaning fluid such as Energine can be applied to a damp sponge and blotted with a paper towel.

Coffee - Saturate a cloth with a mild liquid detergent and blot the stain with it. It that doesn't work, blot the stain with an equal mixture of white vinegar and water. Let it dry and repeat if necessary.

Lipstick - Dampen a cloth with dry cleaning fluid which is available at most grocery or drug stores. Dab it on the lipstick. Another way to remove lipstick is to rub the stain with a solution of non-chlorinated bleach and water.

Crayon - Like lipstick, it's water-based. Spray WD-40 light-weight oil and wipe off. Otherwise use the lipstick method.

Blood - Soak the spot in cold water. Make a paste of water and laundry powder. Rub the paste into the stain and then rinse. Repeat until stain is removed.

If the blood has dried, clean off as much as possible then cover the area with equal parts of meat tenderizer and cold water. Let it sit for a half hour and then sponge off with cold water.

Ink - Rub the spot several times with rubbing alcohol. Rinse the stain with a mixture of dish detergent and water. If the ink is still wet sprinkle on salt and let the salt absorb the ink.

Red Wine - Make a paste of table salt and white vinegar. Apply the paste to the stain. Allow it to dry, then brush it off or vacuum it.

White Wine - Apply ginger-ale or 7-up to the stain. Sponge off the area.

Marble - Try lemon juice and salt on the stains.

Pet Stains - Flush the spot with a mixture of water and mild dish detergent. Let the mixture sit for a few minutes, then sponge it up. Don't brush the carpet because you might damage the fabric.

WATER CONSUMPTION

The most common repair for landlords, as well as lost revenue if you're paying for water, revolves around plumbing. A dripping faucet or toilet flapper that won't seal tightly can drain away your cash flow.

How Much Water Do You Use?

The average household uses about 300 gallons of water per day with the average daily use per person at 110 gallons a day. Here is how some of our most commonly used items break down per day as reported by the U.S. Environmental Protection Agency.

Activity	Typical Use
Washing Machine	40 gallons
Bath	35 gallons
5 Minute Shower	25 gallons
Doing dishes in sink with water running	20 gallons
Running dishwasher	11 gallons
Flushing toilet	4 gallons
Brushing teeth with water running	2 gallons

Think very strongly about replacing old toilets with the new 1.6 gallons per flush toilets. If the average toilet uses 4 gallons, you should be able to cut your water bill in half just from toilet flushings. It will pay for the toilet the first year. Even if the tenant is paying for the water, change over anyway and save many precious gallons. If you decide not to change toilets, at least put a plastic container or a few bricks in the tank so it will fill with less water.

A fully loaded dishwasher will use less water than if doing the dishes by hand under running water. If washing dishes in the sink, plug it up.

Showers account for one fourth of a home's water use, so consider installing a low-flow shower head which not only cuts down on water costs but also hot water utility bills.

A faucet running at medium flow can send two gallons down the drain every minute. Turn the tap off when brushing teeth, shaving and doing dishes. Aerators on faucets can also decrease water use.

LEAD PAINT

In 1978 the federal government banned the use of lead-based paint in residential buildings, lead in gasoline, and lead in soldered cans. Unfortunately the vast majority of the United States housing stock was built prior to 1978 and so contains some lead-based paint.

This becomes a problem for landlords who own these homes and rent them to families with children. If the child shows high levels of lead in their blood, the chances are very strong that the landlord will be sued and will lose.

When the law first came out a few states said that all housing stock with lead paint had to be abated. This means anything that has paint on it must be removed and replaced. All drywall, doors, windows, and trim had to come out and be replaced. Many inner city landlords quickly discovered that to abate their row home it would cost over $30,000 and the house was only worth $15,000. When landlords started quit claiming their deeds back to the city, the politicians finally realized they had gone to far. Now, in most areas of the country landlords with homes that have lead-based paint must encapsulate (paint over) all areas.

As more information comes out we are learning some very interesting statistics. In July of 1994, the Journal of the American Medical Association reported that "presumptions alleging lead-based paint in older homes had been a leading source of childhood lead exposure were proven wrong." The report found that children with lead in their blood exceeding a level of concern fell dramatically, by 90% over the preceding 15 years. They hailed that "as a major public health success. The major cause of the observed decline in blood levels was most likely the removal of 99.8% of lead from gasoline and the removal of lead from soldered cans," the article concluded.

From 1988–1991 there was a major decline in lead exposure throughout the entire population, among all ages, sexes, races, areas of residence and income levels. Of the 19 million children under the age of six years of age who are most at risk from lead poisoning 1.7 million, or about 8.9% of that group, had elevated exposure to lead. While in the 1970s, before lead came out of paint and gas, about 17 million or 88.2% of all young children had serious lead exposure. It became obvious that exposure to lead-based paint in homes had little do with the improvements that were noted.

The Journal concluded that "the reduction of lead in gasoline is most likely the greatest contributor to the observed decline in blood lead levels during the period of the survey." Since gasoline lead had entered food through multiple pathways, it is difficult to make a quantitative estimate of the reduction in food lead that resulted from decreasing lead in gasoline.

So if children have high levels of lead today and they are not getting it from eating paint chips, where is it coming from? It comes indirectly from the lead that was in our gas prior to 1978. As lead spewed out our exhaust pipes it did not go up to the ozone level of the atmosphere but back into the earth. The half life of lead is thousands of years so it just sits on the surface and waits to be picked up by shoes, and dirty hands. The mud in the shoes dries and falls into the carpet and becomes a fine dust which is stirred up by walking on the carpet, the vacuum cleaner and even the dog. Babies' hands are constantly touching things with this dust and into the mouth the hands go. With proper diet the risk can be greatly minimized. Washing baby's hands as well as one's own hands before eating can also be a big help.

It is interesting to note that in 1978 Japan also banned lead from their gasoline, but prior to and after this ban, the Japanese people never had high levels of lead found in their blood. It has been concluded the reason why is because they take off their shoes before entering the house and children are trained from an early age not to eat anything without first washing their hands.

WORKING WITH CONTRACTORS

Anyone who is involved in rehab projects will someday want to sub-out some of the work. Here are some things to know and get before hiring a subcontractor.

1. Workman's Compensation - In the event the contractor does not have his own insurance, you as the "employer" may be liable for damages in the event there is an injury while the contractors "employee" is working on the job. When in doubt, call your insurance carrier for direction.

2. Know who will be working with the contractor you hire. Are they going to subcontract some of the job? If yes, and those subcontractors don't get paid by the person you hired, you could be subject to liens on the property. A good policy would be to have a written contract that spells out who is doing what work.

3. Don't advance money before work begins. Beware of contractors who say they will not begin work until they have been paid so many dollars. You should only pay for work performed. A contract can spell out partial payments, called draws for work that has been completed.

4. Get everything you want completed in writing. Even the best memories fade. A good policy is to agree on a tentative schedule, agree on the quality of work to be performed and be specific on payment terms.

CHAPTER 6

KNOW THE LAW - DON'T DISCRIMINATE

My goal is to help people make wise financial choices. When you make the wrong choice, you never lose just a dollar. You always lose a dollar plus all future production of that dollar.

— Jimmy Napier

If you first don't succeed, you will get a lot of unsolicited advice from people who didn't succeed either.

The law of Landlord-Tenant governs the rental of commercial and residential property in the United States. It is composed of state statutory and common law. Most states have based their statutory law on either the Uniform Residential Landlord and Tenant Act (URLTA) or the Model Residential Landlord-Tenant Code.

The basis of the legal relationship between a landlord and a tenant is grounded in both contract and property law. The tenant has property interest in the land and the improvements upon it for a given period of time. The length of tenancy may be for a given period of time, for an indefinite period of time, terminable at any time by either party (at will), or at sufferance if the agreement has been terminated, but the tenant refuses to leave (hold over). If the tenancy is for a specific period of time or indefinite, the tenant has the right to possess the land, restrict others, including the landlord from entering upon it. The landlord-tenant agreement may eliminate or limit these rights. This is usually spelled out in a landlord-tenant lease and is subject to the concepts of contract law.

Housing codes were established to ensure that residential rental units were habitable at the time of rental and during tenancy. Depending on the state, housing code violations may allow a tenant to withhold rent. The habitability of a residential unit is ensured by warranties of habitability which are covered by common and statutory law. A breach of the warranty of habitability within the lease may constitute constructive eviction which allows the tenant to withhold rent, repair the problem and deduct the cost from the rent that is owed or recover damages.

Unless the lease says otherwise, the tenant has a duty to pay rent. Rent acceleration clauses that cause all rent to become due if the tenant breaches a provision of the lease are common in both residential and commercial leases. Self-help as a method of eviction is generally restricted. Landlords are also restricted from evicting tenants in retaliation of action the tenant took in regards to enforcing a provision of the lease.

FAIR HOUSING GUIDELINES FOR LANDLORDS

The first federal law to be passed concerning Fair Housing Guidelines was the Civil Rights Acts of 1866, which prohibited all racial discrimination in the sale or rental of real estate both public and private. This law was extended by the Civil Rights Act of 1968 (commonly known as the Fair Housing Act). The CRA of 1968 has the added force of having been upheld by the Supreme Court.

This law prohibits discrimination based on Race, Color, Religion, Sex, or National Origin. The Fair Housing Amendments Act of l988 was enacted to re-enforce the above mentioned items and to extend non-discrimination to include the handicapped and familial status. It is a violation to print or publish any notice, statement or advertisement regarding the sale or rental of a dwelling that indicates any preferences based on the seven categories.

Landlords can no longer write ads specifying no children or ask about children when talking on the phone.

The U.S. Department of Housing and Urban Development (HUD) publishes a list of words, phrases, and symbols they say conveys, either overtly or tacitly, discriminatory preferences or limitations. Using any of these words, phrases, and symbols may violate the act. All newspapers have this list and will not let you use these words when advertising with them.

What are the HUD guidelines for number of people per bedroom? As of this printing, it is two people per bedroom. If a mother with two children wants to rent a one bedroom unit they would be over the limit. If a couple with three children wants to see a two bedroom, recommend that they search for a three bedroom.

The question always arises as to what to do if you have a two bedroom and a couple with two teenagers of the opposite sex call. Must they look for a three bedroom? HUD says no. Mom and Dad could be on a sofa bed in the living room and each kid has a bedroom.

If the building is multi-family you cannot limit families with children to a certain floor or areas within the housing complex. Policies outlining quiet hours and limiting noise should be contained in the rules and regulations and must be applicable to all residents. All tenants, including the children, should be made aware that they are responsible for their actions and all guests actions.

Areas considered dangerous to children, such as saunas, should be listed in the lease as off limits without an adult present. Pool hours should be reasonable for the use and enjoyment of ALL tenants.

Items from a tenant's unit are the responsibility of the tenant and should not be left in common areas or where they might create a hazard to other tenants (stairs, hallways, sidewalks). Be careful about singling out children's toys as not being allowed in common areas, and then allow items such as folding chairs, umbrellas, towels, etc. of adults in common areas.

FAIR HOUSING CREDIT REPORTING ACT

In September 1997 amendments to the Fair Housing Credit Reporting Act took effect. It strengthened provisions for privacy and defined more clearly the responsibilities and liabilities of businesses that obtain consumer reports. The term "consumer report" covers credit, public record searches, employment and residence verification reports.

The old act allowed only the federal government to enforce the act, but under the new law, both state and local governments can investigate and enforce the law. As a result, owners and managers have a greater chance of being prosecuted for any violations. In addition, owners and managers can be held liable for actual and possibly punitive damages if laws are violated intentionally, or employers obtain credit reports without permission.

Here are six points to be sure to use to stay in compliance with the Fair Credit Reporting Act.

1. To run a credit report you need a permissible purpose. For multi-family apartments this means you can only obtain a consumer credit report in connection with the lease application or an attempt to collect a bad debt.

2. Always have the tenant sign the application which gives you permission to run a credit and police check.

3. Do not consider information that is more than seven years old. This covers criminal, credit, and eviction. Credit bureaus will not provide older information except for certain bankruptcies that can be reported up to ten years.

4. You can not pull a credit report on yourself and can be prosecuted for doing so. You may obtain a copy of your credit file directly from each major credit reporting agency for a small fee.

5. Credit reports received in an office should be held in the strictest confidence. Access to these reports should be limited to only a few key employees. Once completed these credit reports should be filed in an area that is secured and locked.

6. Owners and employees should be trained how to read the credit reports, especially considering the sensitive nature of credit data and the civil and criminal liability for misuse of this information.

AVOID RENTAL DISCRIMINATION

How does the government check to make sure you are not discriminating in your rental practices? They hire people called "testers" to try to catch you discriminating. They could be working from complaints about a specific landlord received in their office, or doing cold calls from ads or open houses.

These testers usually work in teams. One team might be a minority looking at your unit in a non-minority neighborhood. If you tell them it was just rented and then tell a non-minority team a half hour later that the unit is available, they will have made their case.

The testers also might call on your ad and disguise their voices the first time to sound like a minority person and then call back a half hour later not as a minority-sounding person and see how the information is presented.

Avoid any chance of someone accusing you of discrimination by complying with what the law requires you to do anyway. Give every one the same information and treat every one equally.

Also be aware that, one out of every eleven people in the United States is classified as handicapped. This group is the largest source of discrimination complaints. If you have any doubts about what might be discriminating, contact a lawyer to learn the law before saying or writing something you will regret later. **Prejudice is a belief, but discrimination is an act or conduct that can be regulated by law.**

Here is a good statement to include on the bottom of your rental application:

This apartment and its owner/managing agent, does not discriminate on the basis of race, creed, color, sex, religion, national origin, handicap or familial status. We do have certain criteria for rental which applies equally to all applicants.

THINGS TESTERS LOOK FOR

If a prospective tenant feels he has been subject to discrimination, he can go to a local, state, or federal fair housing agency. Two testers could be calling and asking questions or be calling to set up appointments to come out to your building. They will pose as prospective tenants, will probably be wired, and will lie when you ask them if they are testers. The job is to see if you are saying the same thing to ALL prospective tenants.

For example, let's say a parent with a child feels you discriminated against them based on familial status. If you do any of the following actions, you may be charged with discrimination. Remember, be consistent. Say the same thing to everyone.

- Married Tester (MT) is not told a credit check or co-signer will be required, but Single Parent Tester (SPT) is, yet they have the same qualifications.
- The SPT must meet tougher guidelines than the MT in order to quality for the same rental.
- The MT is shown/told about more rentals that the SPT.
- The MT is offered an application; the SPT is not.
- The MT is shown a more desirable home, different unit or location than SPT, after each asked for the same type.
- SPT is asked extensive questions about future marital status and length or type of employment. MT is not.
- MT with no children is told a unit is available. A (SPT) with a child is told there are no vacancies, just a waiting list.
- The MT is given a better sales pitch including extra privileges (storage, parking or pool) and the SPT is not or perhaps given information which the ordinary person would interpret as meaning the place is not good for them.
- The MT is told that it takes a day to do the credit check, the SPT is told it takes three days or maybe up to a week.
- The MT is quoted lower rent or deposit prices or better deals than the SPT, yet they have the same qualifications.

Consistency and fairness will help to keep you away from a discrimination charge.

EXEMPTIONS TO THE FAIR HOUSING ACT

Some exemptions to the Fair Housing Act that landlords should know:

1. A private individual who offers single family homes for rent is exempt from this act if the individual owns three or fewer such homes and does not:
   - use discriminatory advertising
   - use a real estate agent to rent the unit
   - sell more than one house during a two year period in which the owner was not the most recent resident
2. An owner who rents units in a two to four unit building, lives on site, and does not use discriminatory advertising.
3. Religious organizations who own and rent units to member of their religion are exempt as long as the religion is not based on race, color, or national origin.

Note that these exemptions apply only to residential dwellings and not to property rented for commercial or non-residential purposes. But some states have passed statutes that have non-residential and commercial rentals falling under the same guidelines as residential leases. As always, check with your local authorities.

FAIR HOUSING QUIZ

See how well you do on these True or False questions:

1. There is no time limit for filing a Fair Housing Complaint.
2. The definition of handicap includes former drug addicts.
3. Ad in paper says Perfect Community for Singles—no kids.
4. Anyone who feels they have been injured as a result of a discriminatory housing practice can file a complaint.
5. Liabilities for non-compliance with Fair Housing Law are limited to actual damages, not punitive damages.

ANSWERS TO FAIR HOUSING QUIZ

1. False - The time limit for a HUD occurrence is one year. Federal Court is within two years of the occurrence, excluding any time that HUD has been processing the claim.
2. True - The term "handicap" does not include current illegal users of or addiction to a controlled substance.
3. False - This ad would be discrimination under the category of familial status because it limits singles and excludes families with children.

4. True - Anyone who believes they have been injured by a discriminatory housing practice can file a complaint.
5. False - If a charge is heard in Federal Court, a judge or jury can impose punitive damages as well as actual damages. There is no limit to the amount of punitive damage awards.

OCCUPANCY QUALIFYING CRITERIA

The easiest way to be sure you will not be caught discriminating is to set up occupancy qualifying criteria that will be used on all prospective tenants. 95% of landlords do not have written qualifying standards and this is why it is so easy for the Fair Housing Council in your area to accuse you of discrimination. The easiest way to avoid this situation is to have written criteria to use to screen all prospective tenants.

Since the law says you must accept the first applicant that meets your qualifying criteria, it makes sense to have your qualifying standards high. If no one qualifies then you can accept the one who comes closest to meeting your criteria, which will probably be the one you want to accept anyway.

This criteria should not be given to prospective tenants with the application. It is an internal document that will appear only if sued for discrimination to prove that all applicants were screened using the same qualification criteria.

Use the Prospective Tenant Checklist form to be sure that all areas of the screening process have been completed. If there are four applications returned, make sure the one you have chosen has the highest number of points based on the written criteria.

The written qualifying criteria and checklist should be modified to meet your specific requirements. This is why blanks have been left on the Rental Standard For Tenant Selection form. Read the form and fill in the blanks with what you would use for standards. Now read some examples of rental standards that would be difficult for any prospective tenant to pass. If they do, you probably will want to rent to them.

RENTAL STANDARDS FOR TENANT SELECTION

A. Income
1. Gross monthly income must meet or exceed 20 percent of the rental amount.
2. Married couples income will be combined. Singles must qualify individually.
3. Singles income not meeting the required income will need a co-signer who owns real estate in the county where the property is located.

4. Same source of income for 60 months with the same company. If same income source is less than two years, previous income sources must be verified.
5. Self employed applicants must provide two years of tax returns.
6. Provide two recent pay stubs to verify the income requirements.

B. Credit History
1. Credit report showing "No Record" will only be accepted if applicant was a student in the past twelve months or if applicant can provide a co-signer who owns real estate.
2. Credit rating must be no higher than a "2" for the past three years. Two is any credit that is 60 days past due. Credit reporting score must be 600 or higher.
3. Must not show any bankruptcy, unpaid judgments or collections.
4. Disputed negative credit due to legal separation or divorce will require verification through an attorney or official court document, relieving the applicant of legal responsibility for the outstanding unpaid debt.

C. Rental History
1. A minimum of five years of acceptable rental history or acceptable home ownership for three years.
2. Verification of rental history or mortgage payment history.
3. Sufficient notice was given to current landlord. No returned checks, late payments, or noise complaints filed with current or previous landlord.
4. No late rent payments or returned checks within a 12 month period.
5. No unpaid damages or outstanding utility bills.
6. Rent at current residence must be within 10% of my rent after adjusting for utility costs.

D. Application
1. Was filled out completely and signed by all parties over 18 years old.
2. Number of occupants is four or less and can prove valid renters insurance.
3. All information is confirmed to be correct.

E. Co-Signer
1. Must be a relative of applicant and live in the county of the property.
2. Must show proof of ownership of real estate (deed) for the property.

3. Must be willing to co-sign the lease.
4. All parties listed on the deed must be willing to co-sign.

PROTECT YOURSELF WITH DOCUMENTATION

Throughout this book there are almost 50 property management forms that have been designed to help leave a paper trail with tenants. When appearing in court with a tenant, you'd better have everything documented because if a decision comes down to your word verses the tenant, the tenant usually wins. As owner of the property, the judge will look to you to be the one required to be more accountable.

Document everything. After a phone conversation with a tenant who promises to repair a broken window or remove a pet in the next 48 hours, have the tenant put that fact in writing. If they don't, then you must document it and get them to sign it. Here is what could happen if it isn't documented. The tenant promises to remove the pet but doesn't, while the landlord continues to receive and cash rent payments. Weeks, maybe months go by, and you are tired of waiting for the pet to be removed and start eviction proceedings. In court the tenant or his attorney will assert that no such promise was made and that you continued to accept rent payments. Since the landlord continued to accept rent payments, his action (or inaction) implied that there was not a problem with how the tenant was fulfilling his lease obligations, even though the actions may be in conflict with the written lease. The tenant feels the terms were acceptable based on the landlord's action. The landlord has now waived his right to evict for reasons that were earlier apparent.

Anytime there is a change to the lease or both parties agree to a change, document it. Send the tenant a letter similar to this one.

> Dear Tenant, This letter is to confirm our conversation last night in which you agreed to remove the dog that is not supposed to be in the apartment. You understand that if the dog is not out within five days, you will pay an extra $10 a day for each day the pet remains. If this is not how you remembered the conversation, please contact me within 24 hours of receiving this note. Send the note regular mail as well as certified mail. Note at the bottom of the letter that it was being mailed regular and certified mail.

HOW TO ANSWER PROSPECTIVE TENANTS' TOUGH QUESTIONS

How would you answer the following questions? How many blacks live in your complex?. Do you have a separate building for children because I work nights and need a quiet environment

---

Rental Standards for Tenant Selection

Income
1. Monthly income must be ____% of the rent plus utilities.
2. Married couples qualify with income combined. Singles must qualify individually.
3. Source of income can be verified and has been the same for ____ months.
4. If current source of income is for less than ____ months, previous income sources must be verified.
5. If self employed, must submit two years of tax returns.
6. Provide two recent pay stubs to verify employment and income.
7. Can pay security deposit and rent requested in full prior to occupancy.
8. Provide a co-signer who owns real estate, if needed to qualify.

Credit History
1. Credit report has no negative entries: late payments, bankruptcy, charge offs, closed accounts, judgments, evictions, or collections.
2. Credit reporting score must be ____ or higher.
3. Can provide ____ credit references.
4. Negative credit due to legal separation or divorce will require documentation from an attorney and/or court records showing applicant is not responsible for any unpaid debt.

Rent History
1. Has resided at current address for more than ____ months.
2. Can provide name and phone number of current and previous landlords.
3. Gave proper notice to current landlord.
4. Has not received written notices of any kind from current or previous landlord concerning neighbor or fellow tenant complaints, police reports, violations of any lease terms, etc.
5. No late payments or returned checks in the past ____ months.
6. Current rent is within 10% of your rent after adjusting for utilities.

Application
1. Filled out application completely.
2. All parties signed application.
3. All information on application is found to be correct.
4. Provided proof of license, tags, shots, etc. for pets.
5. Number of vehicles fits the size of property and parking availability.
6. Number of occupants does not exceed HUD standards for the number of bedrooms.
7. Plans to use premises for other than living purposes.
8. Carries a renter's insurance policy. If there is a waterbed or a pet, a rider must be attached to policy.
9. Provided sources to confirm information requested on the application.

Co-Signer
1. Must be relative of applicant and live in same county as your property.
2. Must show proof of ownership (deed).
3. All persons named on the deed must be willing to co-sign the lease.

39

during the day? Do you have a non-smoking building, because I am allergic to smoke? Do you have a building that is mostly Catholics, so we can pray together? How is crime in this area? Is this a safe neighborhood? Tell me everything you know about the tenants above me and on either side because I do not want to be near someone playing music until 3 AM. If you decided to answer any of these questions you could be in big trouble.

Not only must we be conscious of advertising that might list one of the seven protected classes, but we must also be aware that what we say to prospective tenants questions could also get us into trouble.

Some general rules. Do not volunteer information about race, religion, color, nationality, sex, family status or handicap of residents even when asked directly or indirectly. Remember the person asking the question might be a tester setting you up (legally) for a fair housing lawsuit.

If a prospective tenant asks you questions that you can not answer because of Fair Housing laws, tell them that you or your company is an equal opportunity renter, that you welcome anyone who completes an application, and meets the qualification standards of the company.

If they persist, stand firm. Tell them it would be against, not only your company's policy, but also fair housing guidelines, to discuss racial makeup.

Do not say, "I'm sorry, we do not keep those figures," because then they will ask you to give them a ball park figure. The ball park number could come back to haunt you later. Do not give out names of other tenants who are the same race as the prospect and tell them to contact them. And do not fall for the line "You can tell me—it is just between the two of us."

CRIMINAL HISTORY
OF PROSPECTIVE TENANTS

One of the most misunderstood questions is whether or not a landlord can deny tenancy based on an applicants criminal record. The long and short of it is, you can deny tenancy as long as you are careful and have well established guidelines.

The law that governs this area is the Federal Fair Housing Act. Even though the federal law does not mention specifically "criminal history," as a landlord you will want to ensure that there is no question to the legality of your actions if you choose to deny tenancy based on the applicant's past criminal record.

The most important section of the Fair Housing Act is section 3604(f)((9), which states, "Nothing in this subsection requires that a dwelling be made available to an individual whose tenancy would constitute a direct threat to the health or safety of other individuals or whose tenancy would result in substantial physical damage to the property of others." It is this section that landlords use to deny tenancy based on a person's criminal record.

Before denying tenancy due to an applicant's criminal background, be sure to take the following safeguards:

- Do not automatically deny tenancy just because the applicant tells you that he has a criminal record. Make an "independent and objective" evaluation of the actual threat that the tenancy of the applicant would pose on other tenants and their property, and make the decision to accept or deny on that investigation.
- Do not talk to just the applicant when asking for details of the crime he was convicted of. Contact the police department where the applicant was convicted. Talk to the applicant's parole officer, the prosecutor's office, the prison or jail where the applicant served his sentence for details of the applicant's full criminal history.
- Do not deny the applicant tenancy for every crime they have committed. Several crimes do not fall within the requirements of the Fair Housing Act, including most misdemeanors, simple possession of drugs or other controlled substances, fraud, bad checks, vehicular homicide and DWI. Make sure that the crime the applicant has committed is one that fits within the protective framework of the Fair Housing Act. Examples of crimes that will most often allow you to deny tenancy are murder, assault, robbery, rape, arson, child abuse and sale of drugs.

WHAT CAN YOU ASK ABOUT A DISABILITY?

The general rule of thumb is that you can not ask a person if they have a disability or ask a question that would require the person to disclose a medical condition or medical history. This also applies to asking if an applicant's family member has a disability. Here are some questions NOT to ask.

1. Have you ever been treated by a psychiatrist?
2. Have you ever been hospitalized for a disability?
3. Can you live independently?

Here are some disability questions that a housing provider CAN ask.

1. If the person has applied for housing designated for individuals with a certain types of disabilities, the housing provider may ask the person if they have a qualified disability.
2. If an applicant requests specific adjustments be made to the apartment, the housing provider may ask the person if they have a qualifying disability and the need for the requested accommodation.

3. If during the screening process negative information is revealed about a person's past tenancies, the housing provider can ask the applicant to explain the negative information. The explanation may require the person to reveal information about the existence, nature or severity of their disability. The person may still decide not to say anything about the disability. This is the applicant's right.

4. The housing provider has the right to reject a person for unexplained negative information.

12 WAYS LANDLORDS DISCRIMINATE AGAINST PROSPECTIVE TENANTS

1. Asking a person verbally or in writing about their race, age, what country they are from, religious affiliation, sex, marital status, or disabilities.

2. Telling a person of one group a higher security deposit than a person of another group.

3. Applying different eligibility requirements or income guidelines to applicants based on belonging to a certain group.

4. Informing a person the property has been rented when it has not.

5. Quoting a rent price to one person and a different price to another person based solely on their voice, vocabulary, noise in background, message on tape machine, etc.

6. Processing applications from certain applicants. Examples: Only single mothers, retired couples, married couples, applicants under 40, or of a certain race.

7. Giving different facts to different people such as: vacancy dates, when units are available, financial qualifying standards, move-in costs, length of waiting list, or any other process based on the applicants protected class.

8. Showing the apartment in a way to discourage prospective tenant's from returning the application.

9. Telling applicants the number of occupants they wish to move in exceeds your limit for the number of occupants, when in fact, the number meets or is under HUD guidelines.

10. Encouraging or steering certain applicants to apply for units in a particular section of town.

11. Asking verbally or in your ad for a man to help with maintenance, do yard work, etc. Since women, or people with disabilities could also do this work, state you need a "qualified person" to do these jobs.

12. If you own large buildings, encouraging members of the same protected class to occupy only certain portions of the building. Example: floor for single women, separate buildings for families with children, pets, above certain age, or nationality.

CHAPTER 7

DECISIONS BEFORE ADVERTISING

Your ability to earn is in direct relationship with your ability to solve problems.

The quickest way to success is to fail faster.

To get something you never had you must do something you have never done.

— Mike Murdock

There are many decisions you will need to make before starting to advertise an upcoming vacancy. The type of tenant that you will end up accepting is directly proportionate to decisions you make now before the ad hits the paper.

CHARACTERISTICS OF THE AVERAGE TENANT

What type of tenant will your investment property attract? Let's look at a profile of the average tenant. 90% of the people looking for a three bedroom unit will have children. About 50% of the two bedroom units will attract people with children. Childless couples usually both work. They want, and can afford, the extra room to use as a sitting room or study. One bedroom units will be taken by single or newly divorced people starting out on their own.

A two bedroom duplex (upstairs/downstairs) or townhouse (two story side by side) with a yard, in a residential area, will draw more prospects than a two bedroom of the same price in a large apartment or condominium complex. Efficiencies will attract the same type of people as the one bedroom but on a more limited budget.

Other statistics show that over 50% of all American families have children under the age of 18, and 60% of all homes have some kind of pet. Renters, however, are a little different than the national average with only 50% having a pet. Forty percent of those are dogs and cats, with the remaining 10% being the fish, birds, snakes, ferrets, etc.

This means there is a very high probability that prospective tenants will have children and/or a pet.

80% of tenants will move within a ten mile radius of your apartment with the number one reason for moving being they need more space or are downsizing. The next reason for moving is the one all landlords need to understand. They move because of a problem at the property. It could be repairs are not completed in a timely fashion or there are problems with a fellow tenant that the landlord refuses to address. You must meet the needs of your tenants or they will go elsewhere.

Carpet will need to be replaced on the average every 7 to 8 years. Some carpet will need to be replaced after one year while others might be down for 15 years and still look good because the tenant has taken care of it. The average seems to be 7 to 8 years.

The average length of stay of a tenant is 3 to 4 years. Some tenants move after one year and others will stay with you for long periods of time.

KNOW THE FAIR MARKET RENT FOR YOUR AREA

Knowing fair market rent in your area can be one of the biggest boosts to your cash flow. There is nothing worse than starting an ad for what you think is fair market rent and the phone rings off the hook. Quickly you realize demand is greater than supply and the rent should have been higher.

Knowing who to contact and how to discover the going rent for apartments similar to yours is imperative. This should be an on-going assignment and not something done when a tenant gives notice of vacating. Most tenants' rents are raised yearly, but not in the same month, so this knowledge must always be current.

Start with local newspapers to discover fair market rent. Look for ads in your town with the same number of bedrooms. Call the phone numbers as if you were a prospective tenant. Ask the size of the rooms, condition of the carpet, number of appliances, type of heat, cost of utilities and who pays what, the size of the yard, amount of security deposit, length of lease, age of building, when available, are pets allowed (if yes, any additional security deposit or rent required), is there off-street parking or a garage, etc. Use this information to compare your unit to theirs to determine fair market rent.

When driving by an apartment complex that has a sign showing the availability of a two bedroom unit, stop by the rental office and ask for a tour. Pretend you are a prospective tenant or be up front and tell them you own investment properties and want to compare units. After taking the tour stop back at the rental office and say thanks. If the rental agent is not busy, discuss the rental market, what type leases they use, what credit agency they use to screen tenants, etc. The information you gather will be worth every minute of your time. If you find a complex or fellow landlord with units similar to yours, a networking friendship could develop. When you have two very qualified people return applications, call your new landlord friend and give them the name of the one you will not accept. They will gladly reciprocate the favor and it becomes a win-win for both of you.

A good source is realtors who do property management in the area of your vacancy. They often have people walk in off the street looking for a two bedroom unit. If they have no units available, the prospective tenant could be referred to you. I am presently working with just such a realtor and whenever he refers a prospective tenant to me and they move in, I take him out to lunch. He does the same when I help him. I look forward to our lunches as we compare landlording stories and, of course, compare rental rates!

Often your own tenant can be a source to discover fair market rent. Many times they will give the required notice to vacate and then start looking for a new apartment. After a week or two, they call to say they would like to cancel their notice to vacate. You quickly discover they can find a unit as nice as yours, but the rent is the same or slightly higher and it is not worth the aggravation to move. This concept is covered under Nuisance Rent Increase in the Rent Chapter. Tenants have given me detailed descriptions of what my competition is offering.

Another great source is fellow landlords whom you have gotten to know from answering their ads or from a local real estate investor group. Both are excellent sources for staying current with rental trends in your area. I can't say enough about the great service local investment real estate groups do for investors. They provide an excellent opportunity to network with others with the same interest as you. Take advantage of the many benefits they have to offer.

HOW MUCH SECURITY DEPOSIT TO CHARGE

The simple answer is to get as much as your state law will allow. In most states one and a half to two months of rent is the maximum that can be held as a security deposit. Some states require that anything over one month must be returned after one year. If a prospective tenant checks out and the only requirement that can't be met is the two months security deposit, accept a minimum of one month (get more if you can) and then pro-rate the balance over a six month period. Whatever you do, get more than one month for a security deposit. If you don't, that security deposit will be become the last month's rent payment and if there is damage in the apartment there is no money to cover it. In most states you can't get a tenant evicted in less than three to four weeks, so the tenant knows that if taken to court, he will be in his new apartment before the sheriff arrives to change the locks. This is another reason why the lease should say sixty days notice and not thirty day notice. If they don't pay the eleventh month's rent, you have time to file and get a judgment. If he gives the sixty day notice, but does not pay the last month's rent, you now have an extra half or full month of rent in the security deposit to keep. Charging more than one month in security deposit and requiring 60 day notice to terminate eliminates any thoughts a tenant may have about not paying the last month's rent.

UTILITIES

Prospective tenants want to know, and should be told, approximate costs of each utility they will be responsible to pay. Call the current tenant and ask how much he is paying for electric, water, sewer, heat, cable, and give these numbers to prospective tenants when they call.

Whenever there is an opportunity to sub-meter a utility so the tenant pays, do it. The utility bills may drop over 30% when the bill becomes the tenant's responsibility and not the landlord's.

PETS VERSUS NO PETS

Decide before the phone starts to ring whether pets will be allowed in the lease. Saying in the ad "no pets" will cut down on calls from pet owners, but will not eliminate them. Be ready with a higher number for additional rent if the pet comes along. This could be $100 a month more in rent or even greater. In most cases this figure stops them in their tracks and you won't have to listen to "my pet is the greatest" stories. On the other hand, if they say

"OK," think about how much your cash flow just increased. Keep reading to learn techniques to screen the dog just as you do people.

The pet population in the United States is three times the human population. Remember, 40% of renters will have either a cat or a dog and 10% more have some other type of pet. If you plan not to rent to pet owners, be aware that almost half of all prospects for your vacancy will never respond to your ad. Not accepting pets would be like restaurants banning all customers who smoke. Landlords who accept pets and who have strict rules in place, can use these pet loving tenants to increase cash flow.

There are some caveats. Don't fall for the story about how the dog never barks, only weighs five pounds, and always sleeps. The same holds true for cats that have been declawed and always go in the litter box. I have never had a prospective tenant yet admit they have had trouble with the dog biting kids, or chewing up carpet and woodwork.

It won't happen, so don't fall for "my pet is the greatest" line. Maybe the cat does go in the litter box, but how often do YOU change the litter to keep the smell down?

It is not difficult to tell who is the serious pet owner (where the pet is part of the family) and the casual pet owner ("We got the dog to teach my son responsibility"). Explain, in the initial phone call, that your pet policy requires an additional half month of security deposit and an additional $25 per pet, or whatever amount you care to use, in additional rent. The serious pet owner will gladly pay the extra but the casual pet owner will have his son learn responsibility by performing other chores.

Some prospective tenants will question these additional fees. Explain that you are allowing them to occupy and use your $150,000 investment and that it must be protected. The additional half month's rent is not unreasonable, considering that this money would not even cover the cost of replacing one room of carpet let alone the whole unit.

Some landlords who accept pets write the pet deposit on a separate line and make it a non-refundable fee. I have never understood why a landlord would make the pet deposit non-refundable. When the pet fee is non-refundable, the pet owner will watch his dog chew the molding around a closet door or the cat urinate on the carpet. As soon as the cost to fix or replace reaches the NON-REFUND-ABLE fee, the damage stops. Why not? They were not getting it back anyway! Make the pet deposit refundable and DO NOT list the pet deposit and security deposit separately. The security deposit for a pet is an additional half month of security that makes the total security deposit two months rent. If the lease shows a security deposit of two months rent and the dog does damage, the tenant loses the total security deposit which includes the pet security.

I must admit I learned this lesson the hard way to the tune of $1,000. My very first tenant gave me the story about her perfect cat and I believed her. I never asked to see a letter from the veterinarian showing the cat had been neutered and declawed. I also did not require the extra half month of security deposit and the $25 a month in additional rent. When the lease expired, the carpet was so pungent that a professional rug cleaner could not make it bearable. Three year old carpet, still in half decent shape, was replaced and out of Hip Pocket National Bank flew $1,000.

Screening people is easy, but how do we screen a pet? We can't take a paw print and send it to an FBI lab to tell us the pets habits. The best way to discover if the pet, and for that matter, the tenant, is what you want, visit them at their current residence—unannounced. What you see there is what you will see in your apartment.

If they live close by and have a dog, park in the driveway and observe the back yard. If it looks like a mine field and has not been picked up for weeks, you won't need to come back and see the inside. The outside has told you enough. If the outside looks good, come back when they are at home and knock on the door.

While waiting for the door to open observe the screen door. Is the screen pushed out at the bottom? Is the bottom plate covered with paw prints or scratches and has it been pushed out of its frame? All signs that need to be observed because that is the way your screen door will look when they move out. When the door is opened, can they get the dog to sit and be quiet or must they take him to another room or the back yard? Does he continue to bark the whole time you are there? Red flags should be going up in this situation. If, on the other hand, the dog follows commands, it is obvious who is in control. Once in the house, let your nose do the walking. Whatever smells are there will be in your house if you rent to them. There can be odors even when there is not a pet, so always go on a day you don't have a cold.

I remember having one prospective tenant tell me she had two show dogs. She had no problem with the extra $50 in rent. When I visited her unannounced she invited me right in. I knew instantly that she and her dogs were not going to be a problem. The house was immaculate. We talked in the living room for a few minutes and then she asked if I wanted to meet the dogs. I said yes and she called them by name to come into the living room. In they came and sat at her feet. She told them to be polite and shake my hand which they did with a front paw. After a few more minutes talking she told them they could go back to their room and off they went. I stood up to leave and asked her if she would mind coming over to my house to train my kids!

What is your number one goal as a landlord? Tenant retention. Tenants with pets do not move as often because two thirds of landlords don't accept pets. This makes available apartments hard to find for pet owners. Because of this tenants with pets have a tendency to not move as often, which is exactly what you want. Not only is there less turnover but you are being paid extra for allowing the pet to live in your unit.

Can you deny certain breeds of dogs or limit the weight of a pet? The answer is yes to both questions. If you don't want to allow Pit Bulls, Rotweilers, and Dobermans you can. If you want to limit the weight of a dog to under 20 pounds you can. According to the American Kennel Club this is not the best policy. Most small dogs do not do well in apartment living. The temperament of the dogs rather than the size should be the critical factor. Seven out of ten of the dogs that are under 20 pounds do not do well in apartments. Dogs that are best suited for apartment living are retrievers, collies, golden retrievers and shetland sheep dogs. All these dogs are bred to please their owners and generally can be trained to follow directions. On the other hand the dogs that are least likely to make good apartment pets are chihuahuas, poodles, shih tzus and other so-called lap dogs. All are hyper-active and hard to train. Breed and temperament should be qualifying factors, rather than size.

Breeds That Do Best in Apartments

Breed	Average Weight
Border Collie	37 lbs
Cocker Spaniel	30 lbs
Collie	55 lbs
Dachshund	13 lbs
Dalmatian	55 lbs
English Spring Setter	65 lbs
Golden Retriever	70 lbs
Labrador Retriever	65 lbs
Shetland Sheep dog	22 lbs

Breeds Not Suited for Apartment Living

Breed	Average Weight
Basset Hound	37 lbs
Beagle	18 lbs
Bloodhound	85 lbs
Chihuahua	4 lbs
Chow Chow	55 lbs
Lhasa Apso	14 lbs
Miniature Poodle	18 lbs
Pekinese	9 lbs
Shih Tzu	13 lbs
Terriers (Am. Toy to Pit Bull)	4-8 lbs

Since the average tenant moves every 3-4 years and carpet needs to be replaced every 7-8 years, the best time to put in the pet is after the first tenants. The carpet isn't new but doesn't need to be replaced and will be replaced after the next tenant moves. The dog pays for carpet that you were going to have to replace anyway.

Landlords can require that tenant's animals be spayed or neutered before they are six months old. Neutered male dogs show less aggression, are less likely to bite and do not have the urge to roam and find a mate. Neutered male cats are less likely to mark their territory by spraying urine while spayed female cats will no longer experience noisy heat cycles and won't attract pesky male suitors. Landlords can require proof of sterilization from a veterinarian and also ask to see vaccination records, obedience school diploma and other records. Landlords can also require tenants to carry renters insurance that covers pet-related damage.

An article appeared in a newspaper that showed the letter of a lady who wanted to know if a pet was acceptable at a certain hotel. The hotel's response is printed below with some changes made to fit a landlord. Remember this response before saying no to a tenant with a pet.

```
Dogs are welcome in this
apartment. I never had a dog that
smoked in bed and set the building
on fire. I never had a dog who
played music or the TV too loudly. I
never had a dog get drunk and knock
holes in the walls. So if your dog
can vouch for you, you're welcome
too!!
```

SMOKERS VERSUS NON-SMOKERS

Smokers make up about twenty five percent of the rental market, so if you decide to deny tenancy to smokers, be aware that twenty five percent of possible tenants will not be calling. Sixty eight percent of residents who were surveyed expressed interest in smoke-free apartments, while less than one percent of the nation's apartments are smoke-free.

Can landlords deny tenancy to smokers? Yes they can, because smokers are not protected by the fair housing law. As long as you apply the ban to smokers to everyone, you will not be discriminating under fair housing law. If you have federally subsidized housing, you can not refuse to rent to smokers. You may prohibit smoking in the apartment and allow it in common areas. You are banning the behavior, not the person, just as you would ban loud parties or other infractions to the lease.

If there is more than one building on the property, can one be designated for smokers and another non-smokers? Yes this is possible, but don't set aside individual apartments or parts of a building that are not separate from the rest.

How do you implement a building that has smokers to become a non-smoking building? There are two options to do this:

1. Wait for the lease to expire and have them sign leases stating non-smoking. If they are smokers, move them to another building or they will just move.

2. Another option is to give incentives to those who are smokers to move to the building that will be designated smoking. Paying for moving expenses from one building to the other, or giving a half month rent credit might be enough to cause the smoking tenant to move.

Benefits To Offering Smoke-free Apartments

1. **Fills a market niche.** Carnival Cruise Line came out with the ship "Paradise" which was the only non-smoking ship of the major cruise carriers. I took a cruise on the Paradise and found they strongly enforced the contract that everyone had to sign before getting on the ship. If you are caught smoking, you will be put off the ship at the next port of call. From a marketing standpoint I wondered if this ship would stay full week after week with 25% of potential customers being smokers. At the time of this printing, they have had good success with this concept which shows that it might also work in rental units. One landlord who made a building smoke free advertised the apartments as "smoke-free building." The demand for the units was so great she was able to put a premium on the rents and was getting it.

2. **Reduce Risk of Fire.** We hear all the time about fires in apartment buildings that were started by careless smoking. Not allowing smoking cuts down on this risk which in turn might reduce the insurance premium.

3. **Reduced Damage Caused by Smoke.** Ever wipe down walls before painting in a unit that had smokers? It is not a fun job. Studies have shown that it costs twice as much to clean, repaint, and deodorize an apartment with smokers than non-smokers. Part of that increased expense could also come from having to replace carpets and counter tops with burn marks.

4. **Avoids lawsuits.** There have been cases where non-smokers have won court cases using the reason of second-hand smoke. If smoke from one apartment filters into the next door apartment, that tenant could claim illness from the second-hand smoke.

CHAPTER 8

ADVERTISING

Without advertising a terrible thing happens — Nothing.

Get away from negative-thinking people. They only bring you down to their level. No one can fly with the eagles if they scratch with the turkeys.

— Brian Tracy

Once we have determined the type of tenant that will call, how much rent, additional rent for a pet, security deposit to charge, and the average cost of each utility, it's time to think about how to get the phone to ring.

There are many ways a property can be advertised: A sign on the premises, word of mouth, rental agencies, ads in the newspaper, realtors, and local clergy, a 3 x 5 card on the community bulletin board, housing offices of nearby military installations or colleges. It also a good idea to have a mutual agreement with fellow landlords to refer prospective tenants to each other once your vacancy is filled. The techniques I have found to be most successful are the first four which are detailed below; but I have found tenants from all the sources mentioned.

WAYS TO ADVERTISE
For Rent Sign

Placing a "For Rent" sign on the property, especially in a high traffic area, costs nothing after the initial investment for the sign, and will pay for itself very quickly. It can be used repeatedly.

Try to buy or make the signs with three sections. The top section holds an insert that tells the number of bedrooms. It can easily be removed for the next property that has a different number of bedrooms. The middle and largest section, says "Apartment For Rent" and can be removable or permanent. The bottom section gives the phone number that also can be easily modified if a new number is needed. Have the information printed on both sides of the sign.

Place it perpendicular to the road so people passing from either direction can see it. A perpendicular placement will increase the time available to be seen and read by a passing motorist, more than if it is placed parallel to the road.

Even if the property is in a low traffic area, a sign is still worth while. It is free advertising and when appointments are scheduled, it will be easier for the prospective tenant to find the property.

Word of Mouth

Do not forget the power of word of mouth as a source for finding tenants. Prospective tenants that are recommended by good tenants are much better prospects than dealing with Joe Public whom you know nothing about. I have gone as far as setting up a referral rent credit for present tenants who find friends to move into an empty unit. They are given a half month of free rent after the 13th month of the new tenants' occupancy. This is done to avoid a tenant recommending a friend, getting the half month credit right away and then having the new tenant move out after two months.

Half a month of rent credit might sound like a lot of money, but it is a cost effective move, especially during slow rental periods. Think about the cost of a newspaper ad for three or four weeks, answering phone calls, setting up appointments with times convenient for the applicant, the tenant, and yourself. Remember, the time spent showing the unit, explaining the rules, and processing applications all are costs to you. The prospective tenant usually has been to the friend's apartment, so knows what the place is like. If your tenant is not exactly a model tenant you might not want to use this program. The friend could be like him and not the type to whom you are looking to rent. In this case I would run an ad in the paper and hope someone better qualifies.

Here's one final thought: if you have a strong rental market, consider lowering the amount of rent credit.

Coupons And Rental Business Cards

For non-tenant referrals, give a referral fee of $25-$50. Advertise this fee with coupons or state this fact on the back of your rental business cards. The front of the card might say: "I have apartments/houses for rent. All sizes. All price ranges. Call Don at 555-5555." The back might say: "If you refer a prospective tenant to me and they are accepted, I will pay you $50." Pass them out to receptionists and secretaries in large companies. Leave them with the tip in a restaurant, stick a few in magazines in waiting rooms. Use your imagination and the possibilities are endless.

Rental Flyers

Post them and hand them out everywhere. Visit large construction sites near the vacancy and hand out flyers at lunch break time. Post a flyer on a company bulletin board and a supermarket bulletin board. Give some flyers to local merchants to pass out. If they refer the prospective tenant, you will purchase a $25-$50 gift certificate for the tenant from them. This works well in furniture stores, appliance stores, chain outlet stores, hardware stores, auto repair shops, gas stations, and the like.

Also give a handful to your maintenance man who is fixing up the vacancy. Many times people will stop to inquire about the unit. He will take the time to show and talk about the unit if a referral bonus is being offered. Visit craft fairs, senior citizen centers or a church bingo night. Do not place the flyers on cars of people in a movie theater showing *Pacific Heights.*

Rental Agencies

The rental agency that charges a fee to prospective tenants to find them a place to live, is another good source for free advertising. Give the information about the unit to the rental agency and then wait for the phone to ring. Often, if you have placed an ad in the paper, the rental agency will call you asking if your property can be listed with them.

When a tenant has given enough advance notice (60 days or more) of vacating, call the rental agency two weeks before starting an ad in the paper. You might get lucky and find a tenant before spending a dime on advertising. Remember to call the rental agency when the vacancy has been filled so it can be removed from their records. This stops unnecessary phone calls.

Some rental agencies charge the landlord and give their brochure away free or for a small charge. If the circulation is large enough and if the brochure is distributed in stores around your vacancy, it might be another good, cheap source of advertising.

Newspaper Ads

If the other sources of advertising just mentioned are not working, then it's time to advertise in the local paper. Run an ad for one week. Most newspa-

Advertising Report						
Address	Week of…	Number of Calls	Number of Showings	Applications Returned	Cost of Ad	Notes

pers will allow you to cancel the ad sooner if a tenant is found and you will be billed only for the days it ran. Don't be afraid to call and change the ad, (every day if need be), to try to elicit the most calls. Creating short, concise ads that generate a maximum number of phone calls is indeed a real science.

Most newspapers charge for ads by the line so be sure to ask how the last line of the ad looks. If it only has the last four digits of the phone number, you are paying for the rest of the blank line. Have some words ready to add to fill in the line or see if a word can be abbreviated to move it up one line. Asking this one question when placing ads can give big savings if you have many units and lots of turnover.

WRITING AN AD

There are so many variations and nuances in the English language, you might feel confused trying to find the best way to describe your rental. When starting out, the best way to learn is from fellow landlords and rental agents. Read the classified "For Rent" ads in your paper. Pick up and use catchy phrases that grab your attention. If you notice an ad, it will also be seen by a prospective tenant.

Start by thinking of the positive features of the property. Maybe it has an oversized bedroom or living room. Maybe it is located near public transportation or has cable-ready TV hookup. Other features could be a garage, fenced yard, fireplace, new appliances, and carpet. Pick out the feature that you feel is the strongest and use it in your ad. Try to keep the ad short and to the point. Compare these two ads.

> 2 Bedroom Apartment in Anytown. Wall to wall carpets with refrigerator central air conditioning, close to train and shopping. No pets. Available now. $500 plus utilities. Call 666-6666 after 4 PM.

> ANYTOWN - Spacious 2 B.R., carpets, A/C, refrig. No pets. $500 + util. 666-6666 after 4 PM.

Both ads will generate the same number of phone calls, but the first will cost twice as much as the second. The location and number of bedrooms are the first areas a prospect notices. If the rental amount is in his price range, he will call for the other information. Abbreviations can be used for common words such as BR (bedroom), A/C (air conditioning) and a few others, but be careful not to include too many as it will confuse the prospect.

Many times the newspaper won't allow certain abbreviations. That is even more reason to write a concise ad. It is also a good idea to include items that you will not accept, such as pets or smokers. If these are not mentioned, your time will be wasted talking to people who do not fit the requirements of your prospective tenants profile.

Monitor the response to your ad. Adjust the rental price and/or wording as appropriate. The rental amount will vary according to the time of the year. A vacancy during winter months (in cold climates) sends chills to the hearts of all landlords. Wanting to re-rent the unit as soon as possible might mean having to advertise below true market value. It might be a good idea to lower the rent if the phone isn't ringing.

When lowering the rent, make the lease shorter than a year so it will come due in the strong rental months for your area. During strong rental times start the rent $25 higher than what you think is fair market rent. If the phone doesn't ring, call the newspaper and drop the price $5. Wait a few days and if the phone doesn't ring, call and drop it another $5. Sometimes people who move into the area, don't know rental rates and accept your increased rent. Your cash flow has just increased a few hundred dollars from this one tip alone!

ADDITIONAL ADVERTISING TECHNIQUES

Take a minute and think about who would be the perfect tenant for a one bedroom, two bedroom or three bedroom unit. If your ideal tenant for the one bedroom is a single female with no kids, start thinking about where you could find single females. How about hospitals, health clubs, or businesses that have a large secretarial pool or assembly line work. Place a half page flyer describing the rental on a bulletin board, or desk by the entrance. If the perfect tenant for the two bedroom unit is a retired couple, who spend most of the year traveling to visit the grandkids, where might you find them? Churches, bingo halls, senior activity centers would be some good sources. Three bedrooms usually mean children will be in the picture. Put your flyer in day care centers and churches.

If the one bedroom is near railroad tracks and freight trains go by four times a day, the ideal tenant for this unit might be someone who is deaf. Check the phone directory for deaf schools or colleges in the area and contact them.

RENTING TO THE HANDICAPPED

Don't overlook the possibilities of making a few minor modifications to your building to accommodate handicapped tenants. There is a growing demand for this type housing and not many landlords are making the necessary changes to attract handicapped tenants.

Handicapped tenants will stay longer than the average tenant because of the difficulty locating other suitable housing. Because the demand is high and supply is low, you can command a premium price.

You are not required by law to make modifications to existing structures but some changes to consider are:

- Build a ramp from the exterior to the interior of the building
- Install a stall shower (no tub)
- Install grab bars on either side of the toilet
- Lower kitchen cabinets
- Replace a regular door with a sliding door
- Install a garage door opener

When you have finished, put an ad in the paper that starts "HANDICAPPED RESIDENTS WELCOME" or "HANDICAPPED ACCESSIBLE" and hear the phone start to ring.

CHAPTER 9

QUALIFYING THE PROSPECTIVE TENANT

MANLEY'S SECOND LAW OF LANDLORDING — Over 90% of management problems are solved (or created) before the tenant moves in.

There are two times a landlord can get into trouble—when he's in a hurry and when he feels sorry for someone.

A great pleasure in life is doing what people say you cannot do.

— Walter Gagehot

Mr. Manley's observation is right on the money. Surveys have shown the number one mistake made by over 50% of landlords is trying to take short cuts when qualifying prospective tenants. All admit it was a mistake they will never make again. Learn from their mistakes and follow closely the techniques described in the following chapters. Ignore the steps outlined and landlording will become a time-consuming burden.

Bankers and landlords have a lot in common. A banker needs depositors like a landlord needs renters. The banker holds depositor's money and puts it to work in the form of loans. A landlord buys an investment property and lends it to a tenant. Before granting a loan, a banker requires collateral to guarantee repayment. A landlord receives collateral in the form of a security deposit and a signed lease with a stated promise to take care of the property.

If a loan becomes overdue, the banker uses the collateral to repay the loan. A landlord uses the security deposit to repay what he is owed.

A banker also requires the applicant to fill out a loan application so he can judge whether or not the applicant has the ability to repay the loan. The landlord requires that a rental application be filled out, so he can verify the ability of the applicant to pay for the "loan" of his property.

If these facts are true, why is it that bankers generally receive payments on time while landlords are often faced with overdue rent? The reason is that bankers spend days checking the applicant's credit history and other background information, before giving their approval.

Unfortunately, most landlords use the "first come, first get" or "the first people I like" philosophy in deciding to whom they rent. Can you imagine a banker doing this? Of course they would not, and landlords should not either. If landlords would screen prospects like a banker, their failure rate would be just as low.

The secret to good investing is good landlording. What good is a no money down deal if, after you rent the property, the tenant refuses to pay rent? Take time to screen prospective tenants. Remember, never let a tenant's urgency become your urgency. Good landlords act. They don't react.

In my early landlording days I would let the prospective tenant control the conversation by asking such questions as the location, cost of utilities, amount of security deposit, when available, and when they could see it. I would answer their questions and schedule the appointment. I discovered only 50% were keeping their appointments. I am sure they drove by the unit before the appointment, did not like the location, or looks, and never bothered to call and say they weren't interested. A lot of time was wasted waiting for these "no-shows."

I discovered other problems, as illustrated below, that should have been discussed over the phone before meeting face to face:

1. The husband and wife had three kids, a mother-in-law, and a dog looking at a one bedroom unit.
2. They needed a unit with appliances and this one had none.

3. They thought heat was included in the rent. Finding out that it wasn't, the unit was more than they could afford.
4. They liked the unit but needed to give sixty days notice to their landlord, and wanted me to save the empty unit for them.
5. They loved the unit size, but the carpet would clash with their furniture.
6. Etc., etc., etc., etc.

These potential problems should have been discussed on the phone before showing the unit. From the first hello, you should control the conversation. Don't wait for them to ask about the type of heat, number of appliances, amount of security deposit, or the approximate cost of the utilities. Have all this information written down before the first call. It will only take a few calls before the information sheet is memorized. You can quickly and effortlessly present the basic facts before asking your other questions.

START SCREENING FROM THE INITIAL PHONE CALL

Most phone conversations will start the same. "Hello, I'm calling about the apartment you have advertised. Is it still available?" When you say it is, the most common response will be "Can you tell me about it?" This is the response you want to hear. If they say, "When can I see it?" red flags should be going up. It's probably Monday and the Sheriff is coming on Friday to evict. And when you say it's available, and they say, "I'll take it" major red flags should go up. It is now Friday and the Sheriff is due any minute.

Have your phone screening questions written on a sheet of paper or use the phone screening outline shown in this chapter. Keep it near your desk for easy referral and to make sure nothing is forgotten. After identifying yourself, get the caller's name and phone number. Start with the questions and take notes of the answers given. Keeping this information in a notebook makes it easily accessible for reference and review prior to the initial face to face meeting.

1. Are you familiar with the area? Give the exact address or the closest intersection to the property. Many times people want to move to certain areas so it's good to find this out right away to save time if your unit is not in an area they are interested in moving.

2. How soon do you need to move? Ask this question soon into the conversation. This will save the time of explaining all the features of the apartment to then find out they need something in 14 days and your tenants just gave their 60 day notice. On the other hand, if the apartment is vacant and they don't need something for 90 days, chances are it will be rented in much less time.

3. Who will occupy the unit? State the question this way. Don't ask how many adults and how many children will occupy the unit. Stating it this way could cause discrimination problems later on. If

PHONE SCREENING

Property _____ Show _____ at _____
Date Called __/__/__ They will call back _____

NAME _____ Phones - H _____ W _____
1. How soon do you need to move? _____
2. Who will occupy the unit? _____
3. Do you have a pet? ___ Yes ☐ No ☐ What kind? ___ Size ___
   Is your pet neutered? Yes ☐ No ☐ Declawed? Yes ☐ No ☐ Can you prove it? Yes ☐ No ☐
4. Are you in a lease now? Yes ☐ No ☐ If no, where are you living? _____
   How long at present address? ___ Why moving? _____
   How much notice must you give? ___ Was it given? _____
5. What is your GROSS income weekly, monthly, or yearly? _____
6. What is your current rent? _____
7. What utilities do you pay? _____ How much per month? ___
8. How long been working at present job? ___
   If less than two years, who was previous employer? _____ How long there? ___
9. Have you ever paid rent late? Yes ☐ No ☐ Been evicted? Yes ☐ No ☐ Are you current with rent now? Yes ☐ No ☐
   If no, why? _____ Have you ever filed bankruptcy? Yes ☐ No ☐ If yes, how long ago? ___
10. How did you hear about this unit? _____

Items callers will need to know:
• Unit is located at _____
• It is available _____
• The total monthly utility bill is $ ___. This covers _____
• The security deposit without pets is $ ___. With pets it is $ ___.
• We charge a $ ___ non-refundable application fee.
• Would you like to schedule an appointment? _____

they are not sure who will be living with them, this should be sending up a red flag.

4. How many pets will be moving with you? Notice I did not say do you have any pets? That's a yes or no answer. Asking how many throws them off guard. If they give a number greater than zero tell them the additional cost per pet. Find out what it is, how much it weighs, is it neutered or declawed, and are all shots current? If it is a breed you don't want to accept, tell them you're sorry but the owners don't accept that breed.

5. Are you in a lease now? If they are not in a lease, find out where they are staying. Be cautious if the answer is with relatives and friends and they have been with them for a few years. I want tenants who have rental experience and who are responsible enough with their finances to support themselves.

6. How long have you been at your present address? This one is key. Stability is what I'm looking for, so when they say "we have been here for 6 years and just need something a little larger," I'm already heading for the car keys to quickly show them the unit!

7. Why are you moving? "I need a two bedroom because my wife is pregnant" or "the kids have all moved out so we don't need a three bedroom anymore" are good reasons for moving. Some reasons they will give are for things that you must be sure don't cause you to lose a good tenant. It could be a disruptive neighbor, crime increasing in the area, a divorce, or the landlord won't do repairs are some of the more common reasons given for moving.

8. What is your GROSS income per week? Stress the gross part otherwise they will give you the net income. I prefer to ask it this way instead of telling them the owner's requirements are that one week's gross salary must equal the rent plus utilities. When it is asked this way they have to give a number and an amount per week. They can not just answer, "yes I qualify." Maybe they do and maybe they don't. The first method gets a number out of them.

It is important to stress while on the phone that they will need to show income with two recent pay stubs. If they can't show a pay stub because they are paid in cash, then you will need to see a copy of last year's tax return. If they can't or won't do this, it's time to get off the phone and move on.

9. What is your current rent? How much do you pay for utilities?

These two questions will help to determine if they are making a lateral rent move or a substantial increase in the rent. Be careful if the increase in rent is more than 10% of their existing rent. Example: Tenant is paying $600 for rent and utilities and your apartment will cost them $725 for rent and utilities.

That is more than a 10% increase and unless can prove they have a savings account on the rental application, red flags should be going up.

10. How long have you been employed at your present job? Here is another key question. The longer time, the better, because it shows stability. If the amount of time is less than two years, find out who was the previous employer and how long that job was held.

11. Where are you employed and what do you do there? I'm not interested so much in the company but what position or trade is their specialty. If they are a computer programmer, or a carpenter, or any other type of positions that are in demand, there will be less chance of not being able to find other work in case of a lay-off.

12. How long do you plan to live in this area? Turnovers are cash flow killers. Be skeptical if they respond to this question by asking "How long is the lease?" The longer time given the more excited you should become.

During each phone call I am doing what I call "gut screening." How do I feel about them from this initial phone call? Were they polite, and did they have loud music playing in the background? Did they talk as if they had not made it past third grade English, and did they tell you so much of their life history you know they are losers? There is no way each call could be remembered, but, if listed in the notebook, they are easily accessible.

SCREEN CALLS WITH TAPE MACHINE

Make sure to purchase a machine that allows messages to be retrieved from remote locations by entering a code number. The machine should have a toll saver feature that allows the phone to ring four times for the first call and only two times for subsequent calls. This allows you to check in, but not pay for a call when there are no messages. If the phone rings more than twice, you know there are no messages, so hang up before the fourth ring.

Keep the volume turned up so you can hear the message as it is being recorded. If it is a long distance call, or someone who you need to talk to, pick it up. Let the machine take the calls asking for donations or subscriptions, etc.

Many tape machines also have a button that allows you to record your conversation and another button that lets you leave messages for yourself or a family member. Do not purchase a machine that shuts off after a thirty second message. I gave one to an on-site manager for Christmas and hated my choice of machines after the first day. I could never finish what I needed to say before being cut off.

Consider purchasing a four-voice-box answering machine. This system allows you to record a message that might sound something like this:

```
"Hi, you have reached Don. If you
want to leave me a message, press 1;
if calling about the one bedroom in
Anytown, press 2; if calling about
the two bedroom in Othertown, press
3; if calling about the four bedroom
for sale, press 4."
```

Under each number and message can be recorded about the unit for as long as you wish. Give location, rent, security deposit, appliances included, school district, utilities they will pay, how much they have to gross per week to qualify, what the application fee will be (some hang up here because they are looking for landlords who will not be checking credit), and any other special features of the property. End with: "After taking a drive-by, call back to schedule an appointment." This technique saves hours on the phone because the machine screens the applicants for you.

SCHEDULING APPOINTMENTS

When an appointment is scheduled ask that everyone (including pets) come along. What you see is what you get so why not see it all.

If the appointment is scheduled and it is your only appointment that day, have the prospective tenant call at least one hour before the meeting time to confirm the appointment. Tell them that if a phone call is not received, you won't be there.

Before I started confirming appointments, only about 50% of the prospects would arrive at the appointed time. There is nothing more frustrating than sitting in an empty unit waiting for someone who never arrives.

Try to schedule appointments 15 minutes apart, especially if the unit is still occupied. This is about how long it takes the average prospect to look at the unit. If the timing is correct, the first one should be leaving as the second one knocks on the door. This spacing method allows time to meet the applicants one at a time so that you can answer their questions individually and privately.

PROSPECTIVE TENANTS' QUESTIONS, AND A LANDLORD'S RESPONSE

When the phone rings be prepared to hear the following questions:

1. Why do I need to fill out an application and pay an application fee?
2. Why won't you allow pets?
3. Why do you charge an extra security deposit for pets?
4. Why can't I sign a month-to-month lease?
5. Why must I pay with a certified check when signing the lease?
6. Why must I sign a lease?
7. Why do you charge more than one month's security deposit?

When you do get a call like this, take a deep breath, and politely explain your answers to their questions. The following letter is closer to what I think landlords would rather say to the prospective tenant. I wrote it one day after receiving what seemed like the 100th query about my rental policies.

```
Dear Prospective Tenant,
    Let's get something straight right
away. Just because I own an invest-
ment property, doesn't make me
filthy rich. I know you think I am,
but I'm not. I work for a living
just like you. The difference
between us is, I choose to spend my
hard earned dollars much differently
than you.
    I know this because if you had
saved your money, there would be no
reason for you to be asking me for
the "privilege" of renting my prop-
erty! I sacrificed some material
pleasures to save the money to buy
the home you want to live in. You
have not made such a sacrifice
because you spend it as fast as you
make it. I know this because when
you filled out an application there
was no savings account listed. You
even asked if I would allow part of
the security deposit to be paid off
over the first few months of the
lease. That's another dead giveaway
you have no savings.
    Since you live from paycheck to
paycheck and your job tenure at any
one place is usually short, I must
protect my investment by making sure
I find the most reliable and quali-
fied person I can. About the only
right I don't give up when I rent to
you, is ownership.
    In return for your rights of
leasehold interest, I only ask for
two things; that the rent be paid on
time and that the property not be
damaged.  This property cost me my
hard earned dollars to purchase and
maintain and I am not going to allow
a total, unscreened stranger to
occupy it. Look at it this way. This
is my business, and am treating you
```

as a new customer who wishes to
establish credit with me. I have a
business reason for every question I
ask. If you were in my shoes,
wouldn't you do the same thing?

Have you ever gone to a bank and
asked for a loan when they didn't
require an application or charge a
fee? If you have, I want the name of
the bank! I am doing the same thing
as the banker when I ask you to complete an application.

I use the information you provide
to do a few things. First I run a
credit check which will tell me
about your credit history and if you
are paying your bills on time. I
will call or write your employer to
verify your salary, length of
employment, and work habits.

I also need the application to
have your full name and address so
that I can call the District
Justices' office and the local
police, to see if they have had any
trouble with you.

I charge an application fee for
two reasons: First, if you are not
serious about the property, you will
not waste your money on the application. Secondly, I charge a fee
because if you have something to
hide you won't pay me to find it
out. Your refusal to pay an application fee is a good way for me to
screen out unwanted prospects.

Why do you charge an extra security deposit for pets?

If I am going to allow pets, I must protect myself
with an extra security deposit, and a pet lease that
names your pet, gives it type, gender, weight, color-
ing, etc. I will also want a clause in the lease that
allows me to evict the pet if I find the pet doing any
type of damage (smell or otherwise) to the unit. I
also may come to your present house unannounced,
and let my nose tell me if I want your pet. (This is
also a great way to check on the housekeeping skills
of the prospective tenant.)

Why can't I sign a month-to-month lease?

Why do you want a month-to-month lease? Are
you planning on moving in 90 days or perhaps two
weeks before Christmas?

(Having less than a year's term is a good idea if I
am renting between October and March. This way it
will come due in the spring and summer which is
when 85% of all tenants move.)

If you do take a month-to-month lease, I will
need an additional $30 a month and I'll want pro-
vision for a 60 day (some states may only allow a
30 day) notice to vacate. (You should check with
your attorney to see what is allowed in your state.)
I need the extra money to pay for the added
expenses, including advertising, that I'll incur
when the apartment does not stay rented for the
full term. (This option has its pros and cons, of
course; if you get a bad tenant, they can be
removed quickly by giving the required notice. But
if they're good, you don't want them moving in
less than a year.)

Why must I pay with a certified check when signing the lease?

I require certified funds, prior to, or at the time
you sign the lease. You can give me a check before
we meet and I'll wait until the check clears. I'll sign
the lease if, at that time, I can verify that your check
is good. You can make it simple and just bring a certified check, money order, or cash when we sign the
lease.

Why must I sign a lease?

Believe it or not, a lease protects both of us. It
explains what each of us is required to do and what
we can't do. It is the basis for our agreement, that
will be used by a District Justice if either one of us
thinks we are wronged by the other.

Why do you charge more than one month in security deposit?

A bank will require at least 10% down payment
when making a loan to you. A landlord is loaning
you the use of his unit. What kind of down payment
does the average landlord ask for? On an $80,000
property, where the rent is $800 a month, the land-
lord who charges one month in security gets ONE
PERCENT as a down payment! If he gets $400 a
month in rent and $800 in security, that's still only
TWO PERCENT. Tough to complain about security
deposits now, isn't it?

If I charge only one month in security deposit,
you probably won't pay the last month's rent after
giving me notice of your intent to move. If I find
damage after you vacate, I am out money from my
pocket because you conveniently left without leaving a forwarding address. A month and a half or two
month's security deposit forces you to pay the last
month's rent or forfeit the balance of the security
deposit. Now I have some money to pay for damages but it also makes you think about not doing
damage if you want the balance of the security
deposit back. Under my lease you are not entitled to

that money if the last month's rent has not been paid.

Now that I have answered your questions let me give you some do's and don'ts when calling me or coming to see my property. When calling:

- Don't call me from a pay phone or a bar. If I hear noises I shouldn't be hearing, you have a strike against you right away.
- Don't leave a message on my tape machine that shows me that your IQ is lower than your shoe size. Example: "Hi - I hope this is the person who has an apartment for rent because I need it right away. I will have to call you later from my boyfriend's house because my phone was disconnected." (This is when a tape machine comes in handy. I screen calls and didn't bother to return hers.)
- Don't have a outrageous message on your tape machine when I call back. Example: "Hey dude, You'll have to call me back later. It's party time." I left the following message: "Hi dude, I'm returning your phone call about the apartment for rent. I'm not leaving my phone number because I don't want you calling me back."
- Remember, prospective tenant: YOU NEVER GET A SECOND CHANCE TO MAKE A GOOD FIRST IMPRESSION. Don't come to see the apartment dressed like a slob. I am not saying to come in a coat and tie, but a three day growth of beard, cut off jeans, and no shoes just doesn't make it. Why don't you look at this appointment as if it were a job interview? You should be out to impress me considering I have something YOU want and NEED.
- Don't come in the beat-up jalopy car. If that car is your best, your first impression is not a positive one.
- Don't let the kids play hide and seek in the closets upstairs while I show you the first floor. If you call them down or ask them to stop doing something, I will be watching very carefully to see if they mind. If they do not mind now, I know they won't mind you after your furniture arrives.

Things you can do to impress me:

- Try not to do any of the above don'ts and I'll be impressed already.
- Speak politely, intelligently, and have your questions written down.
- BE HONEST - If you have a bad credit history tell me up front and explain what happened. If you are having trouble with your present landlord or employer, tell me your side of the story. If you try to hide the facts, I will find out anyway, by running the credit check. Your application will not be as strong as the person who was truthful.

PROSPECTIVE TENANT CHECKLIST

This checklist has been designed to make sure you did all your homework before choosing a tenant. Make changes to this list so that it meets the qualifying criteria that you developed.

You will not know if a credit history is good unless a credit check is run. You will not know if the house if clean and neat unless you visit it. You will not know if the present and previous landlords and employer will give good recommendations unless you call them. Check off the facts that apply to your prospective tenant and then total.

Always keep in mind that the time spent researching prospective tenants will be a small fraction of the time needed when evicting a tenant.

CREDIT REPORTS AND WHAT THEY MEAN

Looking at a credit report for the first time often makes landlords say, why did I pay to have this done because I do not understand what these numbers and letters stand for?

Most credit reports will start by showing current address then former addresses. Check to see if the former address matches the one given on the rental application. If not, be ready to ask why. Current and former employer along with dates might be listed next but not always. If it is, check it against the rental application. The model profile section of the report will give an "empirica" rating ranging from 400 as the low score to 800 as the high. Most mortgage companies want to see an average score of credit established around 600. This number will vary slightly depending on the mortgage amount needed which will also vary depending on rental rates. The higher the rent, the higher the "empirica" rating that will be needed. Under "alert" will be a set of numbers whose meanings are established by the three major credit bureaus.

There will also be a "credit summary and total file history" which gives lots of helpful information such as how many accounts the applicant has which includes credit limit, balance due, past due amounts, and monthly payments. It will also show revolving accounts, which ones have been closed with balances and the totals of each.

Another section will be "public records." This will show any bankruptcies, judgments, and criminal information depending on how much information you are asking from the credit bureau that is used.

PROSPECTIVE TENANT CHECKLIST

Each item earns one point unless otherwise noted.

FINANCIAL

1. Monthly income 33% of rent amount ____
2. Monthly income 25% of rent amount ____
3. Monthly income 20% of rent amount ____
4. Current rent is no more than 10% under your rent ____
5. Can pay full deposit and rent to move in ____
6. Paid current landlord promptly each month ____
7. Paid previous landlord promptly each month ____
8. Credit rating over 600 (1.5 pts.) ____
9. Credit rating between 550-600 (1 pt.) ____
10. Credit rating between 500-550 (0.5 pt.) ____
11. Has a checking account ____
12. Has a savings account ____
13. Can provide a co-signer that owns Real Estate ____
14. No judgments from other landlords ____

LONGEVITY

1. More than 2 years at present job ____
2. More than 4 years at present job ____
3. More than 6 years at present job ____
4. More than 2 years at current residence ____
5. More than 4 years at current residence ____
6. More than 6 years at current residence ____

RELIABILITY

1. On time for appointment ____
2. Filled out application completely ____
3. Good response from previous landlord ____
4. Good response from current landlord ____
5. Good response from current employer ____
6. If have pet(s) can prove shots, licenses, etc. ____

VISITATION

1. Condition of current residence excellent (1.5 pts.) ____
2. Condition of current residence good (1 pt.) ____
3. Condition of current residence fair (0.5 pt.) ____
4. Neighbors evaluation of tenant - excellent (1.5 pts.) ____
5. Neighbors evaluation of tenant - good (1 pt.) ____
6. Neighbors evaluation of tenant - fair (0.5 pt.) ____
   TOTAL ____

Date Approved ____/____/____

Date and Reason Not Approved ____/____/____

The section called "trades" will list all credit that the prospect has established and tell you how they are doing with each. It will show the name of the company, when the account was opened, what was the high credit line, past due amounts and then how they have paid in the past two years. There will be 12 spaces so that a number from 1–9 can be entered for each month of the year. An R01, for example, means that it is a revolving account and is current. If it was R02 then the account was thirty days late for that month. An R03 would mean the account was paid 60 days late and so on. R09 are usually charge off accounts, placed for collection, or listed as profit and loss write-offs.

The "inquiries" section will show who has requested a copy of their credit report and on what date. Check this area out closely. If the last three inquiries were management companies or apartment complexes red flags should be jumping out. If they are applying with you they must have been rejected by the other three!

At the end of the credit report there will be the name, address, and phone number of the credit reporting agency. If a tenant requests a written rejection letter, use the form in the forms packet, and give the credit reporting agency address and phone number so if the tenant wishes to contact the them they can. Even if the prospect asks for a copy of his credit report because he paid for it, do not do it. Be careful about what you tell tenants about their credit report. Do not give specific names of creditors. Say, "I see there is a credit card account that was 90 days late" or, "there was a judgment entered in (name month and year) under your name. Can you explain?"

The last items to be listed are usually the names, addresses, and phone numbers of all creditors that can be called to verify any of the information given.

There is much more information that is given on credit reports than I have covered here because each credit reporting agency does their information slightly differently. The bottom line—whichever credit reporting agency is used, do the report and learn how to read the agency that services your area the most.

RED FLAGS WITH PROSPECTIVE TENANTS

Many times prospective tenants will say or do things that will give you a strong indication that all is not what it seems to be. Here are a few of the more common mistakes I have seen tenants make during the screening process:

- The landlord asks to see a copy of their drivers license and the prospective tenant can't produce one, but drove to the appointment.
- A prospective tenant calls and when told the unit is available says, "when can I see it" without asking any questions. That tells me he is probably being evicted on Friday and it is now

Monday. When you tell them it is available and they say, "I'll take it," it is now Friday and the sheriff is on his way to evict.

- The prospective tenant drives up in a rental car, is dressed very nicely, loves to do repairs so won't be calling for you to do them, whips out a wad of bills, and says "here is the first month's rent and one month of security deposit, we'll take it."

- On the phone you were told their names were John and Mary Jones but when you look at the drivers licenses it is John Jones and Mary Smith. When questioned they say they are engaged. Why did you not tell me that on the phone?

- The application is hard to read, many items are not completed or partially completed. The current landlord's name is given but no phone number. The address on the application is different than what is on the driver's license which is different than what is on the pay stub which is different to what is listed on the insurance card. Birth dates and social security numbers on driver's license and pay stubs don't match.

- You are told the prospective tenant has no pets but see and hear one when visiting them—unannounced.

- They park down the street, are driven by someone else, and don't have a phone.

- They arrive poorly dressed. I have something you want, so try to impress me.

- Current landlord tells you they pay but it is partial payments, usually late, and there always seems to be a complaint about something in with the check.

- They list no savings or checking account on the application and their current rent is 25% less than your rent.

- The tenant hands you a copy of his credit report and says he just ran one on himself to be sure everything was OK. Or was it run to cut out some negative items and change some others?

- Signature on the driver's license does not match the signature on the application.

- Applicant is 30 years old and the credit report comes back "no credit found."

- Many inquires on the credit report in the past few months.

CHAPTER 10

SHOWING THE APARTMENT

Trust everyone, but cut the cards anyway.

Make mistakes when you are young. There are fewer zeros on the end.

— Brian Tracy

SCHEDULING APPOINTMENTS WITH PRESENT TENANTS

With some careful planning, showing the apartment does not have to be a traumatic situation for you or your tenants. After receiving their written notification of leaving, call the tenants to confirm receiving the letter. Stress that you want to make this transition as painless as possible and your policy of not entering the unit unless they know you are coming is still in effect. All appointments will be scheduled through them with a minimum of 24 hours notice, which is stipulated in the lease. This "reasonable notice" is appreciated so they have time to make the unit look presentable. If times conflict with their schedule, promise to find another time to schedule the appointments.

This approach helps to ease the tenants' anxiety because they will see that you want to continue to treat them fairly as you have in the past. Because of this, they will try to accommodate your times as often as possible. If you have not taken care of problems when they called throughout the year, good luck. This will make showings difficult.

CONTINUE SCREENING WHEN SHOWING THE APARTMENT

Note the time the prospective tenants arrive for the showing. If they are prompt in keeping the appointment, that is a good indication they will be prompt with rent payments. Try to meet them at their car. Observe the overall condition and especially the tidiness, or lack thereof. Sometimes this inspection will give an indication of their housekeeping abilities. If the car has more rust than paint, all four tires are bald, and the engine sounds like it might die any second, there is a good chance they do not have a savings account.

Since the car is probably their largest asset and on a good day they might get $300 for it, how much do you think their furniture will be worth? Probably less. I'm not impressed when the tenant's "net worth" equals one month's rent!

Don't be surprised when a prospective tenant shows no savings on the rental application. A very small percentage of applicants will have a savings account which tells us most tenants literally live from pay check to pay check. This is another reason why we must be so strict with the screening process.

When they become hurt on the job, expect the rent to be at least two weeks late. That is how long it takes for the workers' compensation check to arrive. This is another reason why landlords should collect the maximum security deposit allowed by your state.

Appearance creates a first and lasting impression. They should be trying to impress me as much as a future boss. Be very leery about renting to people who need massive dental work. I have never had a good tenant that had bad teeth! If they do not care about their own personal hygiene what makes you think they will take care of your property!

Notice how they handle themselves during the walk through and interview. Explaining that their present landlord is a creep, so they stopped paying rent, or allowing their children to run wildly through the house and not mind when spoken to should be telling you lots about these people.

SHOWING OCCUPIED UNITS

If the apartment is occupied, ask to see the drivers licenses of the prospective tenants *before* entering the property. Make them prove they are who they said they are. Don't forget these people are total strangers and you are allowing them to walk through the personal property of your tenant. They could be professional thieves looking to steal jewelry, cut glass, or other items value. They use the front of being a prospective tenant to get easy access to a home.

This is why when showing an occupied property there should always be two people doing the walk through. One in the front and one bringing up the rear to keep them together and watch for wandering fingers and arms. If the tenant won't be home for the showing, find someone else to help out.

It's also a good idea to call back the number you were given after a few minutes. Do this to confirm it's a legitimate phone number and the person is really there. Use the excuse you wanted to call back to confirm the time.

The "guided tour" allows positive features to be highlighted and gives you an opportunity to continue to observe their reactions and to answer their questions. Ask leading questions to discover how they feel about the unit. "Is this living room adequate for your furniture?" "Is the size of the kitchen adequate for your needs?" "Do you think your bedroom set will fit in this room?" "Do you cut the grass where you now live?"

It won't take long to discover who is serious and who is just looking. Remember in the phone screening, to ask that everyone who will be occupying the unit come to see it—including the pets.

Any prospective tenant who looks interested and seems qualified, should be encouraged to fill out an application on the spot. He may not have all the account numbers and phone numbers needed to complete the application, but he can call with the missing numbers when he returns home. The not-so-serious prospects will take the application and say they will mail it back which may or may not occur. Before they leave, be sure to review all expenses they must pay, the amount of security deposit, the date when rent is due, the approximate move-in date, the length of the lease and any special rules that you have.

SHOWING VACANT UNITS

It is still a good idea to have a second person with you for the showing. Get to the property early and open windows to let fresh air in. Bring along a box of toys, games, stuffed animals, and anything that small children will enjoy playing with while you give the parents a tour of the house. This is done because you can tell an awful lot about the parents by observing the kids and, with this simple exercise, can tell lots about who controls who in the family. Invite the kids to play with the toys while you give the parents the tour. Get permission first from the

parents that it's OK for the kids to play with these items. When out of sight of the kids, listen carefully to what is going on in the living room. If the kids are fighting over a toy and when Mom and Dad asks them to quiet down, it gets louder, you have just learned who is in control of this family. If the sounds are of two small children playing together quietly, tell the kids that because they were so good during the showing they can have any item in the box as a gift from me. Get permission again from the parents.

If the kids did not behave in a manner you felt appropriate, move on. If the kids were good and have taken home a toy, we want this good prospective tenant to remember that nice landlord every time they have to pick up that toy to put it back in the toy box and hopefully decide to return the rental application to that nice landlord.

SHOWING UNITS
THAT DON'T SHOW WELL

Your tenant has not damaged the unit but gets a grade of "D" or lower for housekeeping skills. When meeting the prospective tenant at the property, explain before entering the unit, that your tenant is not the most fastidious person in the world so please look at room sizes, color and condition of the carpet (if you can find it) and not at his furnishings and housekeeping standards. Tell them to concentrate on room sizes and the general layout of where they would be positioning their own furniture.

Explain that any items needing replacement or repair will be completed as soon as the tenant vacates, and that they are under no obligation to sign a lease until all work has been completed.

This is not the best approach to use with prospective tenants, but sometimes there is no other choice. Showing to a few people, with the possibility of one returning an application, is better than waiting for the unit to become vacant, and then cleaning, and showing it. The latter method gives no chance of turning the unit over quickly.

Don't be surprised if the prospective tenant's emotional level when you walk through this type of unit is not real high. Put yourself in their shoes. Some of their questions could be: What will we do if this landlord does not have the repairs completed when he says? We have to be out of our unit on a certain date and a new tenant is moving in as soon as we move out. Where will we stay if this unit isn't ready?

One solution to the above situation would be to show a similar unit of a tenant with good housekeeping skills. Approach this tenant about allowing his unit to be shown to prospective tenants, and indicate your willingness to pay for this inconvenience. The pay could be in the form of money each time a prospective tenant is shown; or you could give them a gift certificate to a nice restaurant or a rent credit.

Tell the prospective tenants you were not able to schedule a time to see the unit that will soon be vacant, but another tenant has been nice enough to allow you to show his unit. Stress that no lease will be signed until they have had an opportunity to inspect the other unit. This approach allows you to process the prospective tenant and approve them so that you are ready to go when the unit finally opens. After the old tenant has moved, spend some time getting the place back in shape, before walking the new tenant through and finalizing the lease. After a prospective tenant has been approved, collect a portion of the security deposit to hold the unit but explain that it's fully refundable until they have inspected the unit they will occupy.

MAKE REPAIRS BEFORE SHOWING VACANT UNITS

Expect repairs and realize the better it looks, the higher the rent. A quick way to turn off strong rental prospects is to show them a unit that has holes in the walls, looks like it was painted 30 years ago, has stains in the carpet, dead insects in the medicine closet, a dried up toilet, and a stove that looks like a potpourri of every meal ever cooked. There is still much more for them to see but half the light bulbs are burned out and the other half, the ones that worked, moved with the last tenant. Maybe they won't notice the water stain marks near the refrigerator, the broken screens, or the missing dining room fixtures.

All the landlord can say is, "Everything will be fixed and painted before you move in." He might be telling the truth, but smart shoppers make decisions on what they see, not on what they are promised. Look at it another way. What happens if the unit is shown in this terrible condition, and the prospect says he likes it? What does that say about them? If he thinks the condition of this unit is acceptable, then all he is looking for is another place to spread out his mess! Make the needed repairs before showing the unit. It may take a little work, but this helps to attract quality tenants.

When the unit is vacant, arrive a few minutes before the appointment so outside litter can be picked up and windows opened to air the unit. Placing air fresheners around is helpful if basements are damp or pet odors are present. If any curtains or blinds were left by the old tenant, clean them and leave them up. It will make the unit look occupied from the street and will give a warmer feeling to prospective tenants.

If the new tenants do not need or want the curtains or blinds, remove and store for the next unit that might need them. The curtains are icing on the cake but don't forget the cake!

THE PROFESSIONAL TENANT

There is another situation you might encounter. The prospective tenant shows up in a rented car, even though he lives in the area. He is well dressed, polite, asks good questions. He smiles a lot, and stresses how much he enjoys doing minor repairs around the house. After seeing the unit, he reaches into his pocket and pulls out a four inch wad of bills and, still smiling, says, "My wife and I really love this unit and want to make sure we get it. We'd like to sign a lease right now, and we'll pay for the security deposit and the first two months of rent with cash right now."

When this seemingly innocent, but professional, tenant pulls this move, just remember, the money in his hand is probably three months of rent owed to his present landlord. You are scheduled to be next on his list of victims. The cash so easily flashed now is the last money you may ever see. Unfortunately there are landlords who fall for this scheme and they usually don't last too long as landlords. I have never received a phone call from a fellow landlord inquiring about a tenant I was evicting. That fact alone tells me when a landlord has a vacancy, his number one priority is to get it rented, not rented to the right person.

It is very tempting to sign people like "the flash with the cash" but I urge you to resist the temptation. Stay with the game plan. These tenants know the laws like the back of their hands because they go through the eviction process a few times each year. Each time they learn a little more about beating the system, so postponements become the rule not the exception. A clever tenant can evade eviction for months. Careful screening will save more than money in the end.

YOUR "GUT" FEELING

Everything discussed in this chapter comes down to what we talked about in the last chapter called "gut feeling." Sometimes, what sounds good on the phone, is not good in person. Most times, if they sound questionable on the phone they are definitely a "no go" in person.

In my early landlording days, my instinct would say no. But faced with the persistent applicant, calling three times a day and with no other applicants from which to choose, I would give in and accept them. I usually regretted it later.

If you're not absolutely sure, let the unit sit empty and wait for a better qualified applicant. The money lost by having the unit stay vacant an additional month will be cheap, compared to the cost if the wrong tenant is accepted.

Do not reject a tenant because of your "gut feeling." Reject them on factual information. See the Denial Request For Tenancy form which lists reasons for denial to be checked off if they ask for prove of rejection in writing.

PROTECT YOURSELF WHEN SHOWING UNITS

The following items apply to realtors and landlords who are showing houses:

- Don't show a property by yourself.
- Take your own car to showings.
- When leaving the car, lock it.
- Don't park the car where it can be blocked.
- Don't go in the basement or confined areas.
- Ask the prospective tenant to show you ID before entering the property.
- Have your cell phone turned on and carry it in your hand.
- Leave purses and jewelry at home.
- Arrive early and survey all rooms to determine escape routes.
- Let your office or family know where you will be and the time of the appointment.
- If you're alone, let them explore with you bringing up the rear.
- When scheduling an appointment over the phone get their phone number then call the number a few minutes later to re-confirm the time.

CHAPTER 11

RENTAL APPLICATION

It is not so much making the right decision as making the decision right.

We make a living by what we get, but we make a life by what we give.

PROCESSING THE APPLICATION

Start the screening process by assuming that everything on the application is false and you need to prove otherwise. This approach will make you think long and hard about not verifying information on the application. Tenants know the electricity, gas, cable TV, can be turned off or a car can be repossessed much quicker than you can get them thrown out of the apartment so those bills get paid first. This is why thoroughly screening a prospective tenant is so important. Taking the time to do the following steps will take much less time than it takes to evict, clean, and repair a unit because you didn't do them.

If you only want to be in the landlording business for a just short time, skip this chapter. If you plan on staying in this business a long time, devour everything that is in this chapter!

After receiving an application, call the prospective tenant, to let them know it was received. Use this opportunity to ask additional questions that will help in the screening process.

Most applicants won't lie, and often give more information than would be discovered when calling

Rental Application

For Property at _____ Projected move-in date if accepted ___/___/___

Personal Information - Please Print

First Applicant (First, Middle, Last Name) _____ Birth Date _____

Social Security Number _____ Driver's License # _____

Present Address (street, city, zip) _____ | How long at this address?

Current Phone ( ) _____ Email _____ | _____ Months

Current Landlord's Name _____ Phone ( ) _____ Current Rent $ _____

Why Moving? _____ Was Notice Given? YES☐ NO☐

Previous Address (street, city, zip) _____

Previous Landlord's Name _____ Phone ( ) _____ How long _____

Why Did You Move? _____ Monthly Rental Amount $ _____

Names of Additional Occupants _____

How many pets ? ____ What breed, weight, size? _____

　　 Neutered? YES☐ NO☐ If cat, declawed? YES☐ NO☐ Is pet current with all shots? YES☐ NO☐

2nd Applicant (First, Middle, Last Name) _____ Birth Date _____

Social Security Number _____ Driver's License # _____

Present Address (street, city, zip) _____

Landlord's Name and Phone Number _____

Financial Information

First Applicant Occupation _____ Full Time _____ Part Time (less than 32 hrs) _____

Employer _____ Position _____

Address _____ How long employed? ___ Years ___ Months

Gross Income Month $ _____ (Include copies of two recent pay stubs when returning application)

Person to Contact _____ Phone ( ) _____

Previous Employer _____ How long employed? ___ Years ___ Months

Why did you leave? _____ Gross Income Month $ _____

Additional Employment: Employer _____ Contact Person _____

Position _____ Weekly Hours _____ Income/Mo. $ _____ Phone ( ) _____

Second Applicant Occupation _____ Full Time _____ Part Time (less than 32 hrs) _____

Employer _____ Position _____

Address _____ How long employed? ___ Years ___ Months

Gross Income Month $ _____ (Include copy of two recent pay stub when returning application)

Person to Contact _____ Phone ( ) _____

Previous Employer _____ How long employed? ___ Years ___ Months

Why did you leave? _____ Gross Income Month $ _____

Additional Employment: Employer _____ Contact Person _____

Position _____ Weekly Hours _____ Income/Mo. $ _____ Phone ( ) _____

Credit References - list credit cards and present loans - if you need more room list on separate sheet of paper

　　 Name　　　　　　　Account #　　　　　Balance　　　　　Monthly Payment

Personal References - Please list two with name and phone number _____

Page 1 of 2

35a

employers and landlords. Make notes of their answers on the back of the application and then verify the information by calling the appropriate people.

If there has been a problem, hearing the applicant's side of the story as well as the landlord's, employer's, etc. will help separate truth from fiction. Think about starting each question to a prospective tenant with the words "when." It shows a course of action you will take. Some examples of questions to ask are:

- When I run a credit check, what will I find out about you?
- When I call your present landlord, what will he say about you? (pays on time, keeps a neat unit, no late payments, considerate of neighbors, etc.)
- When I call your previous landlord, what will he tell me?
- When I talk to your employer, what will he tell me about you? (reliable, on time, often sick, and so on)
- Before I begin processing this application, is there anything else I should know about you?

Explain that it will take two or three days to process the application and all information gathered will be given to the partners/owners (make them the bad guys), who will make the final decision as to who will get the unit. You will then call and let them know the owner's decision.

It will not take two or three days to get the credit check back and to do the other work, but this gives more time for other applications to be returned and processed. Of course, if the applicant checks out "A-OK", call them immediately.

CREDIT CHECKS

Running a credit check is an absolute must. Find a company that runs credit checks and open an account.

Run credit checks on everyone applying over 18 years old. If two single adults apply, have two applications filled out and charge two application fees.

Make the application fee non-refundable. This fee separates the serious applicants from the ones just looking. Casual applicants will not spend the money unless they are interested. It discourages the professional tenant looking for the easy landlord who doesn't run credit checks and call references.

Many good credit bureaus, specializing in tenant screening, are surfacing throughout the country. They offer other services such as screening for judgments, criminal violations, and bankruptcy, for an additional fee. This is an excellent way to screen

many areas that might take you days to discover at the local court house. I have found that calling the district justice in the town or area where the applicant lived can do wonders. If the secretary or judge knows who they are, without looking up the applicant's record, that is usually a strong sign you don't want them.

Each credit bureau has a different way of categorizing its information. Learn how to read the printouts to discover if the prospective tenants are current, or not, on bill payments. Are they 30, 60, or 90 days late and have any gone to "collection account" status? Look for bankruptcy and repossession accounts. Mortgage companies require an explanation, in writing, of a one day lateness on a payment, before giving a mortgage. Why should you consider someone who is 60 or more days late on a payment, or has had a car repossessed or has filed bankruptcy?

Tips for Reading a Credit Report

- Compare the date of birth with the first time the person used credit. If there is more than a 25 year gap, the information may not be his. It might be that he was married and the credit is in the spouse's name, or that he was in prison and changed either his name or social security number (not legal).
- Run the credit check on everyone. Husband and wife can each establish credit and you need to look at total debt per month for both of them.
- Look at the public record section to see if there are judgments, liens or garnishments.
- Look to see that the address on the application, drivers license, insurance information, and pay stub all match up
- Verify that the social security number on the application matches the one on the pay stub.
- Look to see if a bankruptcy appears. If one does, make sure that it has been discharged, which should be noted on the credit report. If not, ask the prospective tenant for a copy. If it has been discharged study carefully to see what has happened since the bankruptcy. Hopefully he is not making the same mistake.
- Is there more than one name associated with the social security number?
- Study the number of inquiries listed and when posted. This will tell you who else has been looking at the same information. Is it human services looking for a child support payment or a car dealership which could reveal high payments for the new car just purchased. It could also be a collection agency or fellow landlords doing the same thing you are.

Personal Information Section of the Application

Full Names - Ask for the full name which includes middle names, Jr.'s. If they have a nickname or go by another name get that also.

Current Address - The current address is needed to run the credit report plus it allows you to drive by and check out their neighborhood. How long they have lived at this current address will tell a few more things about them. If they have been at the same address for three years or more, they show stability. If they have been there for a year or less, look very closely at how long they lived with the previous landlord. If this shows a short stay, find out why they move so often.

Do not accept applications that list a post office box as the address. It is hard to drive by a post office box and talk to neighbors, fellow tenants, and look in the back yard. If you have to file for eviction, the sheriff will not serve a post office box. If the tenant is to be subpoenaed it must be done at a residence. These are all good reasons for not accepting post office boxes as the current address.

Previous Address - Check to see if the previous address on the application matches the previous address on the credit report. If there has been a Landlord-Tenant judgment it will probably be listed under a previous address.

Current Phone and E-mail address - The current phone number will be needed to contact them with questions or to tell them if they have been approved or not. The same things could be done by e-mail.

A prospective tenant calls and leaves his phone number and email address on your tape machine (because you asked him to leave both). Five calls that come in give their email addresses. Type in each address in your email program and under subject state: "2 Bedroom Apt. in Anytown is still available." Draw up a standard letter giving all the particulars of the property and paste it in. Also, give your qualifying standards and ask them to write back if they are still interested in scheduling an appointment to see the property. You show it to three of the five who respond back via email and one is accepted.

After receiving their deposit to hold the unit, e-mail them a copy of the lease so they can review it before the move-in day. Then, say, a few days before the lease signing the couple backs out. Since it will take a couple of days to get the ad back in the paper, start sending out e-mail to the other e-mail addresses of people who had inquired about the property. Let them know it's back on the market.

Another scenario. It's the middle of winter and the rental market is slow. The rent at $525 is not working. Many showings, but no applications. Contact all prospective tenants who left e-mail addresses to see if they would be interested in renting at $510 or at the $525 price with some upgrades.

EMPLOYMENT VERIFICATION

From: _____

_____

_____

I authorize you to give the the requested information to:

_____

Signed _____

Date ____/____/____

To: _____

_____

_____

Dear Sir or Madam,

_____ has applied to rent one of our rentals and has given your name as a present or previous employer. We would appreciate you taking a few moments to supply us with the information requested below.

Thank you for your cooperation.

Sincerely,

_____

Job Title of Applicant _____

Length of Employment _____

Full time _____ Part time _____

Average hours per week: _____ Is applicant reliable? _____

Salary $ _____ Week ☐ Month ☐ Year ☐

Additional comments you feel would be helpful: _____

_____

_____

_____

_____

_____
Signature of Employer or Agent

7

Send it out as a personal invitation to tour the "new upgraded apartment."

Social Security Number - This is a vital number the credit agency needs for screening a prospective tenant. Before calling in for the credit report, verify the social security number that is on the application matches the social security number that is on the driver's license and pay stub. This number can also help smoke out tenants who use different names on different documents but write down the same social security number.

Birth Date - Verify from driver's license or pay stub. This date is also helpful when running credit checks.

Previous Landlord - Call the previous landlord first. They will have no reason to lie because the tenant is no longer living there. Here are some questions to ask the previous landlord:

- How many months did he reside with you?
- Did he ever pay late? If so, was the late fee included?
- Did he get along well with fellow tenants and neighbors?
- Did you ever have to send him a notice about anything? If yes, what was it about?
- Did he have any animals? If yes, what?
- Did you ask the tenant to leave?
- Did he leave owing you money?

Current Landlord

The current landlord's incentive to tell the truth is proportional to how good or bad the tenant has been. Your phone call could be the difference in finally getting rid of the bad tenant. This is why visiting prospective tenants at their home, unannounced, will tell if the landlord was lying or telling the truth.

The landlords can be mailed, or faxed the Landlord Verification form. Make sure to verify that the return address on the envelope or phone number on the fax matches what is listed on the application.

If calling the landlord, start the phone call by telling him his tenant has applied for credit with your company (which they have) and you need to verify some information. The landlord, not suspecting a fellow landlord, will be more open from a credit standpoint than if receiving a call from a landlord/tenant relationship. At this point mention that they are also being shown as a current landlord and have them answer these questions:

- Are they current with rent?
- Have they ever paid late? If yes, how often?
- Have they given the required notice to vacate?
- How long have they been renting from you? (Try to get month and year.)
- How much notice must they give you to terminate the lease?

Of course if it's a friend answering the phone pretending to the landlord they will give positive responses as will a real landlord trying to get rid of a bad tenant.

LANDLORD VERIFICATION

From: _____

_____

_____

To: _____

_____

_____

I authorize you to give the requested information to:

_____

Signed _____

Date ___/___/___

Dear Sir or Madam,

_____ has applied to rent one of our rentals and has given your name as the present or previous landlord. We would appreciate you taking a few moments to supply us with the information requested below.

Thank you for your cooperation.

Sincerely,

_____

Rented from you from _____ to _____

Rent amount _____ Ever pay late? _____ How often? _____

Was proper notice given? _____

Number of people living in the unit: _____

How many pets? _____ What kind?_____

Did they call often about repairs? _____

Additional comments you feel would be helpful: _____

_____

15

Current Landlord or Friend - How To Tell?

How will you know if the person on the other end of the line is the real landlord or a friend of the applicant? Here is another angle that works real well. When the landlord, or friend, answers the phone, identify yourself and ask if you are speaking to Mr. Smith who is John and Mary Jones landlord. Let Mr. Smith know that you have received a rental application from the Jones'. Since we are not sure if Mr. Smith is the true landlord or a friend it's time to find out. Start changing information that is on the application. For example: The Jones list their address as 123 S. Main St. Tell Mr. Smith the address they gave you is 128 S. Main St. The real landlord will know his own address but a friend might not. The rental application lists the rent at $500. Ask Mr. Smith if the rent the Jones' are paying is $550 a month. The real landlords will know the correct rent but a friend might not. If they said they lived in the apartment for 2 years tell Mr. Smith they said they have been a tenant for 5 years. Once again the real landlord will know this is incorrect or can look up to verify if he is not sure. Next look on the application under the "do you have any pets?" section. If the Jones listed on the application they *did not* have a pet, ask Mr. Smith if he had any trouble with the dog? I have had people listed as the landlord miss every single one of these questions.

If you are still not sure whether you are talking to a friend or the real landlord, check the local tax records to see that the name and address where the tax bills are being sent matches those listed on the rental application. If there are discrepancies, try to discover the reasons why. If the answers don't satisfy you, let this be a warning to be careful. Another way to verify if it's the real landlord is to look them up in the phone book and see if the phone number matches. A cross directory could also be used to match up a phone number with a street address.

PETS

This topic is covered in-depth in Chapter 7.

WHY MOVING?

Discovering the reason for moving can also be enlightening:
- My landlord is selling, so I must move.
- My landlord is getting a divorce and needs to move into our unit.
- My rent was increased 75% and it's not worth it.
- I can't get the landlord to make repairs.
- I want to be closer to work.
- I am expecting another child and need the extra bedroom.

- I am tired of living with in-laws.
- I like your location better than my present location.

These may not necessarily be the real reasons. Be prepared to ask follow up questions. One applicant stated he was moving due to a job transfer. His present employer, of three months, was a local ski shop. He listed his previous job as a scuba instructor with a resort in Bermuda. He had been there for just three months. I pressed him further, and he told me that before Bermuda he had been a ski instructor, (again for three months), in Colorado. I'm sure if I had asked what he did before Colorado it would have been a life guard in Hawaii—for three months!

CALLS FROM FELLOW LANDLORDS

When receiving a phone call from a fellow landlord inquiring about your tenant, always tell the truth however bad they have been. The landlord is doing his homework by calling, so he deserves a fair accounting. Answer questions that you can give factual information such as: they paid late three times; I had to file for eviction once but they got caught up; the rent is $500 a month; I pay water/sewer they pay the rest. Avoid subjective questions such as: do they keep a nice unit; how well do they get along with fellow tenants; are the kids well behaved.

FINANCIAL AND EMPLOYMENT VERIFICATION
Employer

The employer information can be gathered by using the Employer Verification form which can be faxed to the employer who then faxes it back. Employment can also be verified with two recent pay stubs submitted with the application. Check to confirm that the amount listed for gross salary per week matches what the pay stubs show.

Previous Employer

The "previous employer" section of the application is helpful if the applicant shows a short tenure with the present company but many years with the previous one. The change in jobs usually means a major advancement and/or a big salary jump.

Credit References

If there are loans or credit card balances that must be paid each month, this amount should be subtracted from the weekly gross salary. Mortgage companies normally use 28%-36% as the ratio between the mortgage payment to the home buyer's gross income. My ratio of 25%, or one week's gross salary should equal the monthly rental amount plus utilities, is slightly higher than the mortgage company's.

The amount of alimony or child support received or paid should also be calculated when figuring qualifying ratios. If there is money in a savings account or if they are willing to give extra security the ratios can be modified slightly.

What should you do when applicants have good credit and your gut feel says they are OK, but they fall short in qualifying income? Ask them if someone who owns real estate would co-sign with them on the lease. Stress that their co-signer must sign the lease and if rent is not paid and a judgment is awarded, a lien will be placed on the co-signer's real estate.

It might take years to get the money, but it is just like the commercial says: "You can pay me now or you can pay me later."

Usually a quick phone call to Mom and Dad will produce a check real fast.

Personal Information

Getting personal information about the applicant can also be very helpful. If they must answer yes to any of the following questions, they might decide to look for another landlord that won't ask them these potentially embarrassing questions.

- Do you have renters insurance?
- Have you ever broken a lease?
- Have you ever been given an eviction notice or been asked to move?
- Have you ever been convicted of a felony?
- Have you ever had a judgement entered against you?
- Are you presently an illegal abuser of a controlled substance?
- Do you have any history of drug use or offenses?
- Do you own a waterbed and if yes, and carry an insurance policy?
- Do you have phone service in your name?

Emergency Name and Phone Number

Getting a name and phone number of a person to contact in an emergency is a good idea. If a robbery or fire occurred, and the tenants cannot be located, this person should know how to contact the tenant.

Make and Model of Vehicles

Asking for the make and model of the tenant's cars on the application will help identify different vehicles parked at the house. If a different car suddenly appears, either the tenants bought another car or they have a "permanent visitor".

You can also use the license number and VIN (Vehicle Identification Number) to track a tenant

that "skips out" in the middle of the lease. For a few dollars, the state police motor vehicle department can provide the tenant's new address. They need the tenant's full name, birth date, social security number, and last known address.

It most likely will be a few months before the tenant gets around to changing the address on his driver's license. Be patient. You will eventually get it. The new address will be needed so the court papers can be forwarded. Remember, if you want to collect for rent or damages, it is your responsibility, not the court's, to locate a tenant who has moved.

Visit the District Justice that services the area where they are now living. Take your signed application with you and ask if any judgments have been filed against them.

Another option is to call the local police in the town they are now living and ask them not about the specific tenant, but about the property. Have they been called to this property and if so for what reasons.

Driver's License

Require each applicant to return a copy of his driver's license with the rental application. Most states have photo ID licenses so this will help verify the person's identity, as well as address, date of birth and license number. Some applicants may use stolen credit information to get approved and then deny living in the apartment. If you have the applicant's picture with your rental application, the tenant can't claim you got the wrong person. In most states the driver's license can also be used to get new address information.

Application Fee

Require a non-refundable application fee to cover the cost of running the credit check. Charging this fee keeps the professional tenants who don't want their credit checked from applying. It also quickly separates the serious prospects from the lookers.

VISIT THE PROSPECTIVE TENANTS' HOME

Everything is checking out. The credit report is excellent, employment history and salaries are acceptable and current and previous landlords all say nice things about the prospective tenant. There is no record at the District Justices' office and they presented themselves well when shown the unit.

One of the last things to do in the screening process is to visit them at their home unannounced so they don't have time to clean. If they live within one hour of your home, they should be visited. If the ride will be more than a half an hour, call and say I'm in the area and will be there in a few minutes. Since 80% of all rental applications are not filled out completely it will be very easy to find a signature, a vehicle registration number, a social security number, etc. missing on the application. If every thing is completed on the application then take a blank lease. Say it's your policy to let prospective tenants review the lease ahead of time in case they have any questions. It's only a few sheet of paper and if it helps you get in the front door, then it was worth it.

But how do you get into the house? You don't have a warrant. Get creative. The three cups of coffee you drank on the way over has made for a full bladder and you need to use the bathroom. If it is a hot day ask for a glass of water and then once inside ask to use the bathroom. You need them to sign or complete information on the application. Your main objective is to at least get into the foyer area which should give you a view of most of the first floor.

Look at the walls for holes and crayon marks. Look at the stove for years' worth of accumulated burnt offerings and grease build-up. Is the kitchen sink filled with two weeks' worth of dirty dishes? Does the unit have a pet odor or a poor housekeeping odor? Remember that what you see or smell in this unit is exactly what you will get in your apartment.

Remember what you see here is what your nice clean walls and carpet will look like when they move out. People have said that this takes a lot of time to do. Not when you consider how much time it will takes to rip out carpets, repaint walls, and repair broken items if you didn't do it. Sometimes two applicants will qualify on paper, but visiting both houses makes your choice much easier.

What should you do if they still don't let you in? Explain that you manage the unit for a group of investors (your wife and kids but they don't know that) and they have requirements that you must do before submitting the application. Some of the things they require are to run a credit check,

call previous and current landlords, call employers, etc. One of the items on your check list is to visit them at their house. "If you don't let me in, I won't be able to put a check next to that box. This might cause another applicant to score higher and they would be given the apartment." If they still refuse, you don't want them anyway. Do not use this as the reason for rejecting. Find some other reason from the credit report or application research.

Visit Neighbors

Rental applications gives lots of information but it does not tell who plays his music loud, throws parties every Friday night in the back yard until the wee hours of the morning, or allows the dog to bark outside all night long. It doesn't show who does verbal and/or physical abuse to their spouse and kids. It doesn't show that cars drive up to the

---

RENTAL DEPOSIT TO HOLD UNIT

Applicant 1 _____

Applicant 2 _____

Address _____

City _____ ST _____ Zip _____

Date ____/____/____

The above named applicant(s) has been accepted to occupy the premises listed above. An earnest money deposit of $ _____ has been paid to reserve the sole right to rent the property at the above address. This deposit will hold the property until _____ when applicant(s) agrees to move in.

If applicant does not move in for any reason by the above date, the deposit is NON-REFUNDABLE as liquidated damages. The applicant will also be held accountable for days the property remains vacant that are not covered by the deposit as well as be responsible for additional advertising costs required to re-rent the property.

____/____/____   _____
   Date   *Landlord*

37

house all times of the day or night and only stay five minutes. The people who know this very important information are fellow tenants and neighbors. Approach these people either in person or call them on the phone. Use a cross directory to get the phone numbers. Let them know that the tenant next door or downstairs has given you an application and you would like to ask how they have been as neighbors. It would be a good idea to interview more than one person to be sure the stories match. Sometimes one neighbor or fellow tenant might say positive things just to get rid of the fellow tenant.

RENTAL DEPOSIT TO HOLD UNIT

Once the decision has been made and the applicant has agreed to rent the unit, require a portion of the security deposit to be paid to hold the unit. Ask for one month and settle for nothing less than a half month deposit to hold the unit. Complete the rental deposit form which shows the amount of the deposit and states that if the tenant does not take possession, the deposit is forfeited.

ACCEPTANCE LETTER

When the deposit to hold the unit is received, I mail an acceptance letter which gives the exact address of the property, and the amount of funds due when the lease is signed.

It also includes a copy of the lease. This gives the tenant the opportunity to review the lease with an attorney or professional of their choice before meeting to sign the lease. Don't wait until the day you sign the lease to show it to them for the first time. This does not give them enough time to review it (unless you plan to stay and review each point with them) and could be considered an invalid contract if the tenant could prove you only gave them a few minutes to review and then made them sign it. They should not feel pressured in anyway to sign it.

Review again all rules and regulations so there are no misunderstandings later. Stress that you expect rent to be paid on time and in return you will do repairs in a timely fashion. Explain this is a business to you and if necessary, legal action will be initiated to enforce any of the rules of the lease.

DENIAL OF REQUEST FOR TENANCY

Most times a phone call telling the applicant another person was chosen will be enough to satisfy him. Wish him good luck in finding another apartment and stress you will keep his application on file in case a similar unit comes available in the near future. If he wishes to have the denial in writing, check off the appropriate box on the denial form and put it in the mail. Never give the applicant a copy of the credit report. They can obtain a copy through the local credit bureau if they wish to review the report.

ACCEPTANCE LETTER

___/___/___
Date

Dear _____.

It is our great pleasure to inform you that your application has been approved to rent the property located at _____.

It is our policy to mail your copy of the lease to review before signing. We encourage you to seek professional help in reviewing this information if certain clauses are not understood. Please also feel free to contact us with any questions.

Contact us a few days before the move-in date to schedule a convenient time for us to meet and sign the lease, do the walk through inspection, and pay the balance of money owed.

Be sure to contact the appropriate utility companies to have service started in your name as we will be contacting them to take these services out of our name.

The following funds should be brought with you when signing the lease. If the signing is not during banking hours all money due must be paid with a bank check, money orders, or cash. No personal checks will be accepted.

	PAID	DUE
Pro-rated Rent	_____	_____
Security Deposit	_____	_____
Totals	_____	_____

We hope your stay will be a long and happy one.

_____

```
┌─────────────────────────────────────────────────────────────────┐
│                 DENIAL OF REQUEST FOR TENANCY                      │
│                                                                   │
│                                                                   │
│  Date ___/___/___              From _____             │
│                                      _____             │
│                                      _____             │
│                                                                   │
│  Dear: _____                                          │
│         _____                                          │
│         _____                                          │
│                                                                   │
│   Your request for tenancy has been denied for the following reason(s) below: │
│      ___ Application incomplete          ___ Suit, repossession, foreclosure │
│      ___ Excessive financial obligations ___ No credit on file    │
│      ___ Insufficient credit references  ___ Insufficient credit on file │
│      ___ Insufficient length of employment ___ Insufficient income │
│      ___ Too short a period of residence ___ Previous eviction(s) │
│      ___ Unable to verify residence      ___ Bankruptcy           │
│      ___ Unable to verify credit references ___ Irregular employment │
│      ___ Unable to verify employment     ___ Delinquent credit references │
│      ___ Unable to verify income         _____   │
│      ___ Other _____           _____   │
│                                                                   │
│   OPTIONAL: Disclosure of use of information obtained from outside source was obtained │
│   from: _____                                   │
│                                                                   │
│                                                                   │
│                                                                   │
│                                                                   │
│                                                                   │
│                                                                   │
│                                                                   │
│                                                                   │
│   Under the Fair Credit Reporting Act, you have the right to make a written request, within 60 days of receipt of this notice, for │
│   disclosure of the nature of the adverse information. The Federal Equal Credit Opportunity Act prohibits creditors from │
│   discriminating against credit applicants on the basis of race, color, religion, national origin, sex, marital status, age (provided the │
│   applicant has the capacity to enter into a binding contract), because all or part of the applicant's income derives from any public │
│   assistance program or because the applicant has in good faith exercised any right under the Consumer Credit Protection Act. The │
│   Federal agency that administers compliance with this law concerning this creditor is the Federal Trade Commission, Equal │
│   Opportunity, Washington, DC 20580.                               │
│                                                                5  │
└─────────────────────────────────────────────────────────────────┘
```

• Visit current residence and neighbors.
• Accept or reject the application. If you accept, request a deposit to hold the unit. Try to collect a half to a full month which will be applied to the security deposit.

AFTER THEY ARE APPROVED

• Portion of security deposit received to hold unit
• Lease mailed or reviewed before move-in date
• Renters insurance suggested or required — See a receipt for a one year paid up renters insurance policy with you listed as additional insured before signing lease.
• Inspection sheet filled out, signed, and returned
• All pages of lease initialed and last page signed and dated
• Move-Out Charges given with lease
• Tenant's new phone number
• Maintenance request forms given and reviewed

LEGAL REASONS TO REFUSE TO RENT

The examples listed below will only hold up in court if they are applied to all applicants. They cannot be applied selectively. If you refused to rent to a prospective tenant because he is a smoker, be sure that no existing tenant smokes, or has taken up the habit since they moved in.

TENANT MOVE-IN CHECKLIST

Some of these items will be completed before a tenant is approved and the rest after approval. It's an easy way to make sure you have not forgotten anything.

• Call the applicant and confirm your receipt of his application. If any information is missing, this is a good opportunity to get it filled in now. Use this as an opportunity to ask questions about what you discovered from the credit report and your calls to employers and landlords.
• Are the verification forms signed to mail to employer and landlord.
• Run a credit check.
• Call employers, landlords, references, district justices, and any other references.

1. Bad credit
2. No credit
3. Not previously employed
4. Unstable employment history
5. Cannot verify income
6. Cannot provide two forms of identification- one with picture
7. Fails to sign rental application
8. Fails to fully complete the rental application
9. Gives information that cannot be verified
10. Falsifies information on any form
11. Fails to provide name of present landlord
12. Fails to provide name of previous landlord
13. Has waterbed but no documentation of having waterbed insurance

14. Does not meet your minimum income requirements
15. Has a pet
16. If you do accept pets, the applicant cannot prove the pet has been neutered, declawed, and had its shots
17. Has criminal convictions, civil and/or eviction judgments
18. Has a judgment or liens filed against them
19. Owns a vehicle(s) or objects that cannot be stored on the property
20. Owns excessive number of vehicles
21. Has a history of damaging property
22. Has a history of disturbing neighbors
23. Owns items too large to be stored on the premises
24. Has a contagious disease (other than AIDS)
25. Filed bankruptcy
26. Is a smoker — only use this one if none of your tenants are smokers.
27. Not given notice to current landlord
28. More than the number of persons allowed by occupancy guidelines
29. Can not pay the first month's rent and security deposit in full
30. Use of premises for purposes other than living purposes
31. Application fee or deposit check to hold the unit bounces
32. Previous and/or current landlord not given proper notice
33. Unacceptable debt to income ratio
34. Is a minor with no responsible adult to co-sign on the lease

TRAITS OF FRAUDULENT APPLICATIONS

The following fraud characteristics should be considered as alerts and they are good cause for further investigation. Any combination of these traits is an indication of the possibility of fraud; however, they should not be considered as absolute proof without additional investigation. Think about the effect on your business if you do not follow up on the hints you have been given.

TENANT MOVE-IN CHECKLIST

Tenant _____

Address _____

Move in date ___/___/___

Application filled out completely _____

If not, what's missing? _____

Verification forms signed _____

Credit report run/received _____

Called employers _____

Called current landlord _____

Called previous landlords _____

Called references _____

Visited current residence _____

Deposit given to reserve rental   Amount $ _____ _____

Security Deposit received   Amount $ _____ _____

First month's rent collected   Amount $ _____ _____

Lease mailed or received before move-in date _____

Move-out charges given _____

Renters Insurance suggested / required _____

Mailing address, phone numbers given _____

Maintenance requests reviewed _____

All pages of lease initialed and last page signed, dated _____

Inspection sheet filled out, signed, and returned _____

Date completed ___/___/___

2002

49

Name

1. Unusual name configuration such as two first names: John N. James, George L. Dennis
2. Names of known personalities; ie, Michael Jordon, George Burns

Employment / Salary

1. Job title misspelled
2. Job title does not appear to fit type of employment
3. Salary appears out of range to fit type of employment
4. Monthly salary includes cents or unusual symbols after base salary
5. Years employed don't correlate with age
6. Amount of established credit doesn't correlate with age

Signature
1. Signature scrawled or unintelligible
2. Signature is written over as if mistake was made the first time
3. Signature is underscored and angled off signature line

Miscellaneous
1. Home/business addresses is a P.O. Box
2. Credit references are from unknown companies (use phone book to verify)
3. Credit references are unavailable

Before Buying RE Ask To See Leases and Rental Applications

Remember to ask for leases from owners, before purchasing a property. I purchased a property where the owner swore the leases were month-to-month so I took his word and did not review them. The day after settlement, I discovered they renewed year-to-year. I had bought the property thinking I could raise the tenant's rent $100. I missed the 60 days notice by two days. The tenant paid the lower amount for another year because I trusted the owner without seeing the leases. It is a good idea to get estoppel letters from the tenants you will be inheriting when you buy a new property. These letters are signed by the tenants and state the amount of rent being paid and any special conditions of their lease that might have been arranged verbally with the original owner.

Having the rental applications is important for the same reasons that you want them for your own units. If the seller cannot supply this information, try to have the tenants fill out your rental application. If the seller did not require a move-in inspection sheet, have the tenants complete your own inspection sheet right after settlement.

This inspection sheet will settle disputes as to who caused what damage. Have each tenant sign an inspection sheet after settlement. Granted, there is nothing you can do about damage the tenants caused before your purchase, but they can be held responsible for future damages.

I learned the importance of using an inspection sheet the hard way. I visited a tenant the day after settlement and inspected the unit. The old owner did not have the tenant complete an inspection sheet. I also did not have the tenant complete an inspection sheet. When they moved out, the unit was in worse shape than when I had first inspected it. I subtracted the repairs from the security deposit, and soon found myself in court trying to defend my actions. Since I had not required the tenant to sign an inspection sheet when I assumed ownership, it was my word against the tenant's. They claimed the apartment was left in the same condition it was in when they took occupancy. I obviously lost and learned a valuable lesson. Remember, if a judge must make a ruling from the words of the tenant or the landlord, in most cases the ruling will go for the tenant. My experiences with judges are they know you are the owner and will hold you to a higher standard to provide a paper trail. Without it, your odds of winning dramatically drop . This is one of the reasons I use so many forms and make copies of each before mailing to tenants.

The techniques I have described in this chapter have worked for me, but variations on these ideas might work better for you. Nothing in landlording is written in stone. Always be ready to try different techniques or refine old ones to meet your needs. Talk to fellow landlords, join a local real estate association, and talk to realtors involved in property management. Keep current with market rental rates and share experiences with people in the same business as you. Some of my most memorable evenings have been spent with fellow landlords sharing tenant stories and some creative, but legal, solutions to landlording problems. Learn from as many sources as possible to cut down on landlording mistakes that could be very costly later.

YOU'RE NOT IN THE SUBSIDIZED HOUSING BUSINESS

Too many landlords feel sorry for their tenants when told about their financial difficulties. Most times the landlord will delay starting the eviction because they want to believe the tenant is telling the truth that they will have the rent by a certain date. Unfortunately, most times it backfires and the money promised never materializes.

Another way of looking at the situation is, the longer you allow them not to pay, the further in debt they go. While waiting for the rent, the mortgage must be paid out of your own pocket. This is money that could have been used to make your own mortgage payment, enjoy a trip with the family, or pay some bills.

In sports, every opponent sizes up his competitor to see if a weakness can be found that can be capitalized on to gain an advantage. Tenants do the same thing with landlords. If they discover you are a softy and do not do what is stated in the lease, they will take advantage of this every opportunity they can.

The next time a tenant calls to ask if you will waive the late fee because they will only be a day or two late with the rent, try this approach. Give him your mortgage company's phone number. Tell him to explain his situation to your mortgage company and if they will waive their late fee on your mortgage payment, you will waive his late fee. This approach shows the tenant that you have obligations just as they do and since they know what the reaction of the mortgage company will be, the call will probably not be made.

CHAPTER 12

Lease Agreements

Learn from the mistakes of others. Your cash flow will not last long enough for you to make them all yourself.

Those who don't believe something can be done should get out of the way of those who want to do it because unless you are the lead dog, the view never changes.

— A.D. Kessler

There is much more to owning real estate and doing property management than finding tenants, making repairs, collecting rents, and then ultimately selling the building. You have certain rights in ownership but you grant some of these rights to tenants when you allow them to occupy and use your property. These rights are set forth in laws that come from the national, state, and local governments.

Contact the local landlord, apartment owners, or real estate investment association, to learn about the laws of your state and local government. If you don't know of a group like this in your area, call the National Real Estate Investors Association at 1-888-7NaREIA or check out their website at www.nationalreia.com. for a group in your area.

WHAT IS A LEASE?

A lease is a contract, either written or oral, that transfers the right of possession of the premises to the tenant. A "leasehold estate" is created when the landlord conveys a possessory interest in the property to another for a specific period of time, in exchange for the tenant's payment of rent. When a landlord signs a lease giving a "leasehold estate" he is giving the tenant exclusive possession right of the premises, for an agreed upon term. If the tenant fails to comply with the leasehold bargain, the landlord's only legal recourse is to remove him through eviction proceedings.

MAKE YOUR LEASE A VALID CONTRACT

Most states honor verbal leases of less than three years but require leases for more than three years to be in writing. Verbal leases are not preferable because they are more likely to be open to various interpretations. Leases are a needed legal, as well as psychological, device to explain the terms and conditions of the contract.

In order for a lease to be valid, it must include the five elements of a contract:

1. **Capacity** – The law limits the legal capacity of signing contracts to people at least 18 years old. A person not of legal capacity would be someone under 18 years old or not mentally competent.

2. **Must Be a Legal Document** – An agreement between two parties is not a legal contract if both parties agree to do something that is against the law. An example might be agreeing to commit a criminal act or using a gambling debt as payment.

3. **Must Have Mutual Consent** – All parties must understand and agree to all terms of the contract, or it is not valid. To make sure there are no misunderstandings when signing a lease, mail or hand deliver a copy of the legal section of the lease and the additional terms and conditions to the new tenants at least 48 hours before signing. The cover letter encourages them to seek professional help in reviewing these documents before meeting to sign the paper work. When they do come to sign the lease, ask if they have any questions about the information received and wait for a "no" response. If they have questions, answer them but don't move on until a "no" response is heard.

Review all other documents with the tenant the same way by waiting for the "no" response to questions. Everything must be understood. This is done to ensure the contract will not be thrown out of court because the tenant states he was forced to sign something he did not understand.

4. **Must Be Consideration** – A contract is not binding unless there is an agreement to some sort of consideration. Consideration is whatever both parties agree to exchange as a mutual promise to fulfill the contract. This could be in the form of money, jewelry, gold, antiques, etc.

5. **Must Not Be Under Duress** – If a tenant can prove in court you threw the legal section of the lease in front of him, which he had never seen before, pointed a gun at his head, and said sign, the lease would then be considered invalid because there was duress. Take away the gun and the tenant might still have a strong case. By asking the questions outlined above and mailing the legal part of the lease to the tenant before signing, it will be difficult for him to show duress.

FOUR TYPES OF LEASEHOLD ESTATES:

1. **Term Tenancy** is for a specific time with a beginning and ending date. When the ending date arrives, the estate is terminated without notice required from either party.

2. **Periodic Tenancy** is the one most often used by landlords. It is an estate from one specific date to another, and renews for the same amount of time until ended by either party giving the required notice. Periodic tenancies are usually year-to-year or month-to-month.

3. **Tenancy at Will** exists until either party wishes to terminate. Upon the death of either party, or by the sale of the property, the tenancy ends.

4. **Tenancy at Sufferance** is created when a person fails to vacate or surrender possession of the premises at the end of the leased term. When this occurs, the tenant is called a holdover tenant. This means that the landlord gave adequate notice to vacate, but the tenant failed to leave. Common sense would conclude that if the "contract" has been broken by a holdover tenant, the owner should have the right to gain control of his property by calling the police and having him removed. Not so. The tenant is entitled to "due process" and the normal eviction method for your state must be followed.

PLAIN LANGUAGE LEASE

A few years ago, Pennsylvania passed a law that said leases had to be written in easy to understand language. This means written at a fourth grade reading level, with bold headings, spaces between clauses, using only active verbs, and limiting each sentence to 25 words or less. I welcomed the law and converted my lease to meet the guidelines and had it approved by the state Attorney General's office. I was just as tired as the tenants when trying to understand leases drawn up by attorneys that only attorneys could understand.

I have sold this lease in eight states and have yet to receive a call questioning the legality of the clauses. Outside Pennsylvania, I encourage landlords to review it with an attorney (he will probably want a copy to use) and change clauses to fit the state's requirements such as the 3, 5, or 7 day Notice to Vacate, etc.

Over the past two decades I have tried to make this lease as landlord friendly as possible. I like to call it my living lease because I have "lived" every single one of the clauses. Every time a tenant pulls a quick one that I have not thought of, in goes another clause.

I like to mail a copy of the lease to tenants before moving in and encourage them to seek professional help if there is anything they do not understand. Some have called and said their attorneys have told them not to sign it. The attorney did not find anything illegal, but just said "You better not mess up because you won't win in court with this lease." Another tenant called me the day after receiving the lease to review. I asked what he thought. He said, "I think it stinks." When I asked why, he replied, "Because this lease is 99.9% in your favor." As politely as I could, I asked him to point out the one tenth of one percent that favored him, because I wanted to take it out!

There is no law that says a lease has to be 50-50. If all clauses are legal and all parties agree to the terms and conditions, it is a valid contract. If they tell me they can not sign it on the advice of their attorney, I say that's fine. I'll take the next person in line for the apartment and move on.

Another word of caution. If you have not gotten at least one month of security deposit to clear the bank before signing the lease, do not accept another check for the balance due. Require the tenant to bring certified funds, money orders, or cash. If they bring a check, do not accept it unless it's during banking hours and your cell phone is working. Call the bank to make sure the funds will clear and then when done signing the lease go directly to the bank and cash the check. By waiting a day or two, this gives the tenant time to put a stop payment on the check or withdraw enough funds so that the check won't clear. Avoid this situation by insisting on a money order, cash, or a certified check when signing.

Do not give keys to a tenant without a signed lease showing the date the keys were given. If you allow him in before the lease begins, your liability risk becomes much greater if someone is injured. He is not tenant bound under a contract. Example: Old tenant moves April 1 and new tenant can't move in until April 15. The new tenant agrees to do the painting and cleaning for a half month of free rent. No rent was coming in from April 1–15 anyway so why not give this time as "free rent" for doing painting and cleaning. It gives the new tenant flexibility in his moving schedule, and maintenance you would have had to do, or paid to have done, is being done during the fifteen days no rent would have been collected.

Giving the tenant "free time" for doing the painting and cleaning is not a bad idea, if you feel you can trust him with a paint brush. This can also backfire, so be careful. Go ahead and sign the lease on April l and use this as the beginning date. Write April 1 to April 30 but only show a half month's rent on the line for Rent Due Until Regular Due Date. It also could be listed as April 1 to April 15 – $1.00 and then April 15–30 as a half month of rent. The tenant can start moving in any time once the painting and cleaning has been completed because the lease started on April 1. Many tenants like this arrangement because they are not signing the lease, cleaning their old unit, and moving all in the same weekend.

1. NAMES OF LANDLORD & TENANT(S)

The lease should name the Landlord or Rental agent and give a phone number where he can be reached. It should also include the address where the rent payments are to be mailed. Unless you don't mind your tenants knowing where you live, use a post office box or another address for rent to be received. It is not enjoyable to be sitting down to dinner and have a tenant hand deliver their rent on the fifth day of the month, one minute before 5:00 PM to avoid the late fee charge.

Not all tenants will vacate your property thinking you are the greatest person on the face of the earth. A post office box and unlisted phone number make it more difficult for someone to find you and your family if they have a grudge to settle. Be aware tenants can request your address from the post office by filling out a simple form. Avoid this situation by using an address different than your home, such as another rental property you own or the address where you work.

After filling in the date when the lease will be signed, the following lines are for the names of the parties involved. The owner is always the Lessor and the tenant is always the Lessee. Remember to name all parties over 18 years old and make sure everyone understands their responsibilities under the lease. Always use first and last names, especially when renting to married couples. Do not write Mr. and Mrs. John Tenant. Write John and Mary Tenant. Make sure the wife signs as Mary Tenant and not as Mrs. John Tenant or Mary Smith. Make sure the names on the top of the lease are the same as the names being signed.

2. LEASED PROPERTY

Start by listing the type of property it is that is being rented. Single family, Townhouse, Condominium, Apartment or Other. State the exact address and then list what items will be part of the lease property.

Anything not bolted down or a permanent fixture in the unit should be listed. As the cartoon says, if it is not listed, there is a chance it will disappear and there is nothing you can do about it. Some examples of items to list in your unit: oven/stove, dishwasher, garbage disposal, refrigerator, washer, dryer, garbage compactor, air conditioners, curtain rods, fire extinguishers, special light fixtures, smoke alarms, sump pumps, garage door openers, and, yes, wall to wall carpet. (It is a good idea to list make and model numbers or do this on the inspection sheet.)

Appliances will bring a higher rental amount, but depending on their ages, it might not be worth the aggravation of scheduling and paying for repairs. If appliances are getting old and repairs loom in the future, add a clause stating appliances will no longer be part of the lease. If the appliance breaks, it will be the tenants' responsibility to repair or replace it. See the additional clauses "Appliances" for the exact wording.

3. STARTING / ENDING DATES OF LEASE

When a unit comes available during strong rental months, sign a year-to-year lease. Some landlords may want to start with a month-to-month lease and if things work out, then switch the tenant to a year-to-year lease. If that landlord had done the proper screening, he should know the tenant will be a good one. If the number one goal is tenant retention, why would a landlord want to give a tenant a month-to-month lease? This gives him the option to move with either 30 or 60 days notice with the worst scenario happening in the middle of the winter. After the first year I give renewing tenants the option of month-to-month with sixty days notice with the rent increase being $30 to $50 more per month for this option. If they move in the winter months, I will now have extra money to keep heat in the unit.

What are the best rental months? This depends on the area of the country. Living in the northeast, the best months to find tenants are April to September. People who live in cold weather areas do not move in the winter months unless absolutely necessary. They are inside hibernating in front of a warm fire. They start to come out of the woodwork around March and April, and will usually be looking to move between then and September. The most active moving months are June and July. Many young couples are looking before getting married, and parents with children want to move at the end of the school year.

The landlord who signs a lease between October and March needs to make the term slightly longer or less than a year. This avoids having the lease come due during those off-peak months the following year. If a tenant moves in during November, try to sign a six month lease that will expire May 1. This gives you the opportunity to raise the rent. If the tenant decides to move May 1, you are now into prime renting season and can command top rent. If he decides to stay and has been a good tenant, renew him for one year. If he leaves the following year (May), you are still in prime rental season. With tenants who look very strong and desire a lease longer than sixth months, raise the rent to what you project the rent will be in a year and a half and then charge slightly less than that amount. It is a win-win for both sides. The tenant has the security of a year and a half lease and you have a higher rent than anticipated for the year. If the lease is broken before the end of the term, you are entitled to keep all the security deposit and collect rent until the expiration date, unless a new tenant is found earlier.

The starting date of the lease is the first day rent is paid. In a year's lease, the expiration date should be moved up or back, depending on the move in date, so it expires on the first of the month. Example: One year lease—Starting date is April 10th— Ending date would be April 1 of the following year. Starting date is April 20th— Ending date would be May 1 of the following year.

4. MONEY OWED AT MOVE IN
Total rent owed for entire length of lease

The lease should include the total amount of rent for the entire term of the lease. If it is for one year, multiply the rent by 12 months. If it is for six months, multiply by six. If the total amount for a year is not shown, a judge might say a month-to-month lease has been executed. The total number shows what is owed through the length of the entire contract and that both parties have agreed to divide the total due into 12 equal monthly installment payments.

Security Deposit

How much security deposit should be charged? That's an easy one. As much as the state will allow

under the law. Many times it is difficult for tenants to raise the cash needed to cover two months in security deposit and the first month's rent. Some landlords think if a tenant does not have two months of rent in a savings account as a back-up, he isn't a good candidate to consider. It is known that most tenants live from paycheck to paycheck and have no savings account. Expanded thinking will avoid sitting with many vacancies.

Try this simple but effective compromise if a qualified tenant is coming up short with the required amount of security deposit. Collect a minimum of one month's rent as security deposit. Have the tenant pay the difference that is owed over the first few months of the lease. Example: The tenant is short $400 to cover the full security deposit. Have them pay an additional $100 a month for four months to reach the required security deposit.

Landlords who require 30 days notice and collect only one month in security deposit, often times never see the last month's rent. Tenants have two reasons for not paying the last month's rent. They are afraid the landlord will fabricate needed repairs after they move and they will not see their security deposit returned. They also know it takes a landlord over one month to evict and they will be moved out before the lock-out is to occur.

By charging one and a half month's (or more) in security with 60 days notice, forces the tenant to pay at least the next to last month's rent after giving notice. They know two months is enough time to be evicted. If they fail to pay the last month's rent, the half month of security deposit is yours. The 60 day notice is also helpful if someone must move quickly and can only give 30 days notice. During the extra month it is vacant, the old tenant is still responsible for this rent and it can be subtracted from his security deposit. Use this time to do repairs (with rent still coming in) so it will be ready for the first of the next month.

Be prepared to have prospective tenants ask why the security deposit is more than one month. Most can't fathom why a landlord would need more than one month for a security deposit. Respond by telling them they are being given control of something (your property) that is worth about 99% more than the security deposit. Ask them if they could get a car loan or a mortgage with 1% down?

Rent due until regular due date

Make the due dates of all rent payments the first of each month. Otherwise, it becomes a bookkeeper's nightmare to keep track of when rents are due and late fees start. When signing the lease pro-rate the first month's rent so all subsequent months are due on the first. This will simplify the record keeping. Another reason to have rents due on the first is because most mortgage payments are due on the fifteenth of each month. This gives enough time for the checks to come in, be deposited and cleared before the mortgage payment is mailed. The best way to protect any checks from bouncing is to open a checking account that has overdraft protection. This is a line of credit that can be used if a check does come up short and will keep it from bouncing.

Additional Deposits

Be aware certain cities and towns require a building inspector to inspect each unit before a new tenant moves in. Charge the tenant for this inspection. Remember not to list pets as a separate security deposit. If the pet does no damage but money is owed over and beyond the security deposit being held, you will still have to pay back the pet deposit.

5. RENT

Part a) lists the monthly rental amount and the due date each month.

Part b) & c) state that if rent is not received by a specific date (like the 10th of the month) you will begin court action on the 15th day. The 10th and the 15th dates are just examples. Use whatever dates work for you. Part d) says the postmark date of the letter is the date the payment is received. This means if rent is due by the fifth and late on the sixth, and the check is mailed on the fifth but does not get postmarked until the sixth, the late fee is owed.

6. ADDITIONAL RENT CHARGES

This just a fancy way of saying late fee but it sounds better. How much to charge as a late fee varies from state to state, locality to locality and from landlord to landlord. Here are some examples of late fee techniques.

- Charge $2-$5 a day for each day late after the fifth of the month. The drawback to this approach is that late fees become ridiculously high very quickly and the tenant loses all incentive to pay or try to pay.
- Charge a percentage of the rental amount (usually 3-10%). This type fee also causes many bookkeeping headaches because the late fee is always a different amount for each rental property and never works out to an even dollar amount.
- Charge no late fee at all but each time the rent is late the rental amount goes up $10 for the balance of the term of the lease. For example, if the rent is $500 and payment is late during the sixth month of a one year lease, the new rental

amount for the balance of the lease would be $510. If the payment is late the next month the rental amount increases to $520 for the balance of the term. Talk to a real estate attorney or a District Justice to determine if this type of lease is acceptable in your state.

- Charge a flat $30 late fee if they are one day or 20 days late. This simplifies bookkeeping, is easy to explain, and to understand by tenants. Since most tenants paying the late fee will be paying between the fifth and the tenth, why not collect as much as possible and still be reasonable. Starting the late fee less than $20 could make the late fee an advantage in order to get other bills paid first. Make your late fee as high as you think a tenant will accept without balking and moving out.
- Charge $30 late fee if paid between the sixth and tenth of each month. Any rent paid after the tenth causes the late fee to jump to $50. This method will force the tenants who will be late to pay by the tenth to avoid additional late fees.
- Always check with your own attorney when establishing late fee rules and regulations. Some states do not allow flat fee arrangements that effectively exceed a certain percentage of the rent.

I like the two tier late fee where the tenant pays a $30 late fee if received between the sixth and tenth of the month. If they pay after the 10th, the late fee jumps another $20 for a total of $50. This gives them some more encouragement to get the payment in before the tenth day. If there is just one late fee and it doesn't matter if the rent is paid on the sixth or twenty-sixth, most tenants will wait until the twenty-sixth to pay the rent and late fee. There is no advantage to them to pay as soon as possible. Using the $2-5 per day will do the trick here but does the late fee stop on the day the check was mailed or the day you receive the payment? Too much bookkeeping for me.

Another alternative to a late fee is a rent credit. This clause is covered under the Additional Rules called "Discount For Prompt Payments."

7. NUMBER OF OCCUPANTS

Part a) lists the number of adults and children who are allowed to live in the property. Do not list number of people because adults have a tendency to become kids, and kids, adults. If you don't, this situation might happen: three friends decide to find an apartment and live together and know landlords don't like friends (especially male) moving in together. They decide which two of the three have the best jobs and credit rating. They fail to mention the third roommate to the nice landlord and are given the unit. Without this clause the landlord is left with no legal recourse when all three move in a few days later.

It also asks for the names of all occupants under the age of 18. This is helpful when calling the tenant, as you can call the kids by name. It also helps if the school calls and asks if Johnny Jones lives at 123 S. Main St. and you have the child's name as Sammy Smith. Could be a relative's child who lives in a neighboring town, but has moved into your unit because your schools are better than the other town's schools.

Part b) allows the landlord to end the lease if an unauthorized occupant is found living in the unit, requires the tenant to pay a fee per month (I use $100 a month) for each unauthorized occupant, and requires tenant to pay for all damages caused by this person.

Part c) says anyone living in the property for more than _____ days in a row (I use two weeks) is considered an unauthorized occupant.

Our next problem is how do we determine if the person has been there for 14 days in a row? We could drive by each morning and afternoon to see them coming and going which is not practical. The neighbors or fellow tenants could be asked to come to court and testify against the tenant. which is also not practical. Movies could be taken of the person coming and going but don't miss a day or it won't hold up in court. I used to call and schedule a air filter change on the heater and count toothbrushes, but, I discovered some people use more than one tooth brush! Counting beds these days also doesn't work. The only way I have discovered that will hold up in court is to see if mail is being delivered to the unit in the persons name. It is a federal offense to remove mail from a persons mailbox but there is no law that says its illegal to take a bag of someone's trash!

8. UTILITY SERVICES

This section lists the services both parties are responsible for maintaining. If the tenant is responsible for paying the water and sewer, but only the water is checked off, the sewer is now your responsibility.

The yearly furnace cleaning is too important to worry whether the tenant has paid for the contract each year, so pay for it yourself and be assured it is cleaned and serviced on a regular basis. When the furnace breaks, the tenant calls the service contract company who will call you if the problem is not covered under the service contract.

Be aware that the service contract companies give you the contract with the stipulation that you buy

the oil from their company, and rightfully so. Why should they have to make a repair because of someone else's inferior fuel. The problem is, tenants don't care about the service contract company. They want to buy the cheapest fuel they can find. It would be a good idea to include a clause in the lease requesting the fuel be purchased from the service contract company. If they don't, and the heater needs repair caused by inferior fuel, the cost of the repair is their full responsibility. This is usually enough to convince the tenant that saving a few pennies per gallon is not worth a major bill to repair the heater. Another idea might be to split the cost of the heating contract with the tenant and let them pick the company they want to use. You sign a service contract with that company and everyone is happy.

Make cutting the grass and shoveling snow the tenants' responsibility if they rent a single home or duplex. This includes buying the lawn mower and snow shovel. If the grass is not cut or the snow not shoveled, give the tenants a warning it must be done by a certain date. If not, you will pay to have it done and the bill will be sent to them. The amount of the bill should be included in the next month's rent or will be subtracted from the security deposit.

For units larger than a duplex or triplex, try to find a responsible tenant in the building to do this work. This avoids the problem of travel time for yourself or a maintenance person and offers the advantage of an on-site person keeping track of what needs to be done. A tenant will be more motivated than an outside person to do this type of work since he also benefits from a nicer lawn and cleaner building. Do not ask the first tenant you meet after buying the property to do the maintenance. Take a few months to discover who takes the best care of his unit and the building. Does he pick up trash, trim bushes outside his door, and shovel snow on his step without being asked?

When the right person is found, approach him with the idea of doing minor repairs for some rent credit. Stress you are committed to a safe, clean environment for your tenants to live in, and that you want repairs made in a timely fashion. You will compensate him in the form of monthly rent credit and the amount will be determined by how much responsibility he wants.

Start with common things where it will be easy to judge the quality of the work. Offer jobs such as shoveling snow, cutting grass, weeding flower beds, putting out trash, picking up trash, vacuuming/mopping common halls, etc. Whatever jobs he agrees to do, write a contract explaining in detail his responsibilities so there will be no misunderstandings later. Include a clause that either party may cancel the contract at any time. This protects you if he fails to do the work to your specifications, but also gives him an out if the work becomes more than he can or wants to handle. If the work is not done the way you expect it to be done, he must be corrected in a non-threatening manner. On the other hand, lavish praise for his work when it does meet your specifications. No one ever gets tired of hearing "thank you" for a job well done. If everyone is happy after a few months, discuss adding additional responsibilities.

Be aware that many townships will require some or all of the utility bills to stay in the owner's name and not the tenant's, even though the tenant is responsible for paying them. The bills are mailed to the owner and then forwarded to the tenant. There are two ways to make sure these bills are paid if the utility stays in your name. Mail the bill to the tenant for him to pay. If it is not paid, the following month's bill will reflect the non-payment. The second way is to mail a copy of the bill to the tenant who reimburses you in the next month's rent payment. This way you pay the bill on time and your good credit history remains intact. I would highly recommend using this last approach with condominium fees. The late fees assessed by the condo association will be to you, if the tenant "forgets" to make the payment.

9. INSPECTION

Part a) talks about the inspection sheet needing to be completed and turned in when signing the lease OR **Part b)** returning it within five days so time can be given to run all appliances through a full cycle. If not returned by certified mail in five days - **Part c)** tenant agrees the property is in satisfactory condition. I think it's best to do the inspection at the lease signing. The longer they have the inspection sheet the more little things will be noted.

Take your camera or movie camera and get some pictures of your tenants standing in your nice clean kitchen. Get more shots in the living room and bedroom. If they are in the picture, they can't claim you gave them a unit in poor condition when they are in a picture that everything looks great.

On the inspection sheet make sure the make and model numbers of all appliances are listed. The reason that spurred me to use inspection sheets was a tenant who "stole" a one year old frost free refrigerator from me. Under this section of the lease I wrote, refrigerator, washer, dryer, garbage disposal, etc. but did not list any make, model, or serial numbers. I had installed a brand new 22 cubic foot frost free refrigerator before this tenant signed the lease. When he moved out at the end of the year, I was left with a 15 cubic foot non-frost free refrigerator that looked 20 years old. When I asked the tenant to return my 22 cubic foot refrigerator his response was "I don't know what you are talking about." In court, I showed my receipt for the refrigerator which

---

INSPECTION SHEET

UNIT ADDRESS _____ Move in Date ___/___/___

If any number is OK, put a check next to it. If not, be specific on the lines.

1. ☐ PLUMBING - Any leaks in faucets, toilets, etc. _____

_____

_____

3. ☐ DRYWALL - Any holes or cracks?_____

_____

4. ☐ PAINT - Check walls, ceilings, woodwork, and trim. _____

5. ☐ FLOORING - Cuts or streaks in carpet or tiles. _____

6. ☐ APPLIANCES - Are all working? Any chips or cracks? _____

_____

_____

7. ☐ HEATING AND AIR CONDITIONING. _____

_____

8. ☐ BATHROOMS - Condition of sinks, tub, toilets, vanities, mirrors, and floors. _____

_____

9. ☐ LIGHTING - All fixtures and outlets working? _____

_____

10. ☐ HARDWARE - Do all doors open and close properly, all door knobs, stops, magnetic catches, closet rods,

counter tops, towel bars, toilet paper holders, soap dishes, etc. work properly? _____

_____

11. ☐ SMOKE DETECTORS - Do they work properly? (Replacement of batteries for smoke alarms will be the

responsibility of the tenant.) _____

LIST MAKE AND MODEL OF ALL APPLIANCES

Refrigerator _____   Dishwasher _____

Washer _____   Dryer _____

Garbage Disposal _____   Oven/Stove _____

Signature of Tenant(s) _____ Date ___/___/___

---

was dated one day before the lease was signed. The tenant countered that I must have put it in another unit because it wasn't in his apartment. The judge asked to see an inspection sheet, a picture, anything to prove that the new refrigerator had been installed in the tenant's unit. I could not because all I had listed on the lease was "refrigerator." The tenant had left me a refrigerator! That was a very costly mistake and maybe another reason why I do not supply refrigerators to any of my units.

Do not skip this step or consequences will be paid. A few examples:

A landlord is buying a single family row home and inherits a tenant that has kept the property in great shape. At settlement the old owner has a lease to give the landlord but has no rental application or inspection sheet on the tenant. When the tenant moves out the landlord finds numerous holes in the wall and deducts the repair cost from the security deposit. In court the tenant tells the judge that the holes were there when the landlord bought the property and were there when he moved in. The judge asked the landlord for pictures or an inspection sheet noting the damages. Of course, the landlord did not have proof and the tenant won the case.

In another case the landlord and tenant did a quick walk through and the tenant told the landlord VERBALLY everything was acceptable. The landlord never took pictures or had the tenant sign that everything was acceptable. When the tenant moved out with lots of minor damage and dirt the landlord again lost because he could not prove the condition of the unit when that tenant moved in.

Here is an example that happened to me in my early years as a landlord. I learned many lessons from this one situation as you will see. I had just bought a 30 unit complex and was doing some outside cleanup. A tenant approached me, introduced himself and asked if I was the new owner. I said yes, (remember I was still a rookie and had not learned to say "I manage this for a group of investors"—they just don't know the group of investors were the wife and kids) and asked if there was a problem. He invited me in his unit to show walls that were definitely in the need of paint. He claimed the unit had not been painted when he moved in and would be happy to do the painting if I would supply the paint. I agreed and gave him eight gallons of paint with the color we used in the complex. Six months later I had to file for non-payment of rent on this tenant. When he appeared at the District Judge hearing with a grin on his face, I knew there was a problem. The judge asked the tenant if he owed the rent stated in the complaint.

He said he did not because of a letter he had sent to me the previous month stating that if I did not paint his apartment as promised and repair the damaged walls he had shown me when I came into his unit, he was going to withhold rent and do the repairs himself. At this point he pulls out a series of Polaroid pictures showing his hammer induced holes and the discolored walls.

I told the judge I had not received this letter, had given the tenant paint six months ago because he said he would paint, and there were no holes in the walls when I inspected the unit. The tenant admitted sending the letter by regular mail so couldn't prove that I received it "but I sent it your honor." What recourse did I have? I had no proof I gave him eight gallons of paint. I had no contract that he would do the painting and had no inspection sheet from the old owner, nor did I do an inspection after purchasing the property.

The judge gave me two weeks to paint his unit and repair the hole damages. When I went to the unit to ask for the 8 gallons of paint I had given to him earlier, he replied with a big smile, "What 8 gallons of paint?" I did the hole repairs, painted the unit and took pictures of the completed work.

I was ready for the next hearing with the pictures. He didn't show because he knew I had the pictures. I was awarded the judgment and finally the eviction day was set. My on-site managers confirmed he was moving the night before and I went to bed relieved this headache tenant was finally going to be gone. But it wasn't over. He needed to leave me with one more "Let me stick it to you."

The constable and I arrived at the same time the next morning. As we opened the door, we saw water gushing from the living room ceiling onto a sofa in the middle of the living room. As we waded through totally saturated carpet we quickly discovered the float ball in the toilet upstairs had been removed. The flow of water into the tank was faster than the overflow tube could take it out causing the toilet to overflow throughout the night. The sofa had been moved into the middle of the room so it would be under the water flow, saturated, and be very heavy to remove.

I hope I have made myself very clear that everything needs to be documented, and when possible, photographed. Learn from my mistakes or you will lose thousands in lost cash flow as I did.

10. CHANGES TO THE LEASED PROPERTY

This clause lets tenants know they are not to do any redecorating without written permission. They can not paint walls, hang wallpaper, or drill holes in ceilings, floors and doors. If something is approved in writing it becomes part of the property and can't be removed unless landlord and tenant agree otherwise in writing. When a wall in a bedroom is painted or borders put up in the kitchen or bedrooms, they must be repainted or removed when moving out.

11. INSURANCE

Part a) lets the tenant know that I carry insurance on the building but not on their personal property.

Part b) they are strongly encouraged to carry a renter's insurance policy and I want to be listed as additional insured on their policy. There is no additional charge to the tenant but it gives you protection under their policy for liability claims. This concept is explained in detail in Chapter 23.

Part c) talks about if there is a loss of property by fire, theft, burglary, or other means, tenant does not hold landlord liable and will pay for any loss or claims filed.

12. LANDLORD NOT RESPONSIBLE FOR TENANT'S PROPERTY AND TENANT'S GUEST INJURY

It is again stressed that landlord is not responsible for loss, theft or damage to property of tenant or tenant's guest. The landlord will also not be liable for any injury to anyone on the property and that any belongings left by the tenant after moving out becomes Landlord's property to remove and keep as abandoned property. The cost to dispose is charged to the tenant.

13. BAD CHECKS

Tenant will pay a fee of $_____ (put in whatever your bank charges for bounced checks). I also reserve the right that if future payments bounce, I can require the tenant to pay by cash, money order or certified check.

14. ADDITIONAL SIGNERS TO THE LEASE

When a tenant is borderline qualifying insist they must get a co-signer that owns real estate or their application will not be approved. This clause states that all signers are responsible for all financial obligations, makes the co-signer aware that if a court judgment is won, a claim or lien can be put on real estate owned by him, and lists the address of the property. It further states that unless payments are received each month on time, the co-signer will stay on the lease for another year.

15. ILLEGAL ACTIVITY

This clause informs the tenant that if anyone is found storing, selling, using, manufacturing, or distributing illegal drugs or any other illegal activity under State and Federal laws, the lease automatically ends.

16. CARE AND USE OF THE LEASED PROPERTY

Primary Residence - Tenant agrees to use the property as a private residence for authorized occupants only.

Use of Leased Property - Tenant agrees not to use the property for

CO-SIGNER AGREEMENT

I, _____, understand that I will be required to meet all financial obligations, which includes but is not limited to: rent, late fees, and damages in excess of the security deposit if my co-signer(s) fail(s) to pay, as agreed in this lease agreement.

Landlord will give me written notice of delinquent payments which I agree to pay within fifteen days of such notice. If landlord has not received my payment within fifteen days, I agree to allow landlord to place a lien on my property located at _____.

___/___/___
Date   _____
Co-Signer

any unlawful or hazardous purposes and must have written permission from the landlord before using the property for a business or profession.

Obey all laws - Tenant agrees to obey all local, state, and federal laws that apply.

Keep safe and clean - Tenant agrees to keep the property safe from fire and water damage, and will remove trash, garbage and other waste in a safe manner.

Heating sources - Tenant agrees to use only the heating source provided in the property and maintain a minimum temperature of 60 degrees. When the landlord pays for the heat, the minimum temperature will never be a factor but if the tenant pays the heat you don't want them taking a vacation in the middle of a cold winter and turn off the heat.

This is another one of those "living" clauses that is here because of a problem that happened that was not covered in my lease when this happened.

A tenant renting an inside condo unit took a week off to go skiing. They decided that since there was heat coming from the two units on either side they would turn off their electric heat and save some money. A pipe split in the laundry room on an outside wall when the outside temperature never got above ten degrees for five days in a row. I found out about the problem from the condo association who thought it was odd that kids were ice skating on my patio!

17. TENANT'S RESPONSIBILITIES

No Noise - This clause is very important. In many leases it will be listed as "quiet enjoyment." It puts responsibility on the tenant to control the behavior of all people, either living there or visiting so as not to disturb neighbors. If your town has local noise ordinances or times children must be in on school nights and weekends, include them here.

Payment of Utilities - Tenant agrees to pay all the utilities they are responsible to pay as listed under clause 8.

Pests - When I give them the keys to the property I will guarantee the property to be free of insects, rodents, and pests for ten days after move-in. After the tenth day, if you see mice or ants, buy traps, bait, or spray just as I would do if it was in my house.

A four-plex building, which has never had an pest problem, all of a sudden is infested with cockroaches two weeks after a new tenant moved in. It is very obvious who brought the critters. In this case you can charge the new tenant to have their unit sprayed, but just eat the cost of the other three tenants who are just as upset with the problem.

Locks - Tenant agrees not to change locks or put additional locks on any doors without landlord's permission. Landlord may remove locks put on by tenant and tenant will pay the cost of the new lock that I will install.

Phone Numbers & E-mail addresses - Tenant agrees to give landlord a current home and work phone number and e-mail address. Tenant will tell landlord of any change in these numbers.

How can email help with existing tenants? Tell them how they can get free email service with Juno.com. Order a copy and give to it them or download it. Encourage them to send in maintenance requests via e-mail. They can print out a receipt for their records and you know right away of a problem instead of having to waiting for them to send in a written request via snail mail.

Send reminder notices to tenants about installing the glass for the storm doors in the winter, or a reminder to check the air filters on the heater. Keep tenants informed of what is happening with a newsletter that can be sent e-mail. Use e-mail to remind tenants of your referral fee for friends that are approved and move in. Let them know about upcoming inspections or congratulate them on the birth of a child. Consider sending rent increase notices and have them print it out and mail in with the rent check.

Use your imagination to come up with many more ways to use e-mail to streamline your management in increased efficiency which results in saved time and money.

18. LANDLORD'S RESPONSIBILITIES

Government Regulations - Landlord must keep the property and common areas as required by law.

Good Repair - Landlord must keep all electrical, plumbing, heating, sanitary, air conditioning and other services in good working order. The tenant will be responsible for notify the landlord if any of these items are in need of repair or are not working. Landlord is not responsible for damage caused by tenant negligence or intentional acts.

19. LANDLORD'S RIGHT TO ENTER LEASED PROPERTY

Part a) gives the landlord permission to put a rent or sale sign on the property.

Part b) says that with "reasonable notice," which most courts say is 24 hours, the landlord, or person chosen by the landlord may enter the property to inspect, show, make repairs, and do maintenance - and here is the key part - even if the tenant is not home.

There were many times, before I added this clause, when I called to schedule a repair or to show the property to a prospective buyer, the tenant would say, "Those times are not good for me." Now, with this clause in place a landlord can say, "I understand these times are not good for you, but I am giving more than 24 hour notice which you agreed to in our contract." "My repair man can only make it during these hours so I'm letting you know we will be there at X time to do the repair"

Part c) says if there is an emergency, the landlord has the right to enter the property without notice but will contact the tenant promptly to explain the visit.

20. DAMAGE TO LEASED PROPERTY

Part a) covers if there is a fire in the unit but the property is still livable. The tenant will be responsible for paying rent according to the percentage of livable space that remains. If one sixth of the unit is not usable, the tenant will pay five sixths of the rent.

Part b) says if the building is not habitable, the lease ends immediately and the landlord is not responsible for finding other housing for the tenant.

Part c) If there is damage and the tenant is allowed to occupy the unit, the tenant must give landlord access to the property to make the needed repairs.

Part d) If the fire or other mishap was caused by tenant or tenant's guest, it is tenant's full responsibility, which includes full payment of rent.

Part e) says that if windows are left open, tenant is responsible, plus any windows or screens broken or doors damaged by anyone is tenant's responsibility.

Part f) says that landlord will not be responsible for damage or injury caused by water, snow or ice that comes onto the property.

21. LOST KEYS

Part a) talks about the cost to unlock a door for a tenant. It is one price during business hours, but is more if after hours.

Part b) says if the tenant decides to have a locksmith change a lock, the landlord must be supplied with a key immediately.

Part c) covers if a key was lost and the cost to replace it.

22. REPAIRS

Part a) The tenant is to immediately inform the landlord of any dangerous or defective conditions. If he fails to do so he is responsible for all injuries or mishaps caused by these conditions.

Part b) This differs from most leases. Most landlords put clauses in the lease that say the first $50 or $100 of any repair is the tenant's responsibility. My clause says that *any* repairs needed *above normal wear and tear* will be corrected paid and for by the

tenant. If a twelve year old electric burner gives out one month after a tenant moves in it will be replaced at no cost to the tenant. If faucets start dripping from just being turned on and off, they will replaced at no cost to the tenant.

Having the first $50 or more of any repair to be paid by the tenant sure does cut down on the number of phone calls, but it does not save a landlord money in the long run.

When I used the first $50 of any repair clause, I found the tenant would decide to do the repair himself or have a friend do it. After the job was totally botched, I would get the call. If they had called me right away, the repair might have cost $100 but now it costs $200. They pay the first $50 whether my cost is $100 or $200, so what did they care the job was botched? Other times they would just remove the broken "J" trap for example, and place a five gallon bucket under the sink and hope they could remember to empty it every day. Others would just not use the dishwasher. In all of these examples when the tenant moved out I still had to make the repair.

When things begin to break because of normal wear and tear, and tenants are told they must pay to have it repaired, they stop caring about up-keep to the property. At some point, enough things will not be working and since they don't have the money to pay for the repair, they give notice and move out. How has making the tenant pay the first $50 of a repair helped ? It hasn't, because the repairs still need to be made and now there is a vacancy. When is the most money lost?

A few years ago I bought a 32 unit apartment complex that had seven appliances in each unit—a refrigerator, garbage disposal, dishwasher, oven/stove and three wall air conditioners. That's 224 potential problems. The seller used this repair clause very effectively. He didn't mind deferring maintenance as long as possible. In fact, he "deferred" it to the eventual buyer of his property, me! When tenants called about a broken appliance he would instruct them to call a repair person, pay the first $50 of the bill and he would send them a check for the difference. Many times the check to cover the difference never materialized. The tenants stopped calling repair people and went without.

When I took over ownership, the tenants wanted to know when the appliances would be fixed or replaced. I adopted a standard that if the repair was normal wear and tear, I would not charge the tenant. This was a positive step. It showed the tenants I wanted to keep the units in good shape because I cared about their needs as well as the needs of the property. This policy gave me an opportunity to get inside the unit to inspect every time a repair was needed (which should be done every six months to a year anyway.) I did not pay for repairs to things damaged by tenants.

Since my tenants know they will not be charged for normal wear and tear items, they quickly pick up the phone and call if there is a problem. I want them to do this for a few reasons. It gives me a chance to get inside the house to check the condition, look for pets or extra people that shouldn't be there, and make the repair in a timely fashion. They see that I care by my willingness to make improvements. Tenants don't move because their needs are being met. No vacancy, means more cash flow, and yes, less headaches in the long run.

Part c) Tenant is responsible for opening all clogged drains, toilets, sinks, and traps caused by tenant's actions. While doing the inspection, all faucets are run, and toilets flushed to show there are no blockages. Normal wear and tear is not removing tinker toys from toilets, hairpins, toothbrushes, and hair from sink drains. If the blockage is outside the walls, then it is the landlord's repair.

Part d) This was added because I had a tenant whose refrigerator gave out sometime during the night. She called first thing in the morning and said she would be home after 4 PM for the repair man. The repair man could go at noon but not at 4 PM. The tenant said no to going in without her being there, which caused the repair to be moved back to the following day. Here is another reason why you want to have permission to enter the property without the tenant being home. (Clause # 18) If I had that clause in the lease when this situation occurred, we would have done the repair at noon because it was an emergency.

The tenant subtracted $250 from the next month's rent for replacing all the food in the 12 cubic foot refrigerator and freezer. She had no receipts so was told I would give $125 in rent credit for the food. This caused me to add this clause to the lease which says that the landlord is not responsible for any "inconvenience" or loss that needed repairs might cause.

Part e) covers replacing filters to the furnace and air conditioning units every six months if the property is a single family, townhouse, or condominium. If damage is caused because the filters were not changed, tenant will pay the cost to repair the furnace, including the service call charge.

23. TENANT MAY NOT TRANSFER OR SUBLEASE

A sublease is a separate lease between the Tenant and another person who agrees to lease all or part of the property. This clause says a tenant may not transfer, sublease, or allow anyone else to occupy the property without the landlord's permission. Any new tenant must first meet landlord's approval before being accepted as a tenant.

24. WATERBEDS

Waterbeds don't seem to be the craze they were a few years

WATERBED AGREEMENT

Property Address: _____

This agreement is hereby attached to and becomes a legal part of the rental agreement dated ___/___/___ between

_____   _____
Tenant   *Landlord*

WHEREAS the above named tenant desires to keep a waterbed on the premises but the current rental agreement prohibits said waterbed to be installed without permission of landlord, landlord does hereby grant to tenant permission to use a waterbed in said premises subject to the following conditions:

DEPOSIT: Tenant agrees to pay to landlord an additional security deposit of $ _____. At the termination of the lease, landlord will inspect for damages caused by the waterbed and will return all monies not needed for repairing, cleaning, or replacement within thirty days of inspection. Tenant agrees to promptly pay to landlord any cost exceeding the amount of the deposit.

INSURANCE: Tenant will furnish to landlord a valid certificate of a waterbed liability insurance policy before installation that will show landlord as the beneficiary or additional insured of the policy. This policy must be for a minimum of $50,000. It will be the tenant's responsibility to keep the insurance policy in force at all times and to provide a copy of the renewal policy.

DEFAULT/BREACH: Tenant agrees to not intentionally, willfully, or maliciously damage the waterbed or allow a visitor to do the same and agrees to become personally liable for any and all damages. Failure to comply with any of the terms and conditions mentioned above allows landlord the right to revoke permission to keep the waterbed and to end the rental agreement.

_____   _____
Tenant   *Landlord*

_____   ___/___/___
Tenant   *Date*

ago, but some people still have them and you need to protect yourself. The two parts to this clause say a tenant is not allowed to have a waterbed unless landlord agrees in writing and, he must show proof of waterbed insurance that lists the landlord as beneficiary or additional insured on the policy.

Being listed as additional insured on the policy helps in another way. The tenant will not be able to sign up for the policy, show a one year paid in full receipt, and then cancel a week later. If he did this, the landlord would be notified of the cancellation as the additional insured and would also be notified when the policy is up for renewal.

To further protect yourself include the Waterbed Agreement form as an addendum to the lease.

25. SMOKE DETECTORS

It is not a federal law that all homes must have smoke detectors but it should be. They save lives and minimize property damage because of the early warning.

Part a) Tenant is informed that the landlord has supplied him with a smoke detector and the tenant is responsible for its operation and replacing batteries as needed. I don't want to be responsible for replacing batteries, especially when they are taken out and used in the kid's toys, or taken out because of smoke from cooking.

Part b) Tenant agrees to notify the landlord if a smoke detector fails for any reason other than the battery.

Part c) The tenant learns the consequences for disconnecting the battery; he is responsible for any injuries, damages, or loss suffered because it was disconnected for any reason.

26. VEHICLES

Part a) Tenant is allowed to park cars, trucks, or motorcycles in the parking area and must have current registration, license plates, and inspection stickers. If he does not, he will be given five days, after written notice is received, to comply with these requirements. If he does not comply, the vehicle will be towed at tenant's expense.

Part b) Tenant may not park or store motor home, camper, trailer, boat, boat trailer, or other recreational vehicle without written permission of landlord.

Part c) Tenant may not paint, repair or service vehicles anywhere on the property.

27. LEAD BASED PAINT NOTICE

This is a federal law which needs to be included in the lease.

Part a) The Federal Environmental Protection Agency requires all landlords who wish to rent property built prior to 1978, to give the tenant a Lead Based Paint Pamphlet called *Protect Your Family From Lead in Your Home.* It explains the hazards of lead to young children, and pregnant women.

Part b) Landlords are required to tell tenants if they know, or do not know of any lead in the home. The tenant may hire, at their expense, a certified lead paint inspector, to inspect the property and notify landlord of the name of the company doing the inspection.

Part c) The tenant has five days from moving in to have the inspection done and the report back in ten days. Tenant gives permission to have the results sent to the landlord in writing.

Part d) The tenant has two choices if lead paint or lead hazards are found. He can end the lease and move out within 90 days of the inspection, or continue the lease and agree the landlord is not responsible for any future health problems due to the lead paint and lead hazards.

Part e) The tenant is required to initial that they received the "Lead Based Paint Pamphlet" before signing the lease.

You can download the Lead Based Paint Pamphlet in Adobe Acrobat PDF format from the following website addresses:

For English booklets:
http://www.hud.gov/offices/lead/outreach/leapame.pdf

For Spanish booklets:
http://www.hud.gov/offices/lead/outreach/leadpdfs.pdf

28. PETS NOT ALLOWED

If you plan to make pets a cash flow generator as discussed in Chapter 7 take out this clause and add in the PETS ALLOWED clause found in the Additional Clauses part of the lease. If you're not allowing pets then keep this clause here.

Part a) Tenant agrees not to have any pet or animals on the property without written permission of the landlord. If a pet or animal is found the landlord can:

1. end lease with thirty days notice
2. start new lease with increases in rent and security deposit
3. remove any animal found on the property that is not approved by landlord to an animal shelter or other such location at tenant's expense.

Part b) The tenant agrees to pay landlord for any damages caused by the animal.

Tenants' memories about what they signed in this section become very short when they see a cute puppy or kitten. It is not uncommon for a tenant to sneak in a pet and not notify the landlord. The existence of a pet may not be discovered until the tenant has moved out, and you find the damage it caused. An easy way to discover "unknown pets" is to buy a silent dog whistle at a pet shop. Before knocking on your tenant's door try a sharp, crisp blow on the whistle; if there is an animal inside, you'll know it!

Be aware that recent court rulings could prevent a landlord from evicting a tenant with a pet. The dog can stay if:

- the tenant can prove the dog is needed to provide security because of living in a high crime area.
- the landlord originally allowed the pet and then changed his mind.
- the dog is needed for a blind or disabled person.

Don't be surprised to receive a phone call from a fellow tenant one day telling you a pet is living in the unit next door. Confirm this information with another tenant or confirm it yourself. Use your dog whistle and look in the back yard.

On some occasions tenants will call about a repair and the pet will great you at the door. When the tenant is asked did they sign a "contract" that said no pets allowed, the response will be "Yes, but look. There is no damage or smell." Remind them of the options listed above, especially the one about taking the pet to an animal shelter at their expense. Use the Pet Violation form to notify the tenant in writing that the contract has been violated and what options are available.

29. TOGETHER AND INDIVIDUAL LIABILITY

This is a must clause if renting to people that are not married. If it is a man and a woman, or two women, or two men, the odds are good that they will not be together two years later. When one moves out, he/she stops paying the rent. The one remaining pays his/her half, but that sticks you with half a month missing rent. This is why all singles need to be qualified individually and not together.

For example, if the going rent is $500 I want to see $500 in gross income a week from both parties and,

if one or both comes up short, in order to qualify, they will need a co-signer who owns real estate. I also need separate rental applications returned with the non-refundable application fee.

This clause specifically states that if more than one tenant signs the lease, each is responsible individually or together for making a full rent payment. This means that if one tenant moves out, the landlord can make one or both responsible to pay the full rent. It also means the landlord can sue any one tenant or all tenants for breaking the lease.

When one roommate moves out, I tell the remaining roommate it is his responsibility, not mine, to find and get the money from the roommate that moved. As stated in the "contract," I am going after you for the full amount of the rent, so don't send half. Most of the time this is enough to con-

---

PET AGREEMENT

This agreement is attached to the lease agreement dated ___/___/___
between _____, Landlord, and _____, Tenant

TYPE OF PET _____ BREED _____ COLOR _____
NAME OF PET _____ AGE _____ SEX _____ NEUTERED: Yes ☐ No ☐
HEIGHT _____ WEIGHT _____ DECLAWED: Yes ☐ No ☐

Tenant agrees to the following terms and conditions:

1. Tenant agrees to pay an additional security of deposit of $ _____. This deposit is subject to all terms and conditions of the security deposit mentioned in the lease. It does not limit the tenant's liability for property damage, cleaning, deodorization, defleaing, replacements and/or personal injuries. All dogs and cats must be "house-broken". Cats must be litter-box trained.

2. Tenant agrees not to leave his pet unattended for any unreasonable periods of time. Tenant further agrees to keep pet(s) on a leash not to exceed four feet in length and only in areas designated by Landlord. At no time will the pet be allowed to be left unattended while outside. Any pets found unattended will be presumed a stray and disposed of by the appropriate agency as prescribed by law.

3. Tenant agrees that if at any time the pet becomes annoying, bothersome, or in any way a nuisance to landlord or other tenants, landlord reserves the right to revoke permission to keep the pet. Should landlord revoke permission, said pet shall be permanently removed from the premises within 48 hours after receipt of written notice.

4. Tenant agrees that Landlord will not be responsible for the injury, harm or death of the animal, and agrees to hold landlord or landlord's agent harmless and to indemnify for any damages suffered as a result of any harm inflicted on the animal or by the animal upon another tenant, guest, or employee.

5. Landlord and Landlord's agent shall not be liable for any damages to person or property caused by the pet and tenant hereby agrees to hold landlord harmless from liability. Tenant shall be liable for the entire amount of all damages caused by the pet as well as the entire amount of any injury to individuals or property. Tenant is hereby encouraged to obtain a Pet Liability Policy which can be added as a rider to most renter insurance policies.

6. Tenant agrees to dispose of his pet's droppings PROPERLY and immediately. This applies to common areas as well as designated areas.

7. Pets must wear the appropriate Local Animal License, a valid Rabies Tag and tag bearing the owner's name, address, and phone number. All licenses and tags must be current. Tenant certifies that his pet has a current rabies vaccination.

I ACCEPT FINANCIAL RESPONSIBILITY FOR THE ENTIRE AMOUNT OF ANY DAMAGES OR INJURY TO PERSONS OR PROPERTY WHICH MAY OCCUR BECAUSE OF MY PET. I UNDERSTAND THAT VIOLATIONS OF ANY OF THESE RULES MAY BE GROUNDS FOR REMOVAL OF MY PET AND/OR TERMINATION OF MY TENANCY.

_____   _____
Tenant   *Landlord*

_____   ___/___/___
Tenant   *Date*

27

PET VIOLATION

To: _____

_____

_____

Date: ____/____/____

Dear _____:

It has been brought to our attention that you are in violation of your rental agreement by allowing a pet to occupy the premises.

You are hereby notified that the pet must be removed by _____. I have checked below the option I will exercise if the pet is not removed.

☐ If the pet is not removed, your lease will be terminated with 30 days notice as stated in your lease.

☐ I would be willing to re-negotiate your lease with rent being raised to $ _____ per month and the security deposit raised to $ _____.

We will be expecting a phone call as soon as possible to inform us of your intentions concerning this matter.

Sincerely,

_____

28

vince him to move which is exactly what you want to happen. Get a new tenant who will pay a full month's rent, not half.

30. TAKING BY THE GOVERNMENT

This is the eminent domain clause that says if the government decides to take the landlord's private land for public use, the lease ends as of the date of the transfer.

31. BINDING ARBITRATION

If you stay in this business long enough, some day someone will try to sue you for something. This clause allows both the tenant and the landlord to submit any dispute concerning the lease to the American Arbitration Association. In doing so both parties give up the right to a jury trial, punitive dam-

ages, tort damage, attorney's fees, and other costs and expenses. The decision of the arbitration panel is final.

32. NO JURY TRIAL

Everyone in this country has a right to a jury trial unless BOTH parties are willing to waive this right in a contract. I wanted this clause in for one simple reason. If a tenant sues me and it goes to a jury trial, my chances of winning are 50/50 or worse. The reason why? There is a much better chance that there will be more tenant's on that jury than landlords! I'll take my chances with the judge and hope he owns some investment real estate.

33. LANDLORDS RIGHT TO MORTGAGE THE PROPERTY

If there is a mortgage on the property, the mortgage company's rights are stronger than the tenant's rights against the landlord. If the landlord fails to make mortgage payments, the mortgage holder has a right to sell the property.

The mortgage company contacts the tenant and instruct him to make the rent payments to them and not the landlord.

34. SALE OF THE PROPERTY

Part a) If the property is sold, the landlord will transfer all security deposits and interest due, to the new owner. The landlord will notify the tenant of the sale and provide the name, address and phone number the new owner gives him. Sometimes the new owner will contact the tenant which relieves the former landlord from doing this.

Part b) The new owner is now responsible for returning the tenant's security deposit when he sells the property or when the lease is terminated.

Part c) The landlord has no more responsibility to the tenant after the property is sold to the new owner.

35. TRUTHFUL APPLICATION

If it is discovered that the tenant has given false information after moving in, the landlord may end the lease immediately. This does not mean the tenant will move out the next day or that the landlord has the right to change the locks. If he does not move on his own, the landlord must go to court and proceed with a normal eviction action.

36. LAWN CARE AND SNOW REMOVAL

This clause comes in handy for single family homes, duplexes, and multi-family units. Assign the responsibility of lawn maintenance and snow removal onto the tenant. Do not buy the lawn mower, or snow shovels, or snow blowers. If you do, and the tenant is injured, you can be sued. Part of the tenant's responsibility of occupancy is to maintain the exterior grounds. If the tenant fails to do this work, landlord will complete it and bill the tenant, which becomes additional rent to be paid with next month's rent. This "additional rent" term is also included in the late fee clause and also the repair clause. What does "additional rent" mean in these clauses? In all three cases the tenant is being told that if he does not pay the late fee, repair bill or maintenance bill with next month's rent, it will be subtracted from the next month's rent payment. If the bill charge is not included in the next month's rent, it will be subtracted from the rent, which then makes that month's rent short and causes the late fee charge to kick in. Without this clause, a landlord has a problem. If the tenant doesn't pay the bill, but does pay the full rent on time, the only recourse is to go to court to collect on the bill.

37. NOTICES

Part a) Any notices sent by the landlord to the tenant will be by regular mail or certified, or delivered in person.

Part b) The tenant agrees to send all notices to landlord by certified mail, return receipt requested. This is the only form of notice permitted in a court hearing as evidence of notice given. This prevents a tenant from writing a post-dated letter saying rent will be withheld if certain repairs are not made (which they broke). He makes a copy, shows the judge the letter during the hearing. Of course, you never received it, but how do you prove it? You prove it by inserting the last sentence under Part b).

38. PHONE

The need for additional phone lines to handle business and personal calls along with fax machines and the internet has never been greater. Without a clause explaining who is responsible for what it can open a can of worms. Supply one phone jack that you will be responsible for and any additional lines and phone jacks can be installed at tenant's expense after written permission is granted from landlord. If additional lines or jacks are installed, tenant is responsible to carry the Wire Maintenance Plan offered by phone companies.

39. CABLE

Everything just described above also applies to cable. Supply one junction box and if the tenant wishes to install additional lines for cable or internet access, it will be at the tenant's expense after written permission is granted from the landlord.

40. DEATH DURING LEASE

It is hoped this will not happen, however, it is better to be prepared. When a tenant dies, what happens to the lease? The same thing that happens if you die. The lease becomes the responsibility of the heirs or the executor. The lease does not become null and void.

Part a) The lease will end two months after the death of the tenant but the two months doesn't begin until all furniture is out, the unit has been cleaned and ready for move-in of a new tenant. Once this is done then the notice of cancellation can begin.

Part b) The return of the security deposit is contingent on several things. All rent and other charges must be paid, furniture and personal belongings removed, property cleaned and a replacement tenant found who will take occupancy at the end of the two months.

Part c) If the lease is signed by more than one person, the surviving tenant(s) who signed the lease is responsible to complete the lease.

41. LANDLORD DOES NOT GIVE UP RIGHTS

If the landlord fails to enforce any clauses, landlord may enforce these clauses at a later time without penalty.

42. SURVIVAL

If the courts find any clauses against the law, all other clauses that are legal are not affected.

43. CHANGING TERMS AND CONDITIONS OF LEASE

Landlord must give tenant at least ____ days notice before the end of the lease if any terms or conditions are changing. I like to use 60 days notice because this gives me plenty of time to find a replacement tenant if he decides to move. Since the tenant has to give the landlord 60 days notice of what he plans to do, it is a good idea to mail the tenant your notice 75 days in advance. This gives him

15 days to make up his mind and return the notice with the eleventh month's rent.

44. RENEWING LEASE

The renewal term is one of the most important lines in the lease. Always renew month-to-month and not year-to-year for the renewal period. Having the lease renew year-to-year requires the landlord to remember to send the rent increase notice 30 or 60 days before the lease expires. If the required notice is not given in time, the lease renews at the old rent for another year. The month-to-month renewal period gives much more flexibility. If the notice is missed by a few days it means the rent increase will be moved back one month—not twelve months.

45. TENANT BREAKS LEASE

Tenant loses the protection provided in the lease if he:
- Does not pay rent or other charges when due;
- Moves out before the end of the lease;
- Does not follow the terms and conditions of the lease.

The last part of the clause states that if the tenant does not move out at the end of the lease period, he will be charged a daily fee. Charge five times the daily rate. This daily fee must be high enough to get his attention and realize it will be cheaper to stay in a motel and rent a truck for a few more days than stay. Example: If the rent is $600, divide by 30 days = $20 a day X 5 = $100 a day. If he must stay an extra week he would owe $700.

There have been a few instances where this extra money has come in handy.

One tenant called to say he couldn't be out on the first because his new landlord needed three more days to get his new unit ready. I had a new tenant already on the road expecting to move in that night. When he arrived, I explained the situation and told them that I would put them up in a motel for three nights and pay for any additional truck rental charges. I was able to

do this because I had the $100 a day coming from the "holdover" tenant.

46. TENANT MOVES BEFORE END OF THE LEASE

Sooner or later a tenant will call to ask if he would be allowed to move a few months before his lease expires. The reasons will vary and are usually legitimate, however, it places you in a very awkward position. If you agree to end the lease early and cannot find a suitable replacement tenant right away, you lose rent. If you say no to the early departure, the tenant can make life miserable if they decide to do some of the following:
- Stop paying rent and force you to take time and money to do the eviction.
- Turn up the heat and open the windows in the winter if you pay this utility.

LEASE CANCELLATION AGREEMENT

To: _____, Tenant in possession of
_____
_____
_____

Landlord has agreed to allow Tenant to cancel the Lease agreement prior to expiration if the following conditions are met:

1. Pay a sum equal to two months of rent prior to vacating.
2. Provide a forwarding address in writing before vacating.
3. Leave the unit in a clean condition with no damage beyond normal wear and tear on or before ___/___/___.
4. Pay all final utility bills and return keys to Landlord by move out date.

- Tenant understands that the security deposit will only be returned if the above mentioned conditions have been met.
- In the event the undersigned is in default to one or more of these conditions, Landlord has the right to keep the security deposit as liquidating damages or make this agreement null and void. If Landlord decides to make this agreement null and void, all terms and conditions of the lease agreement will be enforced.
- Tenant understands and does hereby forever release Landlord, his officers, employees, or agents of any legal action arising from the aforementioned lease.

_____   _____
Tenant   *Landlord*

_____   ___/___/___
Tenant   *Date*

16

- Leave faucets or the toilet "running" if you pay this utility.
- Not report needed repairs. Any repair that involves water can do lots of damage.
- Hold a lease breaking party. Use your own imagination as to what happens here.
- Be excessively noisy. This disturbs fellow tenants and might cause good tenants to move to get away from the problem tenant.

When the tenant calls to explain his dilemma, explain this situation is addressed in the lease. There are two options. Let him decide which one he cares to exercise.

Option #1. Allows him out of the lease if he can find a suitable replacement tenant, but he must do the following:

1. Call the ad into the paper after you tell him what you want said.
2. Screen prospective tenants over the phone. Show him a copy of the telephone questionnaire sheet he will need to use when people call. Stress the importance of getting all the required information as well as screening out the people who don't qualify. This will save him time and effort because he won't be showing units to people not capable of meeting your standards.
3. Show the unit. Some sacrifices will need to be made by the tenant to schedule a convenient time for the prospective tenant. He will need to keep a list of names of people who kept the appointment and give a brief description about them.

When applications are returned, run the credit check. If a suitable tenant is not found by the time the tenant moves, rent is still due until a replacement tenant is found or until all security deposit is used up.

Option # 2. Sometimes tenants will say that a friend would be interested in taking over the lease. Have him complete a rental application and see if he qualifies. If he does, signing on the new tenant is better than letting the existing tenant sublet to his friend. There are too many things that can go wrong with the subtenant that the tenant will be responsible to pay. Examples:

- Any rent not paid by subtenant is tenant's responsibility.
- Any utilities not paid by subtenant is tenant's responsibility.
- If subtenant moves out, tenant is responsible for finding a replacement tenant and paying the rent while vacant.

After seeing what his risk is in subletting to his friend, most will take Option #1. This allows time to find a suitable replacement tenant for two months

of additional rent and the tenant will be happy to pay the two months of additional rent so as not to be responsible for the subtenant.

Once he agrees, have him sign the Lease Cancellation Agreement, then start advertising and showing the unit. The best circumstance would be to have a new tenant ready to move in the day the old one moves out. In this situation you have actually taken in an additional two month's rent minus the advertising costs. The tenant will think twice about damage because his security deposit will be in jeopardy. The worst circumstance (and it is a possibility, especially in a slow market) would be that a suitable replacement tenant cannot be found within two months after the old tenant has moved. This could occur in a slow economy and during the cold winter months. Use the creative vacancy filling ideas presented in this book. You should have no problem finding a qualified replacement tenant quickly.

47. WHAT TENANT OWES LANDLORD IF TENANT BREAKS LEASE

If lease is broken, tenant owes to landlord:
- All rent and other charges;
- All legal fees, court costs, collection agency fees, sheriff and constable fees, moving and storing costs, and any other expenses;
- Cost of repairing and replacing any damage caused by the tenant.

48. LANDLORD'S RIGHTS IF TENANT BREAKS LEASE

If the tenant breaks this lease, landlord has the right to:
- End lease, go to court to take back possession;
- Hire an attorney to start eviction;
- Start eviction without an attorney but since you're not paying an attorney, pay yourself. The lease has a blank line here to fill in an amount. Attorneys charge 15% of the judgment amount so using anything from 10% to 15% of the amount that is due should work. The key words are: Tenant will pay Landlord (give the amount) as "collection costs."
- Go to court to recover all rent and other charges due until the end of the lease.
- If landlord wins in court, use the court process to take tenant's personal goods, motor vehicles, and money in banks.

Judges usually will allow landlords who win cases to include attorney fees in the judgment total. Since I don't use an attorney when I go to court with a tenant, I build in a fee of $100 for my time and have found most judges accept this.

Why do I want to be able to recover rent until the end of the lease, even if the lease has not ended? I want to get the Internal Revenue Service involved if I don't get paid. Let us assume a tenant stops paying the $500 a month rent after the sixth month of a one year lease. When the Landlord Tenant Complaint is filed, list the total amount due as being $3,000. ($500 a month X 6 months remaining on the lease.) After receiving the judgment, inform the tenant that if he would pay the actual amount that is due, IRS will not be contacted. When they ask how that would happen, I explain that if he does not pay, under Internal Revenue code 68 and 108, which covers Debt Forgiveness, I can forgive the debt, which will now become income to him. Since he will not pay what is owed, he might as well pay some of what is owed to our Uncle Sam. Explain that the Internal Revenue Service form Misc. 1099C will be sent to IRS showing the $3000 judgment and remind the tenant that this $3000 must be claimed as income when he files his tax return. As you can see, whatever his tax bracket, a $3000 charge judgment is going to hurt more than filing for one month's rent of $500.

Another side benefit for landlords with this plan is when the tenant is on some sort of public assistance. Having this additional income might cause him to be removed from the program or his monthly payments drastically reduced. It is amazing how fast most tenants find the money, especially the ones on public assistance!

49. NOTICE TO END LEASE

A 60-day notice to end the lease protects the landlord much more than a 30-day. It is especially helpful if a tenant gives notice during the winter months when fewer people are looking and moving. The extra 30 days might be needed to find a replacement tenant.

Do not collect one month in security deposit and require only 30 days notice. Most tenants whose leases are written this way do not pay the last month's rent because they know the landlord can't get through the court evic-

tion system in three to four weeks. By the time the sheriff arrives to evict, they have already moved on. Using 60 days notice and requiring one and a half or two months in security deposit will help to avoid this situation.

If the tenant is on a month-to-month lease, this clause states that both the landlord and the tenant must give each other 60 days written notice.

The key part of this clause is part c) which states that if the landlord or tenant notifies the other after the first of the month, notice does not take effect until the first day of the next month. This helps to avoid the situation of tenants calling in the middle of the month saying they have been transferred and will be out 30 or 60 days from that date. It is more difficult to find a replacement tenant in the middle of the month because the new tenant usually can not get out of his lease until the first of the month. If

---

DISTRIBUTION OF SECURITY DEPOSIT

Property Address _____ Date ___/___/___

To: _____

_____

_____

Dear _____.

Pursuant to the terms and conditions of your lease agreement, you are hereby advised that your security deposit will be disposed of as follows:

Total Security Deposit Paid	$ _____
Interest Due	$ _____
Less:	
Past Rent Due	$ _____
Damages to Unit	
_____	$ _____
_____	$ _____
_____	$ _____
Damages from breach of agreement	
_____	$ _____
_____	$ _____
_____	$ _____
Rent due through balance of lease	$ _____
NET REFUND DUE TENANT	$ _____
BALANCE OWED LANDLORD	$ _____

2002

6

the tenant has to move, that's fine, but the security deposit will be used to cover the remaining days until the first of the month.

50. NOTICE TO LEAVE THE LEASED PROPERTY (NOTICE TO QUIT)

Most states have a clause like this which gives the landlord the option of waiving a period of time that notice must be given to a tenant before filing for eviction. This can save days and weeks of down time with a non-paying tenant.

51. REPORTING OF PAST DUE RENT OWED

This clause allows the landlord to report rent owed, damages, or other costs owed by the tenant to a credit reporting agency.

52. SECURITY DEPOSITS

Part a) If the lease is broken in any way, the security deposit is not refundable.

Part b) Tenant agrees to give landlord a written forwarding address and return all keys before moving from the property. If they don't, landlord is entitled to keep the full security deposit.

Part c) Within 30 days of moving, landlord will forward the balance of the security deposit after subtracting any outstanding charges or repair costs.

Part d) Lists the order that the security deposit will be used.

Part e) Again re-enforces that the security deposit can not be used for the last month's rent.

53. RETURN OF SECURITY DEPOSIT

This clause lists twelve things the tenant must do in order to have his security deposit returned.

Distribution of the Security Deposit form will need to be used if the tenant gives a forwarding address or not. If no forwarding address is given, mail the form to the last known address (your unit) and if it comes back, file it in case the tenant tries to say you never notified him.

The Post Office has a service called "Delivery Confirmation Receipt" which goes via Priority Mail and has to be signed by the recipient. The best part is you can track the letter on the Post Office web site. By entering the tracking number on your receipt, you can find out the date the letter was sent and the date it is delivered. This information will stay on the Post Office web site for one year. Print out this page which lists all the information you will need in court if the tenant gets nasty and it will have the Post Office logo. If the tenant does not pick it up the Postal Service will send you an envelope with the tracking numbers matching the information on the internet.

Each state has different laws regarding how soon the security deposit must be returned to the tenant. The average seems to be about 30 days or one month from the date of moving. State laws also vary when, or if, interest needs to be paid on the security deposit.

When damage is found beyond what is listed on the inspection sheet, take pictures or record it with a movie camera. Label the back of the picture with the address of the property, in what room the picture was taken, and the date. If the tenant decides to question your expenses or the amount of damage you have listed, the pictures will be worth a thousand words when they are handed to the judge.

Get bids to repair the damage and, if you do the work yourself, keep all receipts. List these items under the Damage to Unit section of the Distribution of Security Deposit Form.

A lease that has been broken or other monetary items that have not been satisfied will be listed under Damages From Breach of Agreement section. This would include such items as : late fees not paid, advertising expenses to re-rent, bad check charges, unpaid utility bills, and unpaid repair bills.

Two other lines on the Distribution of Security Deposit Form cover "Past Rent Due" and "Rent Due Through Balance of Lease." (see clause # 47)

This form should be mailed with copies of all receipts to justify deductions. Send it certified mail to validate the date it was mailed and that it was received within the allowable time limit.

ADDITIONAL CONDITIONS BETWEEN LANDLORD AND TENANT

This clause is blank so you can include clauses specific to your property or area. These additional clauses might be needed depending on the property or any specific arrangements that have been made with the tenant.

Antennas and Satellite Dishes

Part a) The tenant may not install or attach to the building, any antenna or satellite dish without permission of the landlord.

Part b) If the tenant does install a satellite dish or antenna to the building without permission, the lease will end in 30 days.

Appliances

Appliances for landlords is a catch 22. If you don't supply them, the unit is more difficult to rent. If you do, it's your responsibility to maintain and replace when they break. Here is an alternative. Provide the appliances, and state in the lease that they remain your personal property and are not part of the lease.

Tenant's may use the appliances but you assume no responsibility for their operation, repair, or replacement. If there is a refrigerator, washer or dryer in the unit, I want these to be personal property. They can use them, but I'm not responsible if they break. I will include in the lease a garbage disposal, dishwasher, and oven/stove because these items will not cost as much to repair or replace as the other three. Having to replace a refrigerator can wipe out a year's worth of cash flow. If your lease already states that the appliances are included, think about giving a smaller than normal rent increase and tell the tenant that the refrigerator is not part of the lease. The next year do it for the washing machine and so on.

Appliance Insurance

Explain to the tenant that the refrigerator, washer and dryer are your personal property and are not part of the lease. The tenant is welcome to use them but if they need to be repaired or replaced, it is not your responsibility. However, the tenant may purchase appliance insurance to cover the cost of repairs or replacements for certain appliances. You will need to set up a sliding scale based on the cost to replace the appliance. A refrigerator might be $10 a month, a washer, dryer $8 a month, a dishwasher $5 a month, and a garbage disposal $3 a month.

Insurance

This is the same clause as the one in the main body of the lease with the only change being it says that tenant WILL carry renters insurance.

Billing for Utilities That Remain in Landlord's Name

Many cities and towns do not want utilities in the tenant's name. They prefer to keep the landlord responsible so if the bill is not paid, they can lien the property. Utility bills that are mailed directly to the tenant might not be paid for months and the landlord finds out when a lien shows up on the property or the tenant moves out and a final reading is done.

To avoid this, tell the utility company that all bills are to be mailed to you which you then forward to the tenant. This technique gives the opportunity to verify if the last month's bill or quarterly water bill was paid or not. If the payment has not been made, protect yourself and make the payment. Send a copy of the paid bill to the tenant so they know how much to include in next month's rent to cover this utility.

Another way to handle the utilities is to have the tenant pay extra each month to cover the utility costs. If the charges for that month are less than what was paid, apply the balance to next month's bill or write a check for the difference.

Discount for Prompt Payments

Doesn't credit sound better than late fee? When signing the lease show the rent as $30 more than what was agreed and, explain that if rent is paid on time, the tenant may subtract the $30 as a rent credit. If late, then the full rental amount is due.

This technique has some additional advantages. District Judges have been known to throw out late fees. This method avoids that problem. Show the judge the rental amount is $530. If the tenant pays "on time" a $30 rent credit is given and they send $500 as the rent. If the postmark date shows a late payment then the full rental amount is due.

Another advantage of the rent credit comes into play when refinancing a property. Most appraisers, ask to see the first page of the lease because it has the current rent, and the last page showing the tenant's signature. I always make sure that the "rent credit" or "late fee" clause is listed on page two which they usually don't ask to see. Now they will see the rent is $530 not the real rent of $500. For properties that are more than four units, appraisers are required to use three methods to find fair market value:

- Comparables - what price similar buildings are selling for in the area.
- Cost - if it burns down how much would it cost to rebuild?
- Income - total the rents, subtract expenses to find market value from the income stream.

Remember, for everyone $1 rents are increased, the value of the property increases by $100! Refer to Chapter 13: Rents for a detailed description of how this works.

There is a downside to the rent credit concept that can be avoided. Be careful when sending out rent increase notices that the increase includes the extra $30. I had a tenant paying $530 with the $30 rent credit. Each month he paid on time and sent a check for $500. When it came time to raise his rent, I forgot the rent was listed at $530 because he always paid on time. I sent him a rent increase notice showing the rent was being raised to $520. He quickly sent back his increase notice and thanked me for the $10 reduction in his rent! ($520-$30=$490) I never made that mistake again.

Discount for Repairs by Tenant

If a tenant is a certified plumber, electrician, or carpenter for example and the unit they occupy needs work in his area of expertise, consider giving them a discount rent payment in exchange for making repairs. Get bids from other contractors so you know exactly what needs to be done and what it will cost. The tenant might be willing to do it for less because there is no travel time and it can be done in the evenings or weekends.

Military Release from Lease

Military personnel make great tenants. They have been trained to be neat and are trained to take care of obligations in a timely manner. Contact the military bases in your area and let them know you have units available.

The Soldiers' and Sailors' Civil Relief Act ("SSCRA") has a section that relates to real estate leasing transactions. This act gives the tenants who are called to active military service the power to end the lease before the full term has been completed for either residential or commercial leases.

Use the military clause outlined in the lease when renting to military personnel. It says if they are called to active duty and must leave the area, you will let them out of the lease with sixty days notice. This is acceptable because the military will pay for up to two months of rent after they move. This gives plenty of time to re-rent the property.

Only once did I have a problem with a military tenant. He and his wife had just gotten a divorce and he missed a rent payment. I called his commanding officer who had a check to me the next day for the full amount of the rent. I noticed some minor damage that the tenant had caused when he moved out. I contacted his commanding officer again who had a crew of seven in the unit the next day making the repairs. When they had completed the work, I signed their paperwork that the repairs were completed and moved in another military couple the next day.

Pets Allowed

As you already know, I believe pets are a cash flow generator. Inspect the house where they currently live prior to signing a lease. What you see here is what you will see in your own unit if you decide to rent to them. Be aware of pet odors, excessive pet hair, and the behavior of the pet. If they pass inspection, the pet clause can become part of their new lease with you.

This clause allows the landlord to reserve the right to end the pet agreement if the tenant does not maintain the pet properly or the pet becomes a nuisance to others. They must agree to not leave the pet unattended for the more than 10 hours, walk it on a leash and pick up after the pet. The cost of repairing any damage, and deodorizing carpet is tenant's responsibility.

For further protection add as an addendum to the lease the Pet Agreement Form. It spells out the do's and don'ts with pets in much more detail.

Painting

For any tenant who paints or wallpapers, this clause will apply. It is the responsibility of tenant to paint walls back to the original color or remove the wallpaper and restore walls to move-in condition. If landlord agrees to allow the existing paint or wallpaper to stay, it must be stated in writing.

Repairs

For those landlords who still believe that normal wear and tear should be the tenant's responsibility to repair, this clause is for you. It also includes a section that says the tenant agrees to change filters on the heater every three months. If the heater is damaged because these filters were not changed, the repair and service charge will be their responsibility.

Tenant Fails to Move In After Giving a Deposit

If your policy is to sign a copy of the lease when the tenant gives a deposit to hold the unit, this clause should be included. It says if the property is ready for move-in but tenant cancels moving in, landlord may keep all deposit money paid in advance. The tenant is also responsible for days the property remains empty after their move-in date.

Transfer and Lease to Another Person

Your tenant calls to say that he must break the lease but he has a friend that is willing to take move in and take it over. This clause says the landlord will require the friend to complete a rental application and go through the approval process like any other tenant. The lease will remain in the original tenant's name who will still be responsible for damages, needed repairs, and uncollected rent of the replacement tenant. The replacement tenant must accept the property "as is" and pay a nominal fee to the landlord for time spent in processing the transfer.

Transfer of Lease to New Owner

Use this clause when selling the property. The landlord is transferring all his rights in this lease to the new landlord who will assume all responsibilities as outlined in the lease. The new landlord acknowledges receiving the security deposit in the amount of X, all pro-rated rent, and other deposits being held.

Some words of caution. If you are the buyer, don't let the seller tell you that one tenant always pays late but is good for the money. The old landlord is not including that tenant's one month security deposit at settlement saying that the tenant will pay in another two days and you can use that money as the security deposit. Don't fall for this line. The lease and all monies associated with the property go with the property.

Landlords must also be thinking ahead if you are planning to sell a property in the next year. If the tenant renews year to year they are locked into that unit for the length of the contract. The new owner might want to move in but they can't because of the tenant's one year lease. This could cause them to walk from the deal. Avoid this problem by including a clause that says if the property is sold, the tenant's lease switches to month to month with sixty days notice.

Basement / Crawl Space Water Damage

Apartments that have a basement or crawl space that can be used by the tenant to store items should have this clause moved into the main body of the lease. It protects the landlord from unforeseen circumstances to a tenant's personal property such as a heavy rain storm that partially floods the basement, a broken water pipe, a washing machine hose breaks, or a back up in the sewer line to name a few.

Storage Area

This clause will come in handy if you have a building that has a basement with storage lockers for each tenant. If someone enters and steals an item from the locker, make it very clear that the landlord is not responsible for any items stored in these storage areas. That is why renters insurance should be highly recommended to each tenant.

Signatures

All parties over 18 years of age must sign the last page of the lease and initial all the other pages. Collect the pro-rated month's rent and the balance of the security deposit and give the new tenant the keys after the unit has been inspected.

It is a good idea to call the new tenant a few days before move-in day to remind them of the signing date and time, and inform them of the exact amount of money needed when signing the lease. Stress the money should be in the form of cash, money order, or certified check. If the tenant comes with a regular bank check, explain the keys cannot be turned over until the check clears the bank, or is cashed.

If the tenant starts mumbling and breaks into a cold sweat—BEWARE! Think of the possibilities if the check bounces and the tenant has the keys and possession. You will be out the security deposit, first month's rent and however many months it will take to evict and then re-rent. This is not a pleasant thought, so protect yourself with a certified check, money order, or cash.

Common Illegal Clauses Found in Leases

Be aware of using language of this sort in your lease. You may find out the hard way it is illegal. A provision:
- which waives any right given to tenants by the Landlord/Tenant Act.
- that the tenant gives up his right to defend themselves in court against a landlord's accusation.
- which limits the landlord's liability in situations where the landlord would normally be responsible.
- allowing the landlord to enter the rental unit at anytime with no notice.
- requiring a tenant to pay for all damage to the unit, even if the damage is not caused by tenant or guests.
- stating the tenant will pay the landlord's attorney's fees under any circumstances if a dispute goes to court.
- that allows the landlord to seize a tenant's property if the tenant falls behind in rent.

Divorce and Separation

When a couple decides to separate or get a divorce, and one moves out, this situation presents several problems to you as the landlord.

It is best to visit or talk to the tenant remaining as soon as possible to learn his/her intentions. It must be stressed that all parties are still bound by the rental agreement (I like to call it a contract at this point) and that there is nothing you can do about changing locks until the party who has moved out agrees to give up his/her portion of the security deposit and allows the locks to be changed. Under the terms of the lease, without such a letter, you would be breaking the law by changing the locks.

Stress that as long as the current "contract" remains in force, both tenants are legally obligated to pay the rent if they are living there or not. You understand his/her concerns about the "ex" coming back to the apartment and taking or destroying things, but your hands are tied without this letter. If he/she feel threatened they should get a restraining order from a judge. He/she can change the locks, but if the "ex" tries to break in, any damage is their responsibility.

The next step is to get the individual remaining qualified to rent on his/her own. If the lease is more than a year old, new pay stubs should be submitted.

If he/she does not qualify, see if a co-signer is possible. If not possible, give the proper notice of termination and move on.

CHAPTER 13

RENTS

An optimist builds castles in the air, a dreamer lives there. A realist collects the rent from both.

Many of life's failures are by people who did not realize how close they were to success when they gave up.

Like everything else in this world, rents revolve around the basic economic principle of supply and demand. When vacancy levels are low, there is usually a high demand for housing because of limited availability. Landlords can raise rents quickly and still keep units occupied. On the other hand, if vacancy rates are high, (over-development) rent increases will be nominal or non-existent because demand is low. In order to survive the low demand, high supply periods, landlords often run ads giving the 13th month's rent free. Another approach allows a tenant to move in by a certain date and get a bonus, like a microwave oven installed in his unit.

Over the years, the economy of the country has gone up and down like a see-saw. In the long run though, the value of real estate and rental amounts have both increased dramatically. I believe the trend will continue because of the finite supply of land. Will Rodgers said it best. "Buy land. They ain't making any more of it."

As raw land is developed, our finite product called earth gets smaller. As world population continues to grow so does the need for shelter. These simple facts alone will raise the value of land and the improvements upon it by applying the basic economic principles of supply and demand.

RENT INCREASE SCHEDULE

This form records
- the dates tenants' leases expire
- when the rent increase notice should be sent
- the current rent
- projected increases
- if the increase was accepted
- if accepted was it month-to-month or year-to-year

List the tenants by the dates their leases expire and not by properties. This greatly simplifies the sheet because now you can see exactly how many notices must be sent out each month.

Place the tenants whose leases come due the earliest in the year at the top and work down. This form will literally save hours of time pulling individual property folders to discover which lease is up for renewal in sixty days. It also keeps rents consistent with other tenants in the building. Long-term tenants, whose rent should be less than newer tenants, do not appreciate paying a higher rent than a new tenant. It is very embarrassing trying to explain to the long-term tenant what happened when the answer is that you forgot what increase you gave to which tenant. The problem is easily avoided if you record the increase for each tenant on the sheet.

RAISING RENTS

In the advertising chapter we discussed how to determine the rental market after a vacancy occurs. You can do the same thing when a tenant is up for renewal. Before sending the rent increase notice, think about the tenant who will be getting the increase. Do they pay on time, and make minor repairs without calling, or do they bounce checks every other month and are they constantly calling to complain about every drip and rattle?

Nuisance Rent Increase

The good tenants' rents should be kept at market value. If you have a tenant that is not that good, but still not bad enough to not renew, increase the rent $10 over full market value. This is called a nuisance rent increase.

This type of increase forces the tenant to look at other apartments. He quickly discovers what you already know. Similar units are renting for the same as yours or $10 cheaper. The tenant figures a move would save $120 a year. He then starts adding up the cost of a moving truck, the time spent packing, opening a new checking account at a closer bank, sending new address information to friends, stopping the paper, transferring the phone and electric bills. The tenant quickly realizes it is a nuisance to do these tasks to save $120 and will accept the increase. This idea won't work if vacancy levels are high.

Economic Rent Increase

The other type of rent increase is an economic rent increase. This is used when rents are so far below market value, it becomes an economic need to raise them dramatically. After buying a property, I have raised rents as much as $125 because the seller refused to raise rents on his good tenants. He was forced to sell well below market value because of not increasing rents on a yearly basis. Another fact to remember is that 85% of all tenants who move because they say the rent is too high, will move to an apartment that will cost more than your unit.

$1 RENT INCREASE = $100 IN INCREASED PROPERTY VALUE

Increasing rents not only improves cash flow but also increases the value of the property. For every dollar that rents are increased, the value of the property increases $100. Look at an amortization schedule for $100 at $11\frac{1}{2}$% interest for 30 years. It should read $1.00 per month. This means if a friend loaned you $100 at $11\frac{1}{2}$% interest and you promised to pay him interest every month for the next 30 years, your monthly payment to him would be one dollar.

Using this theory, let's raise a tenant's rent $10 a month. This will increase the value of the property, using an income approach to value, by $1,000. Pretend you own a duplex and right next door your best friend owns an identical duplex. You raise each tenant's rent $10 (total of $20) but your friend does not raise his tenants' rent. Your property has just increased $2,000 more than your best friend's property ($20 X 100) because of the rent increase. This means you could sell your duplex for $2,000 more than your best friend and the cash flow from both properties will be identical.

Landlords who understand this concept are aggressive about keeping their rents close to, or at market value because they know it is increasing the value of their properties. If you own 50 rental units and raise each tenant's rent $10, your net worth increases $50,000! The next time your friend tells you about his latest pay increase, tell him about the pay increase you gave yourself by sending a rent increase letter to your tenant.

Rent Increase Schedule

Address	Tenant	Lease Expires	Send By	Current Rent	Raise To	Accepted / Moving

34

MAKE REPAIRS BEFORE SENDING RENT INCREASE NOTICES

Study your Rent Increase Schedule sheet to see when rent increase notices should be mailed. A few months before they are to be mailed, do some repair work on the building or in the apartments. It doesn't have to be major repairs. Re-caulking the tub, painting shutters, or planting bushes, shows you are trying to make improvements and care about the building.

Tenants become resentful when they never see you at the property. They have never called about repairs, always pay the rent before the first of each month; and are justifiably upset when you raise their rent $40 a month. You can be the nicest person in the world, but in one day you will go from a landlord to a slumlord in their eyes. Doing minor repairs will help to make the increase easier to swallow.

A classic example of "out of the mouths of babes" occurred when I decided to paint some shutters I had missed the previous year. My tenant's son was playing in the yard as I arrived. I started painting the shutter just outside this boy's apartment when I heard the following conversation between the little boy and his mother. "Mommy, Mommy, our rent is going up." "What do you mean Johnny?" asked the mother. "The landlord is outside painting the shutters again this year," he exclaimed. "Didn't our rent go up after he painted them last year?" I would have loved to have been a fly on the wall a month later when his parents received the rent increase notice. I can hear Johnny saying it now, "See, didn't I tell you the rent would go up?"

Stagger rent increase notices so they do not all come due in the same month. Most landlords, especially those living in cold weather climates, try to arrange their leases so they come due between April and August. If a unit opens in an off-peak month, consider giving less than a year lease so it will expire in a peak month.

NOTICE TO CHANGE TERMS OF TENANCY

Once the increase has been decided, mail, or hand deliver, the form letter called "Notice To Change Terms of Tenancy." What is the best method to deliver this rent increase notice? Is it in person, certified mail, or regular mail?

"In person" does not mean sliding the notice under the tenant's door but physically handing it to him to be sure it has been received. This is not exactly a fun job especially if you can mail it. Sending the letter certified mail will give proof that it has been received but there is a potential problem. Certified mail is usually perceived as bad news. Often the tenant refuses to sign for it or pick it up at the post office. It will take two weeks or more for the unclaimed letter to be returned and that can effect the critical timing necessary for your notice. Sending it regular mail will mean a higher certainty

---

NOTICE TO CHANGE TERMS OF TENANCY

To: _____, Tenant in possession of

_____

_____

_____

You are hereby notified that pursuant to the provisions of your lease the terms of tenancy under which you occupy the above described premises are to be changed. Effective _____, 20___, your rent will be increased to the amount shown under options One and Two. Please check the appropriate box, have all parties sign, and return it in the self addressed stamped envelope by ___/___/___.

☐ 1. I would like to renew my lease on a month-to-month basis with sixty days written notice required to terminate. The new rental amount will be $_____ per month.

☐ 2. I would like to renew my lease on a year-to-year basis with sixty days written notice required to terminate. The new rental amount will be $_____ per month.

☐ 3. I am giving my sixty days written notice with this letter that I will be terminating my lease and will vacate the premises by _____.

_____   ___/___/___
       Tenant   *Date*

_____   ___/___/___
       Tenant   *Date*

_____   ___/___/___
  Landlord / Rental Agent   *Date*

_____   ___/___/___
  Landlord / Rental Agent   *Date*

2002

24

that it was delivered, but no tangible proof the tenant received it.

Try this method. Send the "Notice To Change Terms of Tenancy" regular mail at least 15 days before the deadline required to give notice of your intent to renew/terminate the lease. Ask that the notice be returned with the next rent check. If it is not included when you get the rent, call the tenant and ask if they received the rent increase notice. If they say no, it must have been lost in the mail, tell them you will mail another. At this point the tenant is rubbing his hands together because the $20 increase that should have happened in April won't take effect until May. Send the second notice for the increase to take effect one month later but raise the rent an additional $5 a month than the first increase! This means at the end of the year an additional $60 will be collected. This makes up for the $20 lost in

moving the lease back one month and still makes you another $40. Over 80% of the time the tenants conveniently find the first notice and mail it back with the lower amount!

As you can see from the "Notice To Change Terms of Tenancy" form, tenants are given three options. Renew for one year, month-to-month, or terminate. Make the month-to-month option $30 more than the year-to-year option. This extra money will be needed if the tenant decides to move during an off season when fewer prospects are looking.

If the tenant chooses the month-to-month option it does not necessarily mean they are moving. A tenant may choose to renew on the month-to-month option every year. He doesn't mind paying the additional money for the peace of mind it gives him knowing he can give 60 days written notice and leave with his full security deposit returned. On month-to-month tenancies, rents can be raised whenever necessary as long as the required 60 days notice is given each time.

Another approach to the rent increase (this idea will also work when placing a new tenant) is to make the lease a month-to-month tenancy, but lock the rental amount for one year. Consider this method for larger type buildings with multiple tenants living above, below, and beside each other. Noise and personality conflicts can cause the loss of good tenants because of inconsiderate tenants. The credit check does not show who will blast music late at night, have a two hour domestic fight twice a week, or refuse to listen to reasonable demands. This approach helps to remove the bad tenant quickly before the good tenants give their notice of moving. Tenants like it because they have the flexibility of a month-to-month lease but the security of no rent increase for a year.

EXCUSES
WHY RENT WILL BE LATE

By far the number one excuse is "I'm sorry my rent is late. I know I should have called but don't

---

NOTICE OF LATE RENT

To: _____, Tenant in possession of

_____

_____

_____

    You are hereby notified that your rent is _____ days past due. You will be given three additional days to pay all rent due. This letter is your notification that if rent is not received by ____/____/____, eviction proceedings will be initiated against you. As stated in your lease, any rent paid after we file for eviction must include the court costs to stop the proceedings.

    May it be further understood that any court judgment entered against you for non-payment of rent will be recorded in the county you reside in and will be given to all credit bureaus. This judgment will stay in your credit history for five years and an additional five years if it is renewed.

____/____/____   _____
   Date

worry, IT IS IN THE MAIL." After that answer, anything goes.

- "I was laid off from my job and it will take a few weeks for my workers comp to start."
- "My roommate was laid off but there is a chance he will be called back soon."
- "My roommate moved out. I'm going to try to handle the rent by myself."
- "Our son has been in the hospital and our medical insurance is not covering it all."
- "My car was stolen and I have no way to get to work. No work—no pay."
- "I gave it to my husband to mail. I'll bet it is still in the glove compartment."

Try to be understanding but stress you will do what the lease provides for if the rent is not received. Each case must be handled on an individual basis. The couple with the son in the hospital had never missed a payment in three years. I felt strongly they would get the money to me somehow, and they did. The man laid off from the job was a tenant for only two months and his rental application showed his last two jobs were also for less than a year. I filed for eviction right away and told him I would stop the court action if he paid in full plus court costs. He never did and just moved out.

You must establish yourself from the very beginning as an enforcer. Be polite but firm and always do what you say you will do. Some examples of the more bizarre excuses and my answers:

- "I'm sorry to hear about the death in your family. Did the town where the funeral was held have a post office to mail the rent?"
- "I'm sorry to hear the family car died but happy you were able to buy a new car. Are you planning to move into the new car since I have not received your rent?"
- "I'm sorry to hear about your sister losing her job and needing some extra money, but you must understand my mortgage company will be asking for extra money too if I don't get the rent you owe me."

Whatever the excuse, you need their rent to make your mortgage payment. Look at these rents as a business. If they are not collected, you will go bankrupt, which is not far from the truth. Explain to the tenant that your number one priority is keeping a roof over your head, and you would hope it would be the same for him.

Ask when the rent can be expected. If he doesn't say tomorrow, find out why. There will be a second time rent will be late if you allow it to happen the first time.

Often tenants will call or include a note with the rent asking you to hold the check a few days past the due date for their deposit to clear. My response is I will gladly hold the check but remember to include the late fee the next month.

Be careful of tenants who have the use of a postal meter machine. I had a tenant who used this meter to mail her rent on the tenth of the month but set the meter to the first (or ran the envelope through on the first and mailed it on the tenth) The envelope would show two postmarks. The red postmarked date from the postage meter said the first but the black postmark from the post office said the tenth. She pulled this bait and switch for six months until I finally asked the post office why they would mail letters with two different postmarked dates? Once I understood what she was doing, I sent the tenant a certified letter stating I would accept only black postmarked dates. From then on the rent was paid on time—with no red postmarked dates!

WAYS OF COLLECTING RENTS

Most landlords have two ways of collecting rents: by mail, or in person. If you use the mail, get a post office box and an unlisted phone number. One is no good without the other, unless you don't mind having your tenants know where you live.

When registering for the post office box do not give them your home address. Anyone can go to the post office and for a small fee request the other address that was listed when registering for the box. Give them your work address or the address of one of your rental properties.

Rents received through the mail show the postmarked date which becomes your evidence for charging or not charging the late fee. It also allows rents to be picked up at your convenience. I tried the "collecting in person routine" once, and never did it again. All four tenants were waiting for me the first Saturday of the month and had me in for coffee. They all wanted to show me minor repairs that were needed and then they moved on to the gossip of the building. A five minute job took two hours to complete.

ADDITIONAL RENT COLLECTING TECHNIQUES
Twelve Post Dated Checks

Streamline rent collection by having the tenant fill in 12 checks, each dated for the fifth of each month (Jan. 5, Feb. 5, etc.) Have the tenant write the checks when signing the lease and in return give him a $5 a month reduction in rent. Explain that he won't need to worry about the check being lost in the mail or paying late fees if the check is lost. No checks will be deposited until the sixth of each month. But, if the check does bounce, the late fee charge must be paid.

Stickem labels

Type your name and address on 12 stickem labels. Place them on 12 envelopes, or let the tenant provide his own. This is inexpensive and will make your operation more professional. This stickem label idea can also be used to address envelopes of monthly bills such as phone, electric, mortgage payments, etc. Keep them together with a rubber band. Pull one out each month, write the check and place it in the ready to go envelope.

Automatic Draft Transfers

Many banks now offer automatic bank draft transfers. The tenant can sign an automatic bank draft agreement which allows the landlord to draft his bank account for each month's rent. Some employers have a system where the tenants can have their rent automatically withdrawn from their paycheck and deposited directly to their account. Check with your local banks for the feasibility of this plan.

Money Orders

Many tenants do not have a checking account and will do their banking business with cash or money orders. If there is a store close to your apartment that offers money orders, make arrangements with the store for you to pay the money order charge for the tenant. This can be a win-win situation for all three parties. The first win is to the tenant because he does not have to pay the money order fee.

The second win is the store owner who appreciates the additional traffic entering his store because he knows that people that come in for only one item often leave with additional items which increases his business. The third win is to you, the landlord. You provide a convenience for your tenants while putting yourself at less risk because no cash is changing hands.

Another advantage can occur if the store owner can be convinced the money order fee should be reduced or dropped because of the extra business you are generating for him.

Deposit Slips

Consider using duplicate deposit slips. The first page is completed like a normal deposit slip but the second page (your copy) can be used to write the tenants' names next to their rent amount. If a dispute arises as to a rent payment being made or not, the deposit slip with their names and bank number should save some aggravation.

BOUNCED CHECKS

In most cases the tenant knows he has bounced a check before you do. The good tenant calls to apologize and says to redeposit the check even before you know it bounced. If no phone call is received from the tenant, call him to ask if it is alright to redeposit the check. Stress you are calling because you don't want the check to bounce again which will cause more bounced check fees for both of you—more them than you. Listen very carefully to the reason the check bounced in the first place and, more importantly, when it can be redeposited. Be more intense with your questioning if the check bounces in the last two months of the lease and they have given notice of vacating. The odds are they are trying to stall to keep you from filing for eviction.

Try this technique the next time a tenant's check bounces. Call the bank and tell them that the tenant has bounced a check for $500 and you want to know if it can be redeposited. If they answer no, ask if a cash deposit of $100 would make it clear. If they say yes, hang up and call another branch and ask if a $50 deposit would make it clear. If they say yes again, try another branch and see if $25 would make it clear. The reason for calling the different branches is because the bank representative will know you are trying to find out the balance of their account and they don't know who you are.

If I have a strong feeling I am not going to get my rent money, I will go to their bank, get a deposit slip and ask the teller how much cash I need to deposit to make a check for $500 clear. If $35 is the magic number, deposit the cash and then cash the $500 check. $465 is better than nothing at all.

One tenant called, furious, after I used this approach. He had given his 60 days notice and bounced the next to last month's rent check. I called his bank three days in a row, and each time I needed to deposit only $10 cash into his account to make the check clear. I deposited the money and cashed the check. He admitted he had no idea how I was able to cash the check when he KNEW there was not enough money to cover the check. I never let on what I had done and enjoyed listening to him complain about how my check clearing made ten other checks bounce at $25 per check!

TYPES OF RENT PAYMENTS

Most rent payments are made by check or money orders. Go to the local stationary store and have a stamp made that says, For Deposit Only to the account of _____. Stamp the checks and money orders as soon as they are received to protect you if they are stolen and cashed.

Try not to accept cash payments especially from the same tenant at the same time each month, because you are setting yourself up for a robbery. Protect yourself by not only giving the tenant a receipt listing the date, amount, for what, and then signing, but also get a receipt from the tenant with the same information.

Learn from another mistake I made. A tenant called to ask if we could meet so he could pay his rent in cash. We met but he was $100 short. I wrote the receipt with the information described above, took the money and went home. He called twice during the month promising to pay the balance due but canceled the appointment both times. Before I knew it, the first of the next month had arrived and he called to pay cash again.

Once again he was $100 short but he had a large refund from his income tax return due any day. Another receipt was written for the amount paid. The $200 owed is promised as soon as the tax refund check arrives. Of course no money is paid so we go to court.

I was surprised to see my tenant at the hearing. I explained to the judge I am owed $200 plus late fees for rent during the past two months. My tenant sat in his chair with his mouth wide open as if I had just accused him of robbing a bank for a million dollars. He proceeded to show the judge "copies" of my receipts showing the $600 rent had been paid in full. As soon as I saw the "copies" I knew he had changed the 5 to a 6 and now it was my word against his "copies." I lost, but learned a valuable lesson. Get a signed receipt from the tenant showing the date, amount, what it covers. An easy way to avoid this situation is to buy a receipt booklet in duplicate form. Now if the tenant tries to change numbers, you have a duplicate receipt to show the judge.

WAYS OF COLLECTING LATE RENTS

The key point to remember here is not to wait until the end of the month (or longer) to start a court action. A tenant's check mailed on the fifth of the month should get to you the next day or by the seventh day, (if local), at the latest. Have the "Notice of Late Rent" letters in the envelope and ready for the stamp if the

check is not in the post office box. I give them three days or until the tenth of the month in this notice. Many times after receiving the notice, the tenant will call explaining why the rent is late. Be understanding but firm. Stress you will be in touch on the tenth if the rent has not been received to explain what will happen next.

Another approach that can be effective, if visiting the tenant, is to show them what a Landlord/Tenant Complaint form looks like. Visit your local District Justice office and ask for a blank Landlord/Tenant Complaint form and make a copy. Type on the copy the tenant's name, address, and the amount owed. Explain to the tenant this is the form you will enter against them, for non-payment of rent, when you file for their eviction. Stress after the judgment has been awarded, another form will be filed in the county seat that allows this judgment to be placed

NOTICE OF LEASE TERMINATION

To: _____. Tenant in possession of
_____
_____
_____

You are hereby advised that you are in default of the material provisions of your lease dated _____, 20___. The particular default(s) are as follows: _____
_____
_____

You are hereby notified that your lease is being terminated for the above reasons and the premises must be vacated by ___/___/___. If you do not vacate the premises within the stated time and pay all sums currently due, appropriate legal proceedings will be initiated against you.

Your defaults, as listed above, do not necessarily include a statement as to damages to the premises for which you may be responsible. At such time as you vacate the premises, it will be inspected and damages noted. Upon receiving a forwarding address, a list of damages, if any, will be provided. It is imperative that you provide a forwarding address in order to facilitate a return of all or any part of the escrow deposit to which you may be entitled.

___/___/___
Date   _____

on their credit report for five years. This means that if they were planning on buying a car, home, or taking out a loan, etc., "forget it"!

NOTICE OF LEASE TERMINATION

When all avenues fail, or when you have just had enough, give this notice and move on to the next tenant. This form can be used for non-payment of rent or for the violation of any other terms and conditions of the contract. Some examples are: additional adults, children, pets, improper use of the premises, etc. Serve this notice by using the same methods described earlier in this chapter.

NOTICE TO VACATING TENANT

Address: _____

Dear _____:

This letter is to confirm that we have received your letter wishing to terminate your lease on _____. We would like to take this opportunity to explain the procedures from now until the termination date.

We will immediately begin advertising for a new tenant. There will be times we will need to show your residence, but rest assured that at no time will anyone be shown your residence without your knowledge and permission. We try to give a minimum of 24 hours notice of any showings. If you wish to be home for the showings, contact us with times during the week and weekends that would be most convenient for you.

We also offer a bonus to vacating tenants. If you recommend someone who qualifies and agrees to rent your residence immediately after you move out, we will add an additional $ _____ to your security deposit.

In order to receive your security deposit back in full, the property must be returned in the same condition it was given to you. Rent will continue to be due, (even if you have vacated) until all keys are returned, utilities paid in full, and a written forwarding address is received. When the keys are returned we will do a final inspection using the inspection sheet you completed when moving in. If repairs are needed, we will contact you by phone with a price to see if you wish to complete the repair yourself, or to have it subtracted from the security deposit.

If your departure date changes, please contact us immediately. If you have any questions feel free to call.

Thank you for your cooperation.

Sincerely,

26

CHAPTER 14

SECTION 8 HOUSING - RENT CONTROL WARRANTY OF HABITABILITY

I believe the tax tables should be reversed. I don't know anyone on welfare that hires people, but I know lots of people who hire people who are on welfare.

— Jimmy Napier

SECTION 8 HOUSING

Section 8 is the common name of the housing assistance program run by the Federal Department of Housing and Urban Development (HUD). Under the program, HUD gives low income residents monthly vouchers that they can use to pay part of the rent on an apartment that they otherwise could not afford.

REASONS TO ACCEPT SECTION 8 TENANTS

In areas where the rental market is soft or a high percentage of the applicant pool receives Section 8 assistance, there is no reason not to rent to these tenants. The amount of money you receive from a Section 8 tenant in most cases will be the same or possibly more than what you would get on the open market and the government guarantees 70% of that rent.

Section 8 tenants must follow the same guidelines for approval as any other tenant. The only difference is part of their income is coming from a government program. If you don't wish to rent to Section 8 tenants, you do not have to. If an applicant doesn't meet one or more of your criteria, such as having a good rental history, you can reject him just like any other tenant.

Since the program is voluntary, you can get in or out of it whenever you want. If you wish to limit the number of Section 8 tenants in any building or area, that is your choice.

REASONS NOT TO ACCEPT SECTION 8 TENANTS

Before renting to a Section 8 tenant, the unit must be inspected and meet specific housing codes. If it doesn't meet the Public Housing Authority (PHA) standards, you will be notified of what needs to be done to bring it up to code.

Some PHA's work better than others around the country. Some have a requirement that leases must start on the first of each month. If your unit is inspected the last week of the month, but the paperwork is not processed until after the first of the month, you must wait until the first of the next month to place the tenant. Fortunately this does not happen in most areas and tenants can be placed right after the unit has been approved for occupancy.

To rent to a Section 8 tenant, you must use the PHA's form lease. It is acceptable to sign your own lease with the tenant, but, if there is a conflict between the two leases, the PHA lease will be enforced. It is still a good idea to have Section 8 tenants sign both leases. Your lease might contain community rules or building restrictions. Attach your lease as an addendum to the PHA lease.

HUD has set Fair Market Rents for each area in the nation. To rent to a Section 8 tenant, you must charge a rent that doesn't exceed this amount. The problem develops when supply and demand allows the open market to charge more rent that PHA is willing to pay. They often are six months behind in updating Fair Market Rents. In my area, between cut backs in subsidy funds and a strong rental market, I can charge substantially more per month in rent on the open market without the hassles of inspections every six months and PHA's restrictions on the leases.

Contact your local PHA office for details of how to get your rentals set up for Section 8 housing.

RENT CONTROLS

Rent controls were first introduced during war times to keep rental rates from soaring during severe housing shortages. During the 70s rent control became the cry of consumer advocate groups as a way of holding down inflation. Landlords were to provide comfortable housing at reasonable rates. However, there have been many more negative side effects than positive. A study prepared by the Institute of Real Estate Management showed rent controls caused:

- Deferred maintenance that resulted in housing deterioration: Landlords could not charge enough rent to keep up with escalating operating expenses;
- Abandonment and demolition of unprofitable multi-family projects;
- No mobility for low-income families and reduction in housing choices for renters;
- Halting of new rental housing construction
- Excessive condominium conversion
- Increased property tax burden for the single family home owner.

If your area ever thinks about implementing rent controls; become a vocal activist and protest before it is too late.

TENANTS CAN ESCROW RENT UNDER WARRANT OF HABITABILITY

Be aware the courts in many areas of the country have given tenants more rights than they had before. One of these rights is called Warrant of Habitability. This little known section of the Tenant Landlord Act says the tenant has an obligation to pay rent and the landlord has the obligation and responsibility to give the tenant a decent and safe place to live. Details of the Warrant of Habitability vary from state to state, in particular in what is "reasonable time to make a repair." Check with your attorney if you're in doubt.

Warrant of Habitability doesn't guarantee that the house must be comfortable and beautiful, but if the tenant feels the landlord did not repair a problem, he can legally deduct rent from future rent payments. The point is, they have the right to do this; but only if certain procedures are followed. The tenant must give you "reasonable time to make the repair" and the request should be made in writing. How much time is reasonable? That depends on the repair. A leaky roof could be a few weeks but no heat would be a day or two. The tenant can "repair and deduct" an amount equal to but not greater than the rent due until the end of the lease. If the tenant is on a month-to-month lease the "repair and deduct" cannot exceed one month's rent.

Remember the tenant's repair request should be made in writing with a reasonably stated deadline date. After this date, the tenant may make the repair and deduct the expense from future rent payments. If the tenant hires someone to do the work, a receipt must clearly state the nature of the repair, the date completed, name of person doing the repair, and the overall cost. Also be aware that a tenant can legally sue the landlord for previous rent paid if this condition or any other condition is not repaired promptly.

Most states require the tenant to open an escrow account and pay the rent money into this account until a judge decides how much rent adjustment, if any, is needed. Check your state laws before acting.

How does a judge determine the proper amount of rent that is to be withheld? Recent court cases have shown a percentage basis is used. If a roof leaks into a bedroom making one fourth of the total unit uninhabitable for a month, the tenant would be entitled to a one fourth credit of that month's rent. If the heater breaks and the tenant must spend six days at a friend's house, he is entitled to a one-fifth reduction for the time out of the house.

An example that happened to me: A well servicing a single family home went dry. The next door, and only, neighbor who was also on a well, was nice enough to allow a garden hose to be attached to an outside line and run to the pump in the basement. We hooked up a coupling to take this garden hose and bypass my well. I promised to pay for any additional electric because of the well pump running more frequently since it was servicing two homes. I called every well driller in the area and the earliest anyone could be there was five weeks away.

One week after this happened the kind neighbor called to say his pump was running almost constantly. He was worried his well might go dry pumping for two families. I could tell from his voice he was not going to allow this to continue for another four weeks. I suggested we put the tenants on a timetable and rationing plan. The water would be turned on from 7–9:00 AM, off till 6:00 PM, and back on till 10:00 PM. I told my tenants to keep flushing the toilet to a minimum, take quick showers, and take the laundry to a laundromat. I would reimburse them for the laundromat. They were not happy with the new arrangement.

I called the well people everyday to see if they had a cancellation and to stress my urgency. I think they got tired of my calls, and they had the new well in four weeks after it went dry. I paid the higher electric bill for the neighbor and gave them a gift certificate to a restaurant. I paid the tenants for their laundry and some bottled water they had purchased and thought that was the end of a bad four weeks. The following week I received a letter from the local district justice saying my tenants had filed to recover the four weeks of rent because the building was "unfit" under the Warrant of Habitability. Before reading on, decide what you think would be fair compensation, if any, if you were the judge.

At the hearing the judge told the tenants they were not entitled to recovery of rent under the Warrant of Habitability. He told them I had in good faith, paid for the laundromat and bottled water, did everything possible to get them water as soon as the well went dry, and got the well digger one week before the promised date. He also concluded the whole house was still "habitable" and the hours the water was turned off was an inconvenience but not enough of a hardship to cause a deduction in rent for the period. They had also agreed to the water rationing (in writing) versus accepting my offer of a motel. I think they realized staying in the house would be easier than putting four small children (all under the age of six) and two adults in a motel room.

Tenants can also legally escrow rent money to force the landlord to make repairs that do not fit into the category of "Warrant of Habitability." An example might be a tub leak that only occurs when someone is taking a shower. Water comes through the living room ceiling and a bucket must be placed on the floor to catch it. Obviously a repair is needed, but it does not make the apartment uninhabitable.

First the tenant should call the landlord and follow it up in writing about the needed repair. If it is not fixed in a "reasonable time" the tenant needs to send another letter stating that the rent will be placed in an escrow account (they must name the company) and mail a copy of the receipt to the landlord. His failure to open the escrow account will make your case much stronger in court. The problem with the tenant escrowing money is how to get it after the repair has been made. The tenant and the escrow agent are supposed to give you a release that states all funds due are to be given to you. The tenant could refuse to do this. This situation can be avoided by having the tenant sign the release contingent on a neutral third party inspecting the repair. If the repair is acceptable, the neutral party will instruct the escrow agent to release the funds.

Knowing the requirements of the tenant before rent is escrowed will help keep your tenants informed of their rights before they take the law into their own hands by refusing to pay rent. If the tenant is willing to do all that is required legally, their complaint is most likely justified. You, as the landlord, have an obligation to handle all complaints as soon as possible. The best philosophy to communicate to all tenants is: I will take care of problems in a timely manner and I expect you to do the same by paying your rent on time.

CHAPTER 15

Alternative Rentals

The difference between ordinary and extraordinary is that little extra.

History has demonstrated that the most notable comers usually encounter heartbreaking obstacles before they triumph. They won because they refused to become discouraged by their defeats.

— B.C. Forbes

This chapter will show some different, but very profitable, alternative type rentals that might work in your area. The student housing concept works best in a college town, resort rentals work best in high traffic resort areas, furnished units rented by corporations work best in large metropolitan areas, senior citizen assisted living facilities, and furnished units rented for fire insurance claims work anywhere.

STUDENT HOUSING

Why would anyone want to rent to college students? They are rowdy, get drunk all the time, will destroy your property and they never have any money. The creative landlord who rents to college students hopes you keep that image because it means there will be less competition for him.

If you live near a college town, start looking for properties for sale within a half mile to a mile radius of the campus. The more bedrooms the better. Remember you are not renting total square footage but square footage based on size of bedrooms.

Submit information about your unit to the college's "residential housing" department. They will publish, at no charge, details about the units you have for rent. Once the word spreads around campus, there will be more phone calls than you can handle. Many times getting just one student to commit will bring in the rest after he/she spreads the word to friends. When students graduate, the tenants not graduating, find roommates to replace the graduates so there is very little advertising.

Generally each student has his own room but if the room is large, two students can share a room with a 25% savings in the rent. Rents should be based on what they would pay if living in the dorm on campus. Utilities are split equally among everyone living in the house. Try to put one student in charge of collecting the money for the utility bills and then pay you.

Rent payments are due before the beginning of each semester. If a student wishes to stay over the summer, (June - August) reduce the rent. Having the unit occupied cuts down on vandalism and gets the utilities paid. Security deposit is split proportionate to the number of students in the house.

The lease should have some additional clauses
• parents co-signing
• inspections monthly
• damages billed to everyone in house - students work out who is responsible
• drinking outside the house or inappropriate behavior will not be tolerated

Since this is the first time away from home for most students, it is a good idea to go over everything with them about the house. What can and can't be put down a garbage disposal, how to light the pilot on the stove, oven, hot water heater, how the appliances work, trash day, what items get recycled, are just a few examples. It is also a good idea to show up at least once a week to pick up trash, cut the grass, trim some bushes so you show you care about the property.

Student rentals are slightly more repair intense but not enough to justify the 40% increase in cash flow that this type rental brings in.

RESORT RENTALS

Resort rentals can come in many different shapes, sizes and lengths of lease. They can be single family homes with an ocean front view to a duplex or condo two blocks back from the ocean. They can also be condos at the base of a ski slope or a four-plex downtown. All will have peak times of the year when rental rates are at a premium and off peak times when it is almost cheaper to close them up than try to rent.

Obviously for shore properties prime rental time is during the summer and resort properties near ski slopes will be the winter months. There are some areas such Florida, Arizona, and southern California that prime time is anytime during the year.

There are four ways most people use to get their units rented. Word-of-mouth, the paper, the internet, and on-site or local rental agents.

Word-of-mouth to friends is an excellent source that you know works the best. There is no agent fee and you know the unit will be well-maintained by your friends. The paper and the internet for resort rentals is more risky because you don't know the people, but a hefty deposit is a good shield. It also saves on agent fees. It is probably best to work with a rental agent in the town or on the premises with the understanding that they do not rent out a week without notifying you first to be sure you have not already rented it. Their commission fees can be over 20% but that's still better than the unit sitting empty for the week.

Since most resort rentals are for one week, cleaning people must be hired to get the unit ready for new renters coming in just a few hours after the last ones have left.

Resort properties can also be rented out for the few months of prime time which will generate enough income to cover the mortgage payments for the year. Anything rented out of prime time just adds to the cash flow. If you live near the area, the off peak times afford you the opportunity to use the property.

FURNISHED RENTALS FOR CORPORATIONS

Large corporations often have middle management employees come into town to work on a project for a month or two and then return home. Hotel rooms with no kitchens and just a bed and phone get boring real fast for these people. Marriott and other hotel chains have seen the need for short term rentals with the conveniences of a small apartment. They will include a small sitting room with a couch, a chair or two, TV, and a desk. Off this room will be a small kitchen with a stove, sink, refrigerator, coffee maker, and a microwave.

If you have a single family home, condo, townhouse, or even a duplex, that is centrally located, look into what it would cost to completely furnish it from beds, sofas, lamps, to pots and pans. Until you see how this works, rent the furnishings to start. If it is a go, the rental companies will have buy out options.

Contact different corporations in your area to assess if there is a need. Another approach is to hang out in the lobby of one of these suites around breakfast time and start up a conversation with people staying there. Find out the companies they work for and then make a presentation to that company. Make up a brochure showing pictures of the property, what furnishings and appliances come with the property along with the rental rates. In a separate column list items that are included in the rent: electric, water, sewer, trash, lawn cutting, snow removal, maintenance of all appliances. Also list options that are available, for an additional fee, such as: cleaning service, doing wash, dry cleaning, meals that are prepared, frozen, and placed in the freezer designed around specific criteria given by the tenant.

Base the rates so they are competitive with the suite rates. If there are extras such as a garage, fenced yard, finished basement, satellite hookup, Jacuzzi, pool, deck, etc. the rate should reflex the additional conveniences.

The ultimate is to find a corporation or business that wants to rent the furnished unit for a full year. If that does not work, find corporations that will take a three or six month lease.

FURNISHED RENTALS - FIRE INSURANCE CLAIMS

Fires displace families from their homes and it becomes the insurance company's responsibility to help find and then pay for a rental until the house can be repaired. Most times the insurance company calls places that have furnished apartments for short term rentals and they are willing to pay out top dollar to take care of this emergency situation.

A friend of mine discovered just how much of a top dollar they are willing to pay. He had purchased a single family home in a residential area and was rehabbing it. Four doors away a similar home caught fire and displaced the family. He approached them and asked if they would be interested in renting his house. It was close, the kids would still be around their friends and they could easily keep an eye on the reconstruction of their home. The going rent in the area was $700 a month. The insurance company was willing to pay him $2,800 a month because that is what it would cost to put the family in a furnished unit. Needless to say it didn't take him long to rent furniture, completely furnish the home, and move the family in.

Contact insurance companies in your area to see if you could be put on a rental list for fire cases. Another way to find fire claims is to read the paper and listen to the news for houses that have been damaged by fire, water, mud slides, etc.

ASSISTED LIVING FACILITY

With the baby boomers quickly approaching retirement age, the demand for adult communities, nursing homes, and assisted living facilities will be at an all time high. This alternative rental is management intense, but the profits can be very large.

These type homes are designed for people who can take care of day to day functions such as bathing, dressing, and eating but need help with taking the correct medicine at the proper times and eating balanced meals. These needs are taken care of by a live in nurse and another person to do the cooking.

Do not start looking for houses until your state has been contacted. Ask them to send the requirements for assisted living facilities. Some states allow up to four individuals per house and will not need to be regulated by the state. Any number over four, the home must meet all state guidelines. They will be looking to see if the house has a sprinkler system, is handicap accessible from both inside and out. The bathrooms, bedrooms and halls must be modified with railings and handles. If there are steps, a movable chair or elevator will be required. The state will want to see a monthly meal schedule and will critique it for nutritional needs.

Victorian homes seem to work well for assisted living facilities. There is usually a large living room where residents can gather to watch TV, play cards, entertain visitors, read, etc. They also usually have large porches that wrap around the building which makes a great place to rock away a summer evening. Rooms are large and with some modifications can be split up and made into two semi-private rooms. The large basement can be converted into an apartment for the live in nurse. Split level homes can also work and save on the number of steps.

It is not unusual for residents to have to pay over $2,000 a month for this type of care. With just four residents or $8,000 a month you can see there is plenty left to pay for staff, food, utilities, and the mortgage. The more you can fit in, the higher the profit margin.

To find residents, design a flyer with pictures that can be distributed to hospitals, churches, and insurance companies. Word of mouth from satisfied families telling friends is also a good source of referrals.

CHAPTER 16

SOURCES OF ADDITIONAL INCOME

Without Cash Flow all you have is a Hobby.

Unless you try to do something beyond what you have already mastered, you will not grow.

— Ralph Waldo Emerson

INSUFFICIENT FUNDS

When a tenant bounces a check, send an Insufficient Funds Notice and charge him a fee. Paying for his mistake twice, (both you and his bank), may get him to change his ways. Furthermore, as you can see from the form, if another check bounces, he loses the "privilege" of paying rent by check.

The first time a check bounces, I charge the insufficient funds fee but waive the late fee even though the rent is also late. I explain that any future checks that bounce will cause both the late fee and insufficient funds fee to be paid plus losing the privilege of paying by check.

LATE FEES

Collecting late fees can be a big boost to your cash flow, and it takes so little time and effort. I had a tenant who could never get his rent money together before the fifth of the month but always had it to me by the tenth. In two years he never paid on time, but each month paid a $30.00 late fee. This meant that my cash flow was $360 higher at the end of the year.

Enforcing late fee payment helps in two ways. First, the tenant knows you mean business and are an enforcer of your rules. Let

---

NOTICE OF INSUFFICIENT FUNDS

To: _____, Tenant in possession of

_____

_____

_____

You are hereby notified that _____ rent payment has been returned to us marked Insufficient Funds. As stated in the Additional Terms and Conditions of your lease, there is a $_____ charge to you for each check returned marked Insufficient Funds. Please include this fee in next month's rent payment. Your lease also states that if any additional checks are returned because of Insufficient Funds, the privilege of paying by check will be terminated. If this does occur, all future rent payments must be in the form of a money order or certified check.

___/___/___   _____
Date

him slide once and there will be a second time because he will expect you to let it slide again. The second reason is that it is such a big return for so little effort. It takes less than two minutes to fill out the form, address an envelope, and drop it in the mail.

COIN OPERATED LAUNDRY MACHINES

Have you ever had a prospective tenant call to ask if there is a washer and dryer in the apartment or if there are laundry facilities on site? If you have to answer no to both questions, there is a good chance you are losing some very good prospective tenants. Consider giving them something they want while improving your cash flow at the same time.

One of the main benefits of installing coin operated laundry machines (in addition to the money they generate) is that they will make you more competitive in attracting new tenants and keeping the existing ones happy. If tenants are happy, they stay longer which means lower vacancy rates, a better cash flow and improved marketability of the property at sale time. Property value is also increased because of the increased positive cash flow.

Coin operated washers and dryers can show a break even with as few as three units in a building. On the average, one washer/dryer combination will be needed for every eight units. Each unit will do an average of 12 loads of wash a month (more with two or more children). You can charge the same or slightly more than a laundromat. If you charge one dollar for a wash and 75 cents for a dry, the average tenant will spend $21 a month.

A good commercial washer and dryer cost approximately $800 which includes the coin boxes and keys. If eight units spend $21 a month, the machines will take in $168. The cost of water, sewer and gas (always buy gas dryers) will be approximately 15% of the revenue for a net amount of $143 a month. (If you do not have gas in the building add an additional 8-10% to expenses for electric dryers.) This means that in less than six months, the machines will be paid for and your cash flow will im-

prove by $143 per month. To top it all off, you are providing a fee generating service for the tenants and they really appreciate it!

Do not enter into a contract with a washer and dryer leasing company. Why share the profits? Most coin-operated leasing companies have two plans. Both plans will install the machines and guarantee repairs but the similarities stop here. In Plan One, the leasing company takes the money out of the machines and sends you a check for a certain percentage, usually 60% (I did this once and always wondered how much was skimmed off the top before figuring my 60%.) The second plan gives you more control because you have the keys and you pay the company a monthly fee for the rental and repairs. Both options are big money makers for the leasing company and very expensive compared to doing it yourself.

NOTICE OF LATE FEE CHARGE

To: _____, Tenant in possession of
_____
_____
_____

You are hereby notified that _____ rent payment was postmarked ___/___/___. This is in violation of the grace period by _____ day(s). The late fee charge of $ _____ is due and should be included in next month's rent payment.

___/___/___   _____
Date

Buy the best commercial machines (Speed Queen and Whirlpool are excellent), that you can find. I have machines I purchased new five years ago and have never had a service call that required a repairman. I have received phone calls for problems such as removing bent coins, lint from dryer hoses, and having to re-light a pilot light on a gas dryer but nothing more serious than this. These problems were solved in less than five minutes.

The only problem I have experienced was vandalism of the coin boxes. Once, after replacing a coin box, I placed a large sign over the machines that said, "The next person to vandalize these machines will cause them to be removed or the cost to operate the machine will be increased to pay for the expense to keep them in working order. The choice is yours." I have not had a problem since I posted the sign.

The positive benefits of coin-operated laundry machines far outweigh any negatives. The best part of owning the machines is providing your tenants with something they want while rewarding yourself by collecting the money from the coin boxes!

WAYS TO CUT HEATING COSTS

Many times large, old, single family buildings are converted to apartments and the original furnace is left in place to service all the units. If the heating type is oil or gas hot air, it will be difficult to convert each unit to a separate heat source, unless baseboard electric is installed.

If the furnace is oil or gas hot water, your options increase. One method is to place a thermostat in each apartment, and add a circulator motor and flow meter for each unit. With some minor plumbing, each apartment now can be metered separately. The flow meter will tell how much hot water each apartment used. By calculating usage on a percentage basis, each tenant will pay his or her own pro-rata share of the total heating cost.

If the first method isn't practical, consider using timers. During peak use, the heat and hot water, if all on one system, are on; but during off-peak hours the temperature in the boiler is lowered.

The thermostats in each apartment do not have an incremental dial; merely an on/off switch. Each tenant can order as much heat as they wish. There is a further refinement. If the temperature in the unit is less than the preset temperature, the heat will not come on. This type of system has cut my heating costs 40%. The savings more than offset the installation costs.

Finally, look for companies that install a system that measures the amount of BTUs going to each apartment. BTU usage is determined by a sensor that is placed on the hot water line going to each unit. The company will read the usage each month, divide it into the total cost that month for the fuel, and bill the tenants for you. The initial costs will be high but it should pay for itself in a year, or less.

STORAGE BINS

Did you ever notice that apartments never seem to have enough closets and storage areas for large items such as grills, lawn chairs, bikes, etc. Why not consider installing individual storage bins in a common basement? All you need are a few 2 x 4s, some drywall, a door, and a lock. Make them different sizes and charge extra rent for the privilege of using them. And be sure to add a clause in the lease that you are not responsible for any lost or stolen items.

PARKING

Many times, particularly in larger buildings, parking is limited to about one to one and a half spots per unit. Since many tenants own two, and sometimes, three vehicles, parking can become a problem. Turn this problem around and make money while doing it. Assign everyone one parking spot which is included in the rent. A second spot can be reserved for an additional $10 a month. After everyone has the opportunity to reserve a second spot, a third spot could be rented.

WAYS TO CUT ELECTRIC COSTS

If you are paying for electric, call the electric company and ask if they offer off-peak rates for electric water heaters. If they do, have a separate house meter installed, and set it so that it will come on only during off-peak hours. I have used this method, and I have yet had a tenant call to say they ran out of hot water.

You can save by installing fluorescent lights in common halls or laundry rooms. A fluorescent bulb uses one-fourth the electric of a standard incandescent light bulb for the same amount of light output.

Here's another way I've used to go from paying the utilities to having the tenants pay. I merely divided the utility bill proportionally among all the tenants in the building. I did not do it based on the number of units in the building, but on the number of tenants living there. This has worked particularly well with college students.

For other types of tenants, you might want to do this on a trial basis. There could be problems if one tenant is home all day using a lot of electricity while others are at work. Further complications can arise when some tenants have more appliances, such as air conditioners, than others.

WAYS TO CUT WATER AND SEWER BILLS

You can cut your water bills by using the same idea as outlined above. Tenants seem to tolerate this better for two reasons: First, it is more difficult for tenants to know how much water each is using and, second, the bills are usually much less per month than electric bills.

DEVELOP A MARKETING PLAN
FOR YOUR RENTALS
"Standard" and "Customized" Apartments

Two main goals in this business are tenant retention, and ways to increase cash flow. These ideas will not be for everyone but hopefully part of the following ideas can be incorporated into your management style.

My wife and I enjoy taking cruises, especially with a few other real estate investor couples. The travel agent will ask if I prefer an inside, outside or balcony cabin, and what level of the ship I wish to be on. There are different prices for each type of cabin and level of the ship so the travel agent can "customize" my accommodations very specifically. If I wish to travel as cheaply as possible, then an inside cabin on a lower deck will do just fine. If I want natural light then I will choose an outside cabin that will have a window and if I want the total experience then the balcony cabin will be chosen. Each upgrade will cost more, but I am getting more for what I have paid.

Landlords need to develop the same type of thinking for their rentals. When a prospective tenant calls about an apartment, tell them your company offers a "standard" unit for $550 a month but any unit can be "customized" to fit their needs. Explain the "standard" unit comes with (these are just suggestions) wall-to-wall carpet, garbage disposal, dishwasher and oven/stove but you can receive some additional upgrades for just a few dollars more a month. Some upgrade options could be:

> ceiling fan with light - $5 a month
> microwave oven - $10 month
> Refrigerator - $15 a month
> Television - $15 a month
> Computer with printer - $40 a month

I have listed ideas for pricing just to give you some ideas. The actual cost should be based on whatever price the items can be purchased for and then divided by twelve. You want these items to be paid off after one year. If the tenant stays longer, it's additional cash flow each month because you "customized" the unit. A ceiling fan and light can be purchased for under $30 so charging $5 a month will have it paid off in six months. Microwave ovens can

be bought new for under $100 so once again the pay back is less than one year. The average life of a refrigerator is more than ten years. Find a used one that is 3-4 years old or buy a new at scratch and dent prices. Payback at $15 a month would mean buying for no more than $180. If it costs more, raise the monthly price. Call around to motels and hotels and asked to be notified when they plan to upgrade rooms and sell off the televisions. $15 a month should more than cover the cost of the TV the first year. Company's are constantly upgrading their computer systems and are glad to find someone to take a few off their hands at really low prices. Use your imagination to come up with additional options - washer, dryer, upgrade on carpet when you replace the carpet, light fixtures, vanity in powder room, etc.

The secret to the customizing program is to supply the item for three to four years and then give it to them! It's been paid off long ago and will be needing repairs soon anyway. This approach also helps us with our goal of tenant retention. If the tenant knows they will own the computer or television if they stay for another year or two they might not move. If the average tenant turnover cost is $1000-$1500 in lost rent and repairs, the cost of these items is cheap if it retains a tenant. The tenant is happy that you are giving them a "rent to own" option that is much more affordable than the companies offering the same programs.

What do you do if the upgrades ceiling fan is left by the old tenant and is seen by the prospective tenant on the first showing? Explain that the last tenant took the ceiling fan upgrade option which they can also take, but if they prefer not to, it will be removed.

RENTAL PRICE RANGE VS EXACT RENT

Try running an ad in the paper that tells location and number of bedrooms but doesn't include the price. When a prospective tenant calls and asks how much is the rent for the two bedroom, ask them what was the price range they were considering? If the going rate is $500 and they say they were looking for something in the $550 range, the price of that unit just went up. Of course, the price range they will quote will vary greatly but it doesn't matter because you know what your bottom line for rent will be.

LONGER THE STAY THE MORE REWARD
OPTIONS AVAILABLE

As mentioned earlier, if the average turnover costs $1000- $1500, and the average tenant stays three to four years, it's in our best interest to "reward" tenants for their loyalty. If these incentives keep them from moving, than it becomes a win-win for everyone.

The "reward options," or what I like to call my "VIT" program," (Very Important Tenant) will be structured by the type of tenant that rents from you. A lower end tenant will not be interested in receiving frequent flyer miles as their bonus and an upper end tenant will not be that excited about a week of free rent as their option.

The "VIT" program needs to be explained in writing and should be included in the second year rent increase notice. You want them to be thinking about not moving well before that third or fourth year when the options start kicking in.

Hopefully after reviewing the options, they will check off which "VIT" program best suits them, sign, date and return with the rent increase notice.

The following are suggestions for lower, middle and upper end tenants. All incentives are built on the principle that if the tenant doesn't move, that's extra cash flow for you. Use part of it to "give back" to the tenant for their loyalty of staying with you. If they move before completing their "VIT" program, they are not entitled to any of the reward. As you will see, the longer they stay on the program the less likely they will move.

Another advantage of this program is that tenants tell other tenants about what you are doing. Friends of tenants want to get in on the program and start calling to see if any units are available. This cuts down on advertising costs because you are calling people that have called you to get on your waiting list!

"VIT" Option # 1

Usually a lower end rental will choose this option. Offer this option when sending the second year rent increase notice. Even though it doesn't take effect for another two years, it will start them thinking about not wanting to move.

This option gives the tenant a certificate for one week free rent during any month during the fifth year of occupancy. The sixth year they receive a two week free rent certificate, seventh year, three week certificate and the eighth year, one month of free rent. If they stay longer, offer one of the other "VIT" options.

"VIT" Option # 2

This option offers a week's vacation in a time share unit anywhere in the world after their fourth year as a tenant. The option should say during the fifth year they can take a one week time share vacation for only $300. If they need airfare that is also their expense. During the sixth year their portion drops to $200, then $100 in the seven year and total-

ly free during the eighth and ninth year. If they renew in the tenth year the deed is transferred to them. They can continue to use it or if they wish, can sell it since they are now the owners.

Show them either an RCI or II time share exchange book which will list all the resorts and give a write-up on each. How do you find the time share unit to buy and do it cheap enough to make this program cost effective? There are several ways to find time share units for sale. Contact real estate franchises such as REMAX, Century 21 or ERA and see if they can locate agents who deal with time share re-sales. The internet can also be a big help. Find companies that specialize in time share re-sales and see what they have to offer. Another source is to advertise in the local paper "Looking to buy a red time share week - cheap." List your number and wait for the phone to ring. Many people inherit time share weeks from relatives that have died or the kids are grown and they don't want to use it anymore. They often are willing to sell them cheap just to unload it. When a call comes in, tell them you're interested in purchasing a "red" week, anywhere, but the most you can spend is $1000. If they say no to this price, give them your name and number in case they change their mind later.

A "red" week is preferable because "red" is prime time. Your tenant can travel in prime time as well as transition weeks which are "blue" and off season which are listed as "white" times. The fees for maintenance for a week time share will run around $300-$350 per week.

After buying a week it will be necessary to join either RCI or II which are the two largest time share exchange companies. They will "space bank" your week which means you give them permission to rent out your time share unit to another member. You can now choose from hundreds of time share units that fellow members have "space banked." The more notice you can give these companies as to the dates your tenant wants to travel, the better chance they have of getting their first choice.

So how is this program cost effective for you? If they stay for the fifth year instead of moving like the average tenant, you have just paid for the $1,000 time share week with the money saved from not having a tenant turnover. The tenant picks up almost all of the maintenance cost with his $300 in year five, then $200 in year six, etc. Your cost will be only a few hundred dollars by the time the tenant reaches year eight which should be another average turnover. The incentive for the tenant to stay to the tenth year is strong because the time share is given to them. Since it was paid for by not having the tenant move after the fourth year you are still ahead of the game and you have a tenant that can't say enough good things about you.

"VIT" Option # 3

Tenants who are renting more upscale housing will usually choose either the time share option or this one featuring frequent flyer miles. They might have relatives that they enjoy flying to visit each year which will give them a strong incentive to choose this option.

By calling any of the major airlines, they will tell you how much it will cost to purchase frequent flyer mile coupons that can be purchased in different miles denominations. It could be 250 miles, 500 miles, 1,000 or more and the cost will reflect whatever denominations you choose.

This option will have the tenant receiving 100 frequent flyer miles for each month starting from the first month of the fifth year. The coupons can be given at the end of each year or a letter could be sent showing the total miles accumulated to date. Whenever they wish to cash them in, they must give you a month's notice.

CHAPTER 17

GOOD WILL PAYS DIVIDENDS

The difference between a highly successful person and one who barely makes it, is in their habits. The successful person has identified what he does well and repeats it.

— Jeffrey Taylor

A smile is the shortest distance between two people.

Put 20 landlords in one room and 20 tenants in another and ask each to describe the other....

Landlords will say tenants:	*Tenants will say landlords:*
Don't pay rent on time	Don't make repairs on time
Are lazy	Are lazy
... Dishonest	... Dishonest
... Apathetic	... Heartless
Cause damage to the units	... Rich
Will do anything to save a dollar	Will do any thing to save a dollar

Both are probably accurate accounts. However, there is one misconception that tenants have, that really hits a raw nerve with landlords. It is the notion that they are filthy rich. In most cases this is not true. A good percentage of landlords are small-time investors with just a few properties. They use their savings to buy additional investment properties, but, from a cash flow position, they are not much different from a tenant.

It is at this point the successful landlord should remember their poorer days when visiting a tenant or showing a unit. Don't arrive at your property driving a Mercedes and dressed in a three piece suit. When visiting a tenant to make a repair, use an old beat up car and dress in work clothes. Psychologically, you become an equal—not the authoritative rich boss. Requests for outlandish improvements will stop because they see you can't afford a nice car or clothes either!

TREAT TENANTS THE WAY YOU WOULD WANT TO BE TREATED

Tenants want to be treated fairly by landlords just as you want to be treated fairly by them. Sending a tenant a Christmas card and including a rent increase notice of $100 is not the best way to say Merry Christmas. Why not start a positive rapport by making the first move to get the ball rolling? Some examples:

- After signing a lease with tenants, mark their birthdays (get from the Tenant Information Sheet) on a calendar and mail them a birthday card.
- Place a basket of fruit, with a bow on it, in their new kitchen.
- Write a short note wishing them a long and happy stay.
- On the birth of a child, send them a bouquet of flowers.
- If you hear about a death in the family or a hospital stay, send a card or call to let them know that you are thinking of them.
- Write a letter to a tenant's employer. Tell the employer Mr. Smith has been a tenant of yours for the past four years and he has always paid his rent on time. He keeps an immaculate apartment and is a real pleasure to have as a tenant. Ask that your letter be put in his personal file to be used as a character reference for any advancement that might occur.
- At holiday time, send all tenants cards.
- Say thanks to long-term tenants by including a gift certificate to a local department store or restaurant. It makes both you and them feel

good, and you know the good word will spread to the other tenants about your kindness and generosity.

• For all tenants who paid on time between January and November, send them a thank you note stating how much you appreciated their prompt payments and that you would like to show your appreciation by giving them a turkey for Thanksgiving. Tell them you will deliver the turkey around lunch time on a Saturday. This day and time should give you the maximum exposure to the other tenants in the building. You want all the tenants not receiving turkeys to see the delivery. After you leave, the empty-handed tenants will ask their happy neighbors why they were given a turkey.

Many times the tenant will start the ball rolling by making a repair on his own and not telling you about it. One tenant replaced rotten wood on the front porch and then painted the whole porch. I drove by one day and it looked great. When I called to say thank you, he played it down as no big deal. He was afraid someone might get hurt if they fell through the rotting wood. That had been a law suit just waiting to happen, if someone had been hurt. I sent the man and his wife a gift certificate to a local restaurant as my way of saying thanks. Just remember that a few extra dollars or some of your time to pat a tenant on the back, will pay dividends more than you ever imagined. Try it and see.

IMPORTANT NUMBERS AND HELPFUL HINTS

Many times tenants are moving into a new area and need to know where banks, supermarkets, the post office, dry cleaners, auto repair shop, drug store, barber shop, restaurants, hardware store, etc. are located. They also need a list of emergency numbers to use for police, fire, water, sewer, gas, electric, cable, ambulance service, plus an emergency number to reach you.

Along with this information give them a "helpful hints" page that will give important locations of shut off valves in the house,

steps to take if appliances stop working, and things to do to make appliances work better and last longer. The more information you can give a tenant about appliances and how they are to be used, the less maintenance calls you will make.

Here are a few you should review when doing the walk through inspection:

• Stress that the strainer in the tub must stay in and will need to be cleaned out after each shower. It will prevent hair from clogging the drain and costly repairs at their expense.

• While in the bathroom show how to remove the toilet tank lid and push down the flapper if it looks like water will overflow the top of the bowl.

• The stopper in sinks should remain in as it prevents tooth brushes, combs, etc. from dropping down into the J trap.

Happy Thanksgiving!

Dear

Too often landlords take good tenants for granted—especially those who always pay their rent on time. This year we would like to honor our tenants who have paid their rent on time every month in 20___.

We would like to say "Thanks" for prompt payments by "giving" you a ___ to ___ pound turkey for your Thanksgiving dinner.

Your turkey will be delivered on _____ at approximately _____. If you will not be home at this time, please make arrangements with a neighbor or friend to be available to receive it.

We hope you enjoy your turkey on Thanksgiving and thanks again for your prompt rent payments each month this year.

Sincerely,

• While in the shower area stress not to over tighten shower faucets. They will continue to drip for a few seconds after they are shut off.

• Demonstrate how to use the stove, especially if there is a timer device. You don't want to get a call that the Thanksgiving turkey is ready to go and the stove won't go on. It turned out that the timer switch had been set and it was just a matter of turning it off to get the stove to work.

• Encourage tenants to remove food from plates before placing in the dishwasher. Demonstrate the different cycles on the dishwasher.

• Demonstrate how to unclog a garbage disposal, with safety being the number one priority. See #7 on the Helpful Hints form.

• Encourage your tenant to drop ice cubes into the disposal and then run it. It helps clean the blades and moves grease particles down the line.

• Replace the furnace filter at least twice a year. (List on the outside of the furnace the size of the filters for easy replacement by tenants and also note the size for your records.) To check the filter, start by turning off the thermostat and removing the filter cover. Pull the filter out and hold up to the light. If you cannot see light through the filter it should be replaced or cleaned. Align the new filter according to the arrows printed on the filter and slide into the furnace. Replace the filter cover, and turn the thermostat back on.

STAY IN CONTROL OF YOUR EMOTIONS

There will be times that you and the tenant will not see eye to eye. Try not to show your anger or be out of control. If the tenant gets the slightest indication you are losing control, you have already lost. A tenant is just like a child. He will keep pestering you until you can't take the aggravation anymore and give in. Be firm and convincing with your answers and there will be no compromising. If you feel yourself losing control, get out of the situation as quickly as possible; tell him you must talk about this with the partners, and you will get back to him. Then go find the punching bag and have a 15 minute workout before doing anything.

Remember tenants are your customers. Without them you have no business. If they perceive you as a fair person, most will treat you fairly. If you scrimp with money for needed repairs or improvements, it shows the tenant you just want to take it in but not pay it back out. Gain their respect by taking care of problems as soon as possible and then follow it up with a phone call to make sure it was done to their satisfaction.

IMPORTANT NUMBERS AND HELPFUL HINTS

IMPORTANT NUMBERS

Police _____	Gas Co._____
Fire _____	Oil Co. _____
Ambulance_____	Phone Co. _____
Paramedic _____	Electric Co. _____
Doctor_____	Water Dept._____
Plumber _____	Sewer Dept._____
Electrician _____	Cable T.V. _____
Manager _____	Emergency # if no answer _____

HELPFUL HINTS

1. The main shut off valve to stop all water in the unit is located:_____
   Individual faucets may be turned off at the supply line under the sink or toilet. Domestic hot water heaters and hot water baseboard heat valves are usually located on the cold water line above the heater.

2. The main gas shut off valve for the unit is located:_____
   The domestic gas hot water heater valve will be located on the bottom third of the tank and should be turned 180 degrees or so the stem is perpendicular to the supply line. This will also hold true for the gas heater line.

3. The electric main for the unit is located: _____
   Check to see if a fuse has blown or a circuit breaker has tripped. Replace fuses with the same amperage as the one being removed (never more) or push the circuit breaker button back to the on position.

4. The fire extinguisher is located: _____
   Most fires in rental properties start in the kitchen. Keep the extinguisher in the kitchen but away from the stove. Point it at the base of the fire and use short quick bursts. Do not pour water on a grease fire. If the extinguisher fails to work, use baking soda or flour to put out the fire.

5. A toilet bowl can only hold one tank of water. If the water does not go down, another flush will cause it to overflow. If you think it is going to overflow, remove the tank lid and push down on the flap that covers the hole. This will stop additional water from entering the bowl. Use a plunger to remove the blockage and then try flushing again. Be ready to push down the flap if the water rises again. With small infants, always keep the lid down.

6. When taking a shower, make sure the glass door or curtain is pulled closed, especially in the corner closest to the shower head. Check the caulk and grout between the tiles for holes or gaps. If any are found contact us immediately. It is amazing how much damage a small amount of water can do.

7. The garbage disposal is to be used for EDIBLE OBJECTS only. This means DO NOT put down large bones, egg shells, grease, fat, cooking oil, or onion skins to name a few. Run cold water before starting and continue to run for thirty seconds after turning off. If you hear a clanking with a metallic sound, or the motor sounds like it wants to start but doesn't, stop the disposal immediately. Use a flashlight to see if a spoon, dish cloth, handi-wipe, etc. might have fallen down. Use the disposal wrench that fits in a slot on the bottom of the disposal. If there is no slot for a wrench use the end of a broom and try to rotate the blades. Push the reset button and try again. If it still doesn't work, then call us. Ice cubes run through the disposal helps clean the blades and moves grease particles down the line.
   Encourage your tenant to drop ice cubes into the disposal and then run it. It helps clean the blades and moves grease particles down the line.

8. Replace the furnace filter at least twice a year. (List on the outside of the furnace the size of the filters for easy replacement by tenants and also note the size for your records.) To check the filter, start by turning off the thermostat and removing the filter cover. Pull the filter out and hold up to the light. If you cannot see light through the filter it should be replaced or cleaned. Align the new filter according to the arrows printed on the filter and slide into the furnace. Replace the filter cover, and turn the thermostat back on.

2002

10

CHAPTER 18

EVICTIONS

There is only one reason tenants consistently pay late. You allow them to behave that way. Evict them immediately. Toleration of chronic delinquents is bad management.

— John T. Reed

When God wants to send you a gift, he sends you a problem.

For every nice story I hear about landlords, I must hear ten bad ones. This can be changed by doing some things mentioned in the last chapter and also by communicating with your tenants (which means being a good listener). Be aware of the tenant's needs and you will be respected as a fair and concerned landlord. When you say you will do something, DO IT.

There will always be complaints and situations where you must assert your authority and be the enforcer of the rules. Confronting tenants is not a pleasant task but it is a necessary one. Create an image for the tenants from the very beginning. Show them you will enforce the rules, but try not to tell them you are the sole owner of the property. Have partners who must be consulted concerning every decision. Make the other partners the bad guys, and you be the good partner who agrees with the tenant but was out-voted.

Here is an example of how a conversation might go when having to call a tenant whose rent is late. "Hello, Mr. Tenant. I talked to the owners/partners today, and they wanted to know when we can expect your rent payment. They are really putting the pressure on me to get your check with the late fee. What should I tell them?" This approach places you as the go between for the tenant and the owners/partners. You understand their problems, but these are tough business people who are not easily swayed. Pinpoint a date the check will be mailed and then tell the tenant this information will be forwarded to the owners/partners. Explain that you are trying to do your job, and if the rent is not received, you could be fired.

Start this process as soon as the rent is late. Do not wait until the end of the month. Surveys show that when landlords are asked what is the biggest mistake they have made over the years, the number one answer is believing the excuses, and then not being tough enough when they realize they have been taken.

Ways to structure late fees have already been discussed, but be aware that if your policy is to charge a flat fee versus a daily fee, the tenant knows the late fee will be the same amount if he pays on the sixth or the 31st of the month. This might cause him to hold the rent until you call, because after the due date the fine is the same. Calling as soon as the rent is late, shows you are on top of the matter, and he will not be as likely to pull his tricks in the months to follow.

Remember this: the incentive for a tenant to move becomes much stronger the longer he is allowed to stay without being evicted. He quickly realizes that this money he owes you can be used as a security deposit and part of the first month's rent on a new apartment. Then for him it becomes more cost effective to move away than to pay the back rent.

REASONS FOR EVICTION

You must have a reason to evict. It must be a violation of your lease or rental agreement and must be legal. Here are some common legal reasons for evictions:

- Failure to pay rent
- Breach of the contract
- Extra people
- Pets
- Subletting
- Refusing to leave after receiving the required notice to vacate
- Conducting an illegal activity on the premises

All will require going to court to start eviction proceedings. Because of the cost, try to work out the problem before filing. If it can't be resolved, then do what must be done; it is better to remove the rotten apple from the barrel before the good apples are affected.

PROMISE TO PAY OR VACATE

Call the tenants to make sure they are home and ask if you could stop by for a few minutes to talk. Take the "Promise to Vacate" form and the "Five Day Notice to Pay or Vacate" but keep the "Five Day Notice" hidden in a pocket. Present the "Promise to Pay or Vacate" letter for their signature. I must stress at this point to talk to local authorities regarding this letter before actually doing what it says. Some authorities will say the tenant has not been given due process and will not allow it to be used. I like to use it to make the tenant show his hand. If they agree to sign the "Promise to Pay or Vacate" form, the rent probably is in the mail or will be paid by the due date. If they refuse to sign, the odds are that it's not in the mail, and they probably don't plan to pay. This is when the "Five Day Notice to Pay or Vacate" magically appears from your pocket and is served upon them.

Alternatively:

- Skip the "Promise to Pay or Vacate" letter and deliver immediately the "Five Day Notice to Pay or Vacate."
- Present the "Promise to Pay or Vacate" and if they refuse to sign, file for eviction the next morning. Remember this can only be done if the "30 Day Notice to Quit" clause has been signed in the "Additional Terms and Conditions" of your lease. This clause allows you to file one day after the rent due date because the tenant has waived his or her right to the notice to evict.

The two best ways to get this letter to the tenant are to hand deliver it as described above or have someone else hand deliver it. That someone else could be a police officer or friend that owes you a favor. This method really gets the tenant's attention. If the tenant is home, have him sign and date the envelope to the effect that he did receive the notice. If he is not home, a witness will be needed to sign and date the envelope stating they were with you, or the server, when the notice was delivered. Calling the tenant on the phone and verbally giving the notice is not acceptable.

Another way is to send the notice certified mail. The drawbacks of certified mail have already been discussed. Have you ever picked up certified mail that was good news? I once hand delivered the notice and told the tenant he had three days to pay up or eviction proceedings would begin. Fortunately for me, this tenant either couldn't read or was not too bright because he packed up and moved out in the middle of the next night, which saved me a lot of money. I was able to get the unit cleaned and re-rented in less time than the court proceedings would have taken.

PROMISE TO PAY OR VACATE

I am presently renting _____ from _____ and I am aware that I am delinquent in my rent payments. To this date I owe $ _____ for which I promise to pay by _____, 20____.

If for some reason I do not fulfill the above promise, I will vacate my unit by the date mentioned above. If I have not vacated the unit by this date, I give permission for the Landlord/Agent representing Landlord to change the locks, remove my furniture, and set it on the street. The Landlord/Agent will hold my personal belongings for no more than 72 hours after the locks have been changed and it will be my responsibility to pick them up. I am aware that I am liable for any damages to the unit from the beginning of the lease to present as well as all court costs and attorney's fees should legal action be needed to collect the above mentioned money.

Dated this ____ day of _____, 20____

_____   _____
          Tenant   *Tenant*

31

FIVE DAY NOTICE TO PAY OR VACATE

The "Five Day Notice To Pay or Vacate" must contain all names listed on the lease, along with address, amount of rent due, for what period of time, and your signature. Usually, this is where the process stops. The tenant knows you mean business, and will pay. He knows that if he lets it go any further, he will be summoned to appear at a hearing he knows he is going to lose. The tenant will be forced to pay the money owed plus court costs. If he doesn't pay, a sheriff's sale of personal property will be held to pay off the debt. His credit rating will be destroyed, and all security money will be forfeited.

PROMISSORY NOTE

When a tenant falls behind in rent, have him sign a promissory note before you file for eviction. Have the note be his admission that a) he owes you money, and b) that he didn't withhold rent because of needed repairs or code violations.

By admitting he owes you, he cannot later say that the non-payment was to offset some horrible thing you did to him. It also protects you if he tries to say you both had a special deal that he didn't have to pay rent for a certain period of time in exchange for maintenance work.

Showing the judge the promissory note when he starts making up lies will cut him right off. The judge will say, "Did you sign this?" If the answer is yes, the judge will say, "Guilty. Pay up. Next case."

Promissory notes are also assumable so you can sometimes sell it to a local personal loan company. It also can protect you when selling the property and the tenant is behind in rent. The buyer will not ask you to assign the back rent to him.

FIVE DAY NOTICE TO PAY OR VACATE

To _____ , who is in possession of

_____

_____

_____

YOU ARE HEREBY NOTIFIED that your rent is delinquent in the amount of $ _____ for the period from _____ to _____ . Within FIVE DAYS after service of this notice, you are required to pay said rent in full or give up possession of the above mentioned premises. Failure to do so will cause legal proceedings to be initiated against you in order to recover all monies owed and possession of said premises. This notice is also to declare the forfeiture of the Lease or Rental Agreement under which you occupy said premises together with any and all court costs and attorney's fees to be paid by you as stated in your Lease Agreement.

Served this _____ day of _____ , 20____

_____

NOTICE TO PERFORM OR QUIT

This form is used to terminate a tenancy because the tenant is performing or not performing acts he agreed to, when he entered into the lease agreement. Some common breaches of the lease that will force this to be used are:

- Allowing unauthorized persons to occupy the premises
- Allowing a pet to move in
- Interfering with the quiet enjoyment of other tenants.

Make sure you not only list what the violations are, but also what paragraph or number in the lease agreement he is violating.

FILING FOR EVICTION

If the tenant does not pay or leave in the three-day period, then papers must be filed against him. The first time you file for an eviction will be the hardest, because you don't know your way around the court system. Find a fellow landlord who knows the procedures, and ask him to help you, or call a lawyer for the first few evictions you do. Small Claims Court will probably be the place to file, and it is the quickest and cheapest. An attorney can be used, but this will take longer than if filing by yourself. Attorneys handle

PROMISSORY NOTE

_____, 20____

I, _____, the undersigned, am a tenant living at _____. Due to outside reasons and uncontrollable events, I have been unable to pay the rent that is now past due on the above mentioned address.

I promise to pay to the order of _____ the sum of $ _____ on or before _____. Interest on the unpaid balance from the date listed above until paid in full will be ____ percent (%) per annum and will be payable upon demand.

Prepayment of this note with interest to date of payment may be made at any time without penalty.

If the Tenant defaults in the payment of the whole or any part of any installment, the entire unpaid balance with interest will become due and payable. In the event of any such default or acceleration, the undersigned, jointly and severally, agree to pay to the Landlord reasonable attorney fees, legal expenses, and lawful collection costs in addition to all other sums due.

Presentment, demand, protest, notice of dishonor and extension of time without notice are hereby waived and the undersigned consent to the release of any security, or any part thereof, with or without substitution.

_____   _____
            Tenant   _Tenant_

_____   _____
           Witness   _Witness_

32

hearing. Bring a copy of the lease in case the judge has questions about amount of rent, security deposits, notice required to terminate or specific wording of a clause. All correspondence with the tenant, either written or verbal, should be dated and recorded in a separate file and brought to court so you can justify any disputes.

If the tenant fails to appear for the hearing, you win. The tenant is given a certain number of days to pay in full, (plus court costs) or appeal. If a tenant files an appeal, talk to an attorney about asking the court to force the tenant to secure a bond for the money owed. Many times a tenant will not be able to post bond money; otherwise he would have paid you in the first place. This will stop his appeal and save you additional court costs and lost rent.

If the tenant hasn't paid rent or appealed, by the due date, you must re-file, at additional costs, to get possession of the property. The notice is served by the court with a date for the lock out. At this time, the tenant will be forcibly removed, if need be, while you change the locks.

I once had an eviction where the tenant called me two days before "E"-day to ask if they left the washer, dryer and refrigerator could they have a two day extension "so we will have more time to clean the unit." I knew the sheriff would tell me to re-file and start over if I agreed to the extension so told the tenant no. After changing the locks, the sheriff and I did a quick walk through and to my surprise, I discovered they had left the washer, dryer, and refrigerator. I couldn't believe my good fortune. Now they could be cleaned and sold to recoup some of my losses. My good fortune turned to rage when I discovered all three were broken beyond repair and now I had the additional expense for a bulk pickup!

large caseloads and they might not be able to get to your case when you need them. They also are not in as much of a hurry to move the proceedings along as you. They know they will be paid when the case is settled. Each day a tenant spends in your unit not paying rent is money out of "Hip Pocket National Bank." That is the one bank that should never be touched unless making deposits. Once the eviction route is decided upon, get it over with as quickly as possible.

File a Landlord and Tenant Complaint after the required notice has been given to the tenant. The court will choose a date, usually 10 days or less, to hold the hearing and will inform you and the tenant of this date and time. You will have to appear, even if the tenant does not, to be awarded the judgment. Don't give the tenant any reason to appear at the

The court eviction process can take from one to three months with court costs running between $100-$200 (depending on the state) to remove a tenant. These court costs and loss of rent will exceed the security deposit very quickly. Remember, time will be spent serving the three day notice, filing for

---

NOTICE TO PERFORM OR QUIT

To: _____, Tenant in possession of

_____

_____

_____

1. YOU ARE HEREBY notified that you have violated or failed to perform the following terms of your lease agreement which states _____

_____

2. You are in violation of that provision(s) for the following reason(s): _____

_____

3. You must perform or correct this violation within _____ days of this notification. If you fail to do so, you must vacate and deliver possession of the premises to landlord.

4. If you fail to correct the violation or vacate as stated, legal proceedings will be initiated against you to recover possession, rent owed, damages, court costs, and attorney fees.

5. It is not our intention to terminate this agreement; however, the rules that you agreed to abide by must be followed. If they are not, Landlord will elect to declare a forfeiture of the lease agreement. You will forfeit any security deposit needed to cover items mentioned above and Landlord reserves the right to pursue collection of any future rental losses.

___/___/___
Date   _____

25

---

do massive damage just to get even.

Wait the stipulated number of days the tenant has to pay after the judgment has been awarded. Return to the court and have the judgment stamped with an official seal and signed by the judge. Take this official paper to the tenant's bank and tell them you wish to place a lien on the tenant's account. They will automatically freeze the account and award you whatever money is presently in the account. In order to get the most money when it is frozen, file the lien when you know they have a high balance. Use the idea presented in the Rent chapter, under Insufficient Funds, to find out the amount in the account. Most people are paid on Friday so calling first thing Monday morning might offer the best opportunity to lien the most money.

Get in the habit of making a copy of all tenant's checks every six months so if the bank requires an account number, you will be prepared. Even though these account numbers are listed on the rental application, the accounts could be closed by the time you need to use it.

This concept may not work in your state, so call your bank before trying it.

initial hearing, attending the hearing, filing for possession, and meeting the sheriff at the property the day of eviction. The total amount of money lost will be determined by how quickly the tenant is removed, the amount of rent being charged and court fees. Be aware that if the real estate is held in a corporate name, some states require the corporation to hire an attorney to file and execute the eviction proceedings.

FILE JUDGMENT AND LIEN TENANTS' BANK ACCOUNT

This method can be used after receiving a judgment but before the tenant vacates. However, I would recommend waiting until after the tenant moves before you use it. When he discovers you have frozen his bank account he might see red and

REQUEST FOR PAYMENT OF JUDGMENT

First get a monetary judgment from the court and then send the late-paying tenant the letter on this page.

In the letter I am requesting payment of the judgment I was awarded. I let them know that if payment is not received by a specific date, the following options may be exercised.

- IRS will be notified so they know taxes are owed in the amount of the judgment.
- IRS could file tax evasion charges if the amount of the judgment is not included as income on the tax return.
- If on any type of public assistance, the appropriate government agency may stop payments and charges of fraud could be filed with possible fines and imprisonment.

REQUEST FOR PAYMENT OF JUDGMENT

Dear Tenant,

This is my final request for payment of the judgment I was awarded by the court in the amount of $_____. Failure to pay may cause the following procedures required by law if the judgment is not paid in full by ___/___/___.

1. The Internal Revenue Service may require payment of taxes due on the amount of the judgment,

2. The Internal Revenue Service could file charges of tax evasion resulting in fines and/or imprisonment.

3. Agencies such as the Social Security Administration, and the Department of Public Welfare may stop any benefits you are receiving and file charges of fraud resulting in fines and/or imprisonment.

In order to avoid this possibility, I will need the full amount of the judgment paid by ___/___/___. It should be mailed to the address listed on the judgment. Again, this is your final notice.

46

file the 1099 Misc. form with the IRS, Department of Public Assistance, and Social Security Administration with the transmittal form 1096. This form tells the IRS how many different organizations the 1099 was sent to.

The IRS has collecting down to a science, so rest assured that at least they will collect the taxes on the debt forgiveness.

This approach can also have an impact on any public assistance program that the tenant may be on. The additional income could be enough to push them out of the program. A fellow landlord used the threat of this idea on a Section 8 tenant. He called and made the tenant aware of what he would be doing and suggested he check to see if this "income" would put him out of the Section 8 program. The tenant told him he would be over in ten minutes with all the rent money.

The tenant's anger at what is happening goes from you to their "Uncle" (Sam) who is the one collecting. Remember, you are the one forgiving the debt and will not be collecting a dime from the judgment. Now you know why the lease clause says you want to go to court to collect all rent that is due until the end of the lease. If they stop paying half way through a six month lease at $500 a month, they will think long and hard with a judgment for $3,000 ($500 X remaining 6 months) verses $500 (one month) at 28% to Uncle Sam.

This will not affect your tax liability because you did not receive the income but will be able to write off the legal expenses. For copies of the forms mentioned call IRS at 800-829-3676 or visit the IRS website..

FILE THE JUDGMENT WITH THE COURT AND NOTIFY THE IRS OF "DEBT FORGIVENESS"

At some point in your landlording career a tenant will stop paying rent and you will have to file for his eviction. After being awarded a judgment by the court, the tenant is supposed to pay. Unfortunately, if they had the money they would have paid you in the first place. Because of this, many judgments go

This letter will get the attention of some tenants but not necessarily all. For those who don't seem to understand, send a copy of the "Notice of Debt Forgiveness" to the tenant, wait a few days and then do the following...

Fill out IRS form Misc.1099-C. This is a miscellaneous income statement called "Cancellation of Debt." The name, address, social security number, and the amount due goes in the block that says "non-employee compensation". Send it by certified mail. If the certified letter is returned because the tenant did not leave a forwarding address, hold on to the letter as proof that an attempt was made to notify the tenant. This will keep you from being fined.

Send a copy of the 1099-C MISC form to the tenant along with the Notice of Debt Forgiveness. Wait a few days and if you do not hear from the tenant, uncollected by landlords. About all that the landlord can do is take the judgment to the Prothonotary Office in the county seat and, for a small fee, record the judgment. The credit bureaus will pick up the judgment and place it in the tenants' credit file for five years. It could keep them from renting another apartment, buying a car, a house, or getting a credit card. Another method is to send a copy of the judgment to your credit reporting agency who will add it to the tenants credit report.

The one I use the most involves the Internal Revenue Service and is called "Debt Forgiveness." The Internal Revenue Code Sections 61 and 108 state that,

> "Except when intended as a gift or bequest, income is realized by the debtor when indebtedness is forgiven or in other ways canceled."

This means if a landlord is willing to forgive the debt after being unsuccessful in collecting on the judgment, the IRS will treat the money owed as income to the tenant.

PAY TENANT TO VACATE

Sometimes it is easier and more cost effective to pay the tenant to move than it is to go to court. Why spend a couple of hundred dollars in court fees, plus invest your time, when it may be cheaper and less time intensive to encourage the tenant to leave with a fifty or a hundred dollar bill. First explain to the tenant what will happen when the judgment is awarded for back rent to you as outlined in the letter Request of Payment/Judgement form. Now that you have his attention, give him some options.

If he would be out of the apartment within seven days, you will pay him ALL his security deposit (if there is no damage) plus $150 cash. If out in 10 days will pay $100, 14 days $50.

The cash could be used to put his property in storage or for a motel. The security deposit could be used as the security deposit on the next apartment.

Tenants will leave the unit in better condition because, if there is damage, it will be subtracted from the security deposit. The tenant being evicted by the sheriff won't care how the unit is left since he is not getting back any of the security deposit. This damage alone could cost more than the $150 cash being used to buy him out.

Be careful using this concept in multi-family units. If one tenant tell another what you are doing it could be used against you if another tenant decides to stop paying.

WAYS TO COLLECT RENT AFTER TENANT HAS VACATED

Most tenants who do not plan to pay back rent will let the court process take its course. They move out the weekend before the sheriff is due to change the locks. When this occurs, it is your responsibility, not the court's, to research and find a forwarding address so the next step can begin. This step

---

NOTICE OF DEBT FORGIVENESS

To: _____, Former tenant

_____

_____

Dear _____,

This letter is to notify you that I am forgiving the back rent and other charges I was awarded with my judgment of $_____.

Because I am forgiving this debt, I want you to know that the INTERNAL REVENUE SERVICE code sections 61 and 108 state that when indebtedness is forgiven, it becomes classified as income and taxes are due on this amount.

I will be submitting a Miscellaneous Form 1099 to the INTERNAL REVENUE SERVICE in your name for $_____.

Be aware that if you are on any form of public assistance, this increase in your income might cause you to lose eligibility in the program or reduce monthly payments to you.

If you care to discuss this further, please call me at _____ or send the amount due to me at _____

Sincerely,

requires additional paper work to be filed which will allow a sheriff's sale of the lessee's belongings. The new address is necessary for the sheriff to serve the paper work and to list the items in the house that will be sold at the auction. If the tenant does not have enough belongings to make this step worthwhile, file the judgment to cloud his credit, or report the loss as income to the IRS and move on.

Here's a trick an ex-tenant used on me. He found a friend who was willing to put in writing and swear in front of a notary that the furniture, TV, cars, stereo, etc. were his and he had loaned these items to his friend the tenant. The sheriff's hands were tied and I collected nothing.

I could have gone back to court to make the friend produce receipts for each of the items. But it was not worth hiring an attorney and taking off from work to go after them. If there are items that are worth going after, here are a few suggestions to find where they've moved.

Start at the post office. In order for the tenants to receive their mail at a new address they must fill in a change of address card. Most tenants are smart enough to know they don't want you or other creditors to find out where they are moving, so they don't let the post office know their new address.

Every once in a while a tenant that owes money does supply the post office with a change of address card. Here is a cheap and easy way to find out if they have given their new address to the post office. Take a sheet of paper and fold it into thirds. Insert it into a business size envelope and address it to the tenant at their last known address (your house). In the upper left hand corner write your return address and underneath it in red ink, write "Return Service Requested." With the same red pen write "Do Not Forward" underneath the stamp. If they have turned in a change of address card, the post office will place the updated address on the envelope and mail it back to you.

If you can't remember where the tenant works, go to his rental application, refresh your memory, and then follow him home from work. If the tenant has changed jobs, make arrangements with the former employer to let you know the tenant's new address when he requests his W-2 forms to be forwarded.

Try talking to people leaving work to find out if he is still living in the area and if so, get an address.

Another method to try is to have a neighbor or fellow tenant follow the moving truck to his new address and pay them for the information.

Contact the Department of Voter Registration. Give them the tenant's name and ask for an address and current employment.

If the tenant worked in a field regulated by the State such as realtor, insurance, or auto salesman, you may be able to get his new address from the agency that regulates his profession.

If all the above methods fail, locate him through the Bureau of Motor Vehicles, Attention License Plate Department. Give them the tenant's name, social security number, birth date, drivers license number, VIN number of vehicles (all this information is on the rental application), and for a small fee they will give you his new address.

While inspecting the vacant unit look for pennies under the heat covers, duct work, and in closet corners. Call the person listed as the personal reference or the person to contact in an emergency and explain that their friend left some money behind in the apartment. Explain you would like to give the money back but you need a forwarding address. If you can't get a forwarding address at least get a phone number. (Don't be surprised if the friend says, "Hang on, he's right here!") The first question the tenant will ask is how much money? Under no circumstances will you let on it is only six cents. Schedule a specific time and place to meet and remind him to bring the keys that were never returned or the fire extinguisher that was under the kitchen sink. If money was also owed, use this opportunity to deliver any legal notices or other documents that may help you to recover what is owed.

TENANT FILES BANKRUPTCY

I have had two tenants file bankruptcy between the time of receiving a judgment and the sheriff showing to do the eviction. The first time it took eight months to get the tenant out and the second time five months.

When a tenant files bankruptcy it acts as an automatic stay on the landlord taking back possessions and collecting back rent. It also tells the utility companies they can not shut off service for back charges due. This means from the time you are notified that the bankruptcy has been filed, you are barred from filing or proceeding with unlawful detainer suits to recover possession of your property or to recover rent that was due prior to the date that the bankruptcy was filed. If you have already received a judgment, you can not proceed with the eviction until the court grants a relief from the stay. You can not send demand letters to the tenant, shut off any utilities that you pay, make an in-person demand for rent or for possession or take any other action to do the same. If any of these actions are taken it would be in violation of the automatic stay and would potentially subject you to action for violation of the automatic stay.

The bankruptcy court does provide relief for the landlord in this situation. Section 362(d)(2) of the Bankruptcy Act contains a procedure for a landlord to get relief from the automatic stay in order to proceed with an action to recover any rent and costs that become due after the filing since the bankruptcy only affects those debts in existence at the time it was filed. Under this section of the Bankruptcy Act a landlord can file a motion for relief from the automatic stay with the bankruptcy court and schedule a hearing on the motion. A copy of the motion and notice of the hearing date must be given to the tenant, his attorney, the trustee in bankruptcy, and to the U.S. Trustee's Office.

The motion must state the facts as to why relief from the stay should be given and allege that the tenant does not have an equity interest in the property and that the property is not necessary to an effective reorganization of the tenant's affairs. The tenant and trustee can oppose this motion and at the hearing.

If you are granted relief from the stay, you can then file an unlawful detainer action in state court or resume the action filed before the tenant filed bankruptcy since debts incurred prior to the filing are covered. It will be discharged under a Chapter 7 bankruptcy, or included in the repayment plan in a Chapter 13 bankruptcy. If the bankruptcy is Chapter 13, file a proof of claim for all rent and charges that became due up to the date the bankruptcy was filed so that you will share in any distribution to creditors.

All of the above takes time and money for lawyers to file the motions. It will be a few days off from work to go to the federal court house with your attorney to keep the paperwork moving. Seriously consider paying the tenant to move. First call your attorney to ask how much it will cost you to have him take this case. Take that number, add in lost rent for the amount of months the attorney feels it will take to resolve and that should give you a good idea of what to consider paying the tenant to move out now.

BE PREPARED WHEN GOING TO COURT

Study the Landlord-Tenant Act for your state to know what you can do and can not do with a tenant. The more prepared you are with a paper trail before going to court, the better chance you will have of winning. Judges put the due diligence on the landlord to prove his case, not the tenant. Because the landlord owns the property and the tenant is only a renter, judges hold the landlord more accountable. Here are some common mistakes made by landlords when they go to court.

• **No documentation.** Judges do not like verbal leases and not having a signed inspection sheet.

They also like to see pictures of the property before and after the tenant because the pictures will not lie. Be sure to use a camera that shows the date the picture was taken. If your camera does not have that feature then be sure the tenant is in the picture.

• **Landlords try to enforce rules that are not covered in the lease.** If it is written down and both parties agree to it and it is not illegal, it will hold up in court. There is nothing that says whatever is written has to be fair or equal. It's your lease and if they do not like the terms and conditions, they do not have to sign. As you will see in my lease in a later chapter, I have very specific items outlined. For example, if a tenant becomes a "holdover" tenant and doesn't move out at the end of the contract, there are additional fees that must be paid. When going to court, build in a "collection costs" fee the tenant must pay you for having to take time off from work to file and attend the hearing.

• **Not being specific about pets.** If you don't want pets then spell out exactly what will happen if a pet is found living in the property. You can charge additional for pets but it must be spelled out in the lease. Having nothing in the lease about pets or no pets allows the judge to rule whatever way he wishes.

• **Waiting too long to file for eviction.** Don't listen to the excuses. Spell out in the lease when rent is due, when it is late, what the late fee will be and what date you will file if no rent is received.

DON'T FEEL GUILTY ABOUT EVICTIONS

When rent is late, keep telling yourself you are not in the business of public housing. You are in the landlording business to make money so you can buy clothes and put food on the table for your family. Tenants must take responsibility for their own personal finances just as you must do the same with your mortgage lender, utility companies, and business partners.

1. Don't wait. File on the date that the lease says you will file. If the tenant really needs more time, the court will give it to him.
2. Keep reminding yourself the tenants eat the groceries for which they pay. Why should they live in a house for free?
3. You don't make money evicting but you do cut down your losses.
4. Ask your tenant if they work for free because that is what they want you to do.
5. When it gets really thick, give them your mortgage company's phone number. Ask them to ask if the mortgage company will waive your late fee because without their rent check, I will be late with my payment.

CHAPTER 19

TENANTS AND DRUGS

The price of greatness is responsibility.

— Winston Churchill

Happiness lies in the joy of achievement and the thrill of creative effort.

— Franklin Roosevelt

A recent survey showed one in every three Americans over the age of 12 has used illegal drugs at least once during the previous year. In the age group 18–25 more than half have used illegal drugs at least once during the previous year. Landlords must be realistic about drugs. People who rent are a cross section of all socio-economic levels, so sooner or later a drug dealer or user will find you. Unfortunately, it is very difficult, if not impossible, to tell who is selling/using drugs from the initial phone call or even after meeting them in person at the apartment.

The rental application also will give no sign of a drug addict just as it will not show who plays their music loudly after 10:00 P.M., or punches holes in walls when they get mad. Try to read between the lines to figure out the applicant's real motivation in wanting to move into your unit.

Years ago the government would arrest people for growing marijuana in their back yards but the house where the plant was grown would not be confiscated. This is not true today. The Comprehensive Crime Control Act (passed 1984) and the Drug Enforcement Act of 1988 gives law enforcement officials the power to seize and sell property considered an accessory to a crime. By law, when people buy a house with money generated from drug sales or use the property to sell, store, or manufacture drugs, they stand an excellent chance of not only being arrested but also losing the house.

Landlords must be aware of these laws and protect themselves and their investment properties from being confiscated. Under the current federal law, owners don't have to be directly involved in the illegal activity for their property to be seized.

According to the Department of Justice Asset Forfeiture Program, "An innocent owner is a party with an interest in the property subject to forfeiture laws, who can demonstrate that he had no knowledge of the illegal activity that caused the forfeiture, did not consent to the activity, and/or took all reasonable steps to prevent the activity."

A landlord in New York had his building confiscated after a drug raid that revealed that narcotic activity was taking place in 15 of the 41 units and that common areas were littered with crack vials. The owner refused to accept rent from the tenants who were arrested, but the federal grand jury ruled he had not taken all reasonable steps to prevent the drug trafficking.

Listed below are some simple steps landlords can use to avoid confiscation of their properties.

1. Always perform screening and background checks as mentioned earlier in the book. A few months ago I had an applicant return the application showing no employer but showed $500 a week as income. I called him to get the name of the employer and was told he was self-employed. When I asked his line of work, he said he would prefer not to say. I followed up the question by asking if his business was legal or illegal. When he said the IRS didn't know about his job, I told him, he was not a candidate for my unit.

2. Make sure on-site managers keep an eye on what is happening. For a smaller number of units without on-site managers, the tenants must be encouraged to turn in offenders. Stress their names and information will be kept confidential. Many times the tenants might not know there is drug trafficking, but their complaints about certain activity should send off a signal. Complaints such as cars beeping horns and people banging on a neighbor's door at three o'clock in the

morning seven nights a week is usually a good indicator. Other complaints could be people loitering, many visitors who stay only five minutes, litter, including disposable butane lighters, liquor bottles, soft drink cans with holes punched in them, and broken lights.

3. Be suspicious if the tenant stops paying rent by check and starts paying with cash.

4. Drive by the property any time of the day or night and become suspicious if people who showed employment outside the home are now always home. Are the blinds always closed?

5. State clearly in your lease that drug dealing on the property will result in eviction.

6. Keep the property well lit and all locks secure.

7. Insist that common entry doors be kept closed and locked at all times. This will restrict access and insure a safer environment.

8. Notice syringes, matchbooks, bottles, candle wax, paper wrappers and small baggies.

9. Remove abandoned and inoperable vehicles.

10. Check to be sure vacant units have not been broken into.

Drug users might be harder to spot because the obvious signs of traffic in and out will not be there. You now have to be aware of behavior. Do they seem anxious, restless, thinner, or very paranoid? Do they repeat themselves four times in a five minute conversation? When you schedule an appointment to make a repair, do they make you stand outside for five minutes while they "tidy up?" Are they not calling about repairs you know are needed?

As soon as a problem is suspected, begin keeping notes of various happenings, with dates and times. If a fellow tenant calls or writes to complain about another tenant, keep accurate information on dates, times, and the reason why they are calling. When the evidence is overwhelming, review your information, then put it in writing and contact the police. You are now on record as having taken all reasonable steps to prevent the activity. It should be noted that when authorities seize real and personal property, they are able to auction the property and keep part of the proceeds for their agency. You must take positive steps to document your innocence. If the lease is about to expire, don't renew it. In most states, you don't need a reason for non-renewal.

If the lease is not close to expiring, find reasons to call and visit the unit as often as possible. Perhaps, they will tire of the constant nagging about minor things and leave on their own.

When dealing with tenants selling or using drugs, remember to position yourself between the tenant and owners/partners. Become the middle man. If it is no rent, late rent, loud parties, visitors at all hours of the night, unregistered vehicles on the property, pets, etc., it is always the owners/partners who have received the complaints. You are just doing your job and are trying to solve the problem.

Landlords should also be aware that under the 1988 Fair Housing Amendments, recovering alcoholics and drug addicts are considered a handicapped, protected class. However, the same law specifically does not protect current users or addicts. The legal distinction between those who are addicted and those who are recovering or rehabilitated is not clearly defined at the time of this printing.

DRUG SNIFFING DOGS

On a TV show, I saw a program about dogs who are trained to help police sniff out drugs. About the same time I suspected I had a tenant dealing drugs from my 20 unit apartment building. The show gave me an idea. I wrote the following letter to all the tenants in the building.

```
Dear Tenants,
    It has been brought to my atten-
tion that the Police Precinct that
is two blocks from our building has
a recent graduate. It is a drug
sniffing puppy who just received his
diploma from drug sniffing school.
The police I am told, are looking
for areas to let the puppy practice
his special talent.
    This letter is to let you know
that I have volunteered our building
as a practice ground for the new
addition to the police force.
    Do not be alarmed if officers are
in the building with the dog. They
have my permission to sniff where
ever they want.
Sincerely,

Don
```

The next day, not one, but two tenants moved out.

CHAPTER 20

RENTING TO COUPLES, RELATIVES, AND FRIENDS

Obstacles are those frightful things you see when you take your eyes off your goals.

Failure is one thing that can be achieved without effort.

The typical family of husband and wife with 2.4 children is no longer the majority but the minority. The divorce rate has reached 50% now, which has caused an increasing number of individuals, not related by blood or marriage, to live together because it is the only way to survive economically. These "odd couples" could be single women or men living together, single parents with children, and single/divorced adults of the opposite sex. All can create problems without proper screening and a strong lease. However, it also can open the door to opportunities for a landlord.

Many of the problems begin when each of the individuals can't afford the apartment on his or her own salary, and need a roommate's income to qualify. If the friendship goes sour, or one decides to get married and moves out, the remaining tenant (and you) are caught in the middle. The remaining tenant refuses (and can't afford) to pay the whole rent. A month goes by, and you are out a full month's rent. You apply the security deposit and now that is gone.

Usually, the roommate who is leaving will give some notice so the remaining roommate can start looking for a replacement. Insist that the new roommate complete a rental application and be approved by you before his name can be added to the lease. Have him pay the old roommate the security deposit, if so entitled, and have the old roommate write a letter stating he has received the security deposit.

Don't get caught in the middle of a fight between the two old roommates about who owes what for the phone, electric, and oil bills.

When neither applicant can afford the apartment on his own, a co-signer is necessary. Have them find a mutual friend (who owns real estate) to co-sign for both. If this is not possible then make both of them find a co-signer who owns real estate. All four must

come to sign the lease and the two co-signers must bring a copy of their deed to be kept on file.

Include a clause under the special clauses of the lease that states: If one party breaks this lease by moving before the expiration date, he is liable for half the rent for the balance of the leased term and forfeits his security deposit. If an acceptable replacement can be found and approved by Lessor before vacating, Lessee will be refunded the security deposit and his name taken off the lease.

Be careful of two people who are not related, and have a large discrepancy between their salaries. Example: "A" and "B" are unrelated and each returns an application. "A" makes enough money to qualify alone and "B" only makes $100 a month.

If "B" cannot find a co-signer, only put "A's" name on the lease. Think of the dilemma you would be in with both "A" and "B" on the lease and "A" decides to move out after a month. Now you would be stuck with a tenant whose gross income is $100 a month! If "B's" name were not on the lease, there would be no valid reason for him to be in the apartment. I am not suggesting that this gives you permission to physically remove "B" and his belongings, but it should be quicker if a District Judge understands the circumstances. State laws vary on this point so be sure to make inquires with local authorities before proceeding.

DON'T RENT TO RELATIVES OR FRIENDS

After purchasing my first investment property, I asked a realtor friend that owned investment real estate for some landlording tips. His first response was "Never, absolutely never, rent to a relative or a friend." "Take my word" he exclaimed, "Your cash flow will suffer and the stress will be greater." I have always remembered his remarks and have taken his advice. Unfortunately, over the years I have met fellow landlords who did not have such a wise friend.

John should have known he was in for trouble when his cousin questioned why he needed to pay a security deposit. He explained the money was needed to cover rent not paid, and possible damage to the unit. The cousin convinced John to waive the security deposit because he would do all the repairs at his expense, always pay on time and, besides, he was family! John reluctantly agreed, but added a clause that no pets were allowed. The cousin agreed because he did not have a pet. He didn't have one the first month but broke his promise (and the lease) the second month by getting a puppy. The dog started chewing the carpet, scratching the door and pulling up yard plants. None of these were replaced or repaired as promised.

John kept quiet because his big-mouth cousin would twist the facts and he knew the family would side with the poor, helpless cousin. As much as John did not want to renew the lease, he knew what the reaction would be if he evicted the cousin. He decided the best plan of attack was to raise the cousin's rent $50 because he needed the money to repair the damage done by the dog, plus he had had increases in his property, water and sewer taxes. The cousin responded by saying he couldn't believe "family" would give such an unrealistic increase. He told John that a $15 increase was more realistic and that he should make up the difference by increasing his other tenants' rent a few more dollars!

Kevin's story is different but with the same results. He rented to his brother-in-law and had some surprises almost immediately. The brother-in-law decided he wanted more sunlight in the kitchen window so he chopped down the maple tree in the back yard without asking permission. He then decided the area where the rose garden was planted was a perfect place for a vegetable garden, so he ripped out the roses.

It continued to go down hill when junk cars appeared all over the side yard. He admitted he was using parts from the cars to repair other family members' cars at no cost to them. The family couldn't thank Kevin enough for allowing the brother-in-law to work on the cars at the house.

Sandy rented her property to a long-time friend who had just gone through a divorce and needed an apartment. To help the friend through a tight money situation she dropped the rent $30 lower than the last tenant was paying. The friend showed her gratitude by constantly calling about needed repairs. First it was a drippy faucet that turned out to be no problem at all. She merely needed to turn the faucet knobs more firmly. The next call was about the drafty windows. She was sure they needed to be replaced or at least re-caulked inside and out. This problem was solved by pulling down the outside storm windows and closing the inside windows tightly.

Another call complained about the heater making a banging noise. A service call showed that the noise was caused by a metal box she had placed against the heater. All of these problems had cost Sandy money to have repair people check what Sandy perceived as things she would have not been able to fix herself. As the months progressed, the phone calls slowed down, but so did the rent payments. Partial rent would be sent with a promise for the rest at the end of the month. A few more months of this and the rent was two months behind. Sandy's friend could never thank her enough for all she was doing to help her through this difficult time in her life.

Why did the relatives and friends take advantage of these situations? All three investors felt they were perceived by the "friends" as rich because they owned investment property. Since they had no money to buy a home, the family member or friend should "help them out." All three investors agreed that the relatives and friends assumed they would never take any steps to try to evict them or collect the rent owed. All three investors also admitted they did worry about what the family would say at gatherings if they had put their foot down. All three ultimately sold their properties rather than evicting their friends/relatives.

There is no guarantee these type problems can't develop with unrelated tenants, but they are much easier to terminate. You do not have to spend Thanksgiving, Christmas, and the kids' birthday parties with a unrelated tenant you have evicted. All three investors admitted they had become pleasers instead of enforcers and avoided conflicts to keep the peace. All of this amounted to undue stress and a larger-than-normal financial setback in their business of investment real estate. The next time a relative or friend asks to rent an apartment from you, tell them it was just rented!

CHAPTER 21

A CONTROL SYSTEM FOR PROPERTY MANAGERS AND ON-SITE MANAGERS

A good property manager can turn a garbage dump into a gold mine. A bad property manager can turn a gold mine into a garbage dump.

— Nick Sidoti

By following the guidelines outlined in this book, there is no reason why you cannot manage your own properties effectively. The secret is to become organized in implementing the techniques described so the properties will be on "cruise control."

It should take no more than a half hour per month per unit to do everything from collecting and depositing the rent, writing the checks, taking phone calls about repairs and scheduling them. This includes the time that will be needed to show vacant units (my average tenant turnover is every three to four years), run credit checks, and write the lease for the new tenants. Doing these things yourself will increase your cash flow dramatically by saving what a manager would charge.

If you plan to own large buildings that will require on-site managers or partial rent credits for tenants helping, it would be in your best interest to learn good landlording skills before hiring people to do these tasks. In doing so, they will rarely present a problem you have not encountered, which will increase your credibility in their eyes.

Another way to manage your properties that is excellent and very cost effective is to hire someone who manages his own properties. Make sure he has established a good track record with his own property management before approaching him with this proposal. Most states require the individual who manages rental properties, other than his own, to be a licensed broker or to work for a licensed broker. Since the individual you are approaching does not have a license, something must be done to make your relationship with him legal. Consider paying him a slightly lower percentage of the gross rent for a management fee in exchange for giving him a small percentage of the equity when sold. The only

disadvantage is a few less dollars when sold, and even fewer tax saving dollars are lost.

The advantages are plentiful. Who will try harder to find a quality tenant and do it as quickly as possible? Who will do repairs and preventative maintenance in a more timely manner? Who will charge less for repairs and will do a better job? The manager who is part owner will be more motivated to do these things. The licensed management company's goal is to keep you happy thinking they are watching out for your best interests. Try offering them a small percentage of ownership, and watch positive things start to occur.

For those of you who decide not to do the property management but want to own real estate, hiring a property management company or a real estate office that has a property management division would be another option. It is a good idea to screen the people you plan to hire as thoroughly as possible. You get bids from three auto body shops before having your cars repaired, three bids before accepting a landscape contractor as well as a list of recommendations from satisfied clients; the same care should be taken when hiring a property or on-site manager.

This task should be taken very seriously, considering the size of the investment and the potential for lost income if they fail to do what they have promised. Before going to the yellow pages of the phone book, ask friends if they know anyone who has his property managed. Get names and phone numbers and call them.

QUESTIONS TO ASK DURING INTERVIEW OF PROPERTY MANAGER

1. How long have you been in the property management business? We are not looking for real-

tors who do listings and sales and property management on the side. We want a person who does property management full time.

2. How many properties/units do you manage?

3. What is the biggest (number of units) and smallest? What are the ratios? (If 90% are large complexes and you own a duplex, you might get lost in the shuffle. Large complexes have on-site maintenance personnel. Who does the maintenance on the 10% of small units?)

4. What percentage of the gross rent do you charge for a management fee? (This percentage will vary with the area and what services are performed.) If they collect the rent and forward it minus their commission, the fee will be one amount. If bills are paid first from the rent money and then the commission is subtracted, they will charge an additional percentage point or two for paying the bills for you. Six to eight percent is an average range for either of these services. Resort areas can be as high as 20% to 30% of the gross rent. Remember, all fees are negotiable.

5. What fee is charged for placing a new tenant (nothing, half a month, full month) and who pays the advertising bill? If a half month or more is charged, they should pay for advertising. If you feel there will be a high turn over rate, it would be better to pay 1% more in the management fee to have them waive the half or full month fee for placing a tenant.

6. How long does our contract last? Make it any length but have a clause that either one of you may terminate the contract with thirty days written notice. This will keep them on their toes to perform all the time and not just produce a few months before renewal time. Don't sign a contract that locks you in for a year but allows them to terminate with thirty days notice if you refuse to allow them to do a repair. Maybe you feel the repair is not needed or the bid is exceptionally high and want to get another quote.

7. How much security deposit do you collect? (If they say one month or less tell them you require a minimum of one and a half months.)

8. When a tenant calls about a repair, where do they call and who receives the call? If the answer is the office and the call is taken by a "skilled" person ask these questions:

9. What happens if the tenant has an emergency after office hours? If there is an answering service that forwards the call, that's good. If they say it goes on a tape machine and is taken care of in the morning, that is not acceptable.

10. What are the procedures this "skilled" person must follow to handle a tenant's complaint? Since this is a very broad question, do some role playing. Example: A tenant calls that his electric hot water heater is not working. It worked fine before going to work but is ice cold now. The automatic response would be send someone right over to check the problem. A better response would be to ask if the fuse box has been checked. There might have been a surge of electricity that flipped the circuit breaker. Will the "skilled" person pick up the phone and call an electrician? The electrician spends less than one minute in the unit, flips a switch, and bills you for $40. One third of calls about repairs are simple enough that the tenant, with some guidance over the phone, can solve the problem without anyone making a visit.

11. If a repair person is needed, does the agency add a percentage to their bill for making the arrangements?

12. After a repair is made, but before the bill is paid, is the tenant contacted to make sure it was completed to his satisfaction, or is the work physically inspected by the agency? If the answer is no to both, make sure one of the two is included in the contract.

13. If a repair is needed, what is the amount they are authorized to spend without the owner's permission? A good company will say whatever you want that amount to be—within reason. The range usually runs from $100 to $500. Anything over an agreed amount, or any capital improvement, needs two or three bids, with your decision being final.

14. How many grace period days are the tenants given before the late fee is assessed and what do you charge for a late fee? Tenants are usually given a five day grace period and the late fee can be a flat fee, daily fee for everyday late, or a percentage of the rent. Check with your state to see exactly what you can charge.

15. Any late fees that are collected are paid to whom? If the late fee is collected, they should make their commission off the total gross rent with the balance mailed to you. They should not keep the entire late fee.

16. How often are units inspected? It should be at least once within the first six months and then once a year. A written report should be made after each inspection, and it should include the overall condition of the interior and exterior of the property. Recommendations for changes or improvements should also be noted.

17. Ask to see a list of present clients who own units similar to yours. Call them.
18. When was the last time you took a property management course and what was it?
19. What professional property management affiliations do you have? Property managers can obtain credits from IREM - Institute of Real Estate Management; NARPM - National Association of Residential Property Managers; NAA - National Apartment Association.
20. End with this question: What can your company give me that other companies cannot?

CONTRACT FOR CONTRACTORS

Whether you use a management company or not, be sure that all contractors sign an independent contractor's agreement. This agreement helps to relieve you of responsibility and liability if an accident occurs during repair work. The contractor should furnish copies of his workman's compensation insurance and a Certificate of Insurance to prove he has liability insurance.

If you are using a management company and they hire the contractors, be aware that some contractors will submit bills higher than the actual bill and then kick back the extra money to the management company for calling them for the repair. One "check and balance" method that will work in this situation is to call the company, request the same repair, and ask what it would cost.

It also would be a good idea to call other companies and get quotes for the repair and compare prices. Make sure the bids include labor and not just material. Another solution would be to have the bills sent directly to you to pay and not the management company. They would be crazy to send a bill for a price higher than you were quoted.

Many times repair estimates for small jobs are not made in advance because they don't know what they will find until they inspect the job. Have them call you with the quote after inspecting. On occasion, it will become necessary to hold the final pay-

ment until the repair can be tested to your satisfaction. A sink that had a drippy faucet can be inspected and tested very easily. A new roof or a patch repair cannot be tested as easily or as quickly until it has rained. Did you ever try getting a repair person back to correct a repair after they have been paid in full? Most management companies will not call the tenant or personally check the repair before paying the bill unless you ask this question in the interview and have it written in the contract.

QUALITIES NEEDED FOR ON-SITE MANAGERS

As your investment portfolio grows, you will probably be purchasing more units under one roof. It will become cost and time effective to have a full or part time on-site manager(s) helping with the property. Screening these people should be done with as much vigor, if not more (if that's pos-

---

MANAGEMENT CONTRACT (ON-SITE)

This agreement is between _____ owner(s) and
_____ manager(s), for management of the property located at
_____.

The manager(s) agree to the following conditions outlined below:

1. Be responsible for the collection of rents, late fees, security deposits, utility bills, eviction notices, and, if necessary, court proceedings.

2. Keep records as requested by owner of each building and apartments, making necessary deposits and forwarding deposits slips as needed.

3. Submit monthly manager's report to the owner detailing: maintenance and time required to do repairs, number of phone calls received and number of times units shown, and dates and amounts of rent received for each tenant.

4. Place ads in the newspaper as units become available, schedule and show prospective tenants through a unit, take applications, and forward them to owner after credit check is completed.

5. Be responsible for landscaping, cutting grass, shoveling snow, maintaining boilers, cleaning roof gutters, sweeping curbs, halls, stairways, painting exterior, and _____.

6. Units that come available will first be inspected for damage done by previous tenant. If any is found, pictures will be taken and noted on their inspection sheet. Clean, change locks, paint, shampoo carpets, repair and _____ as needed to prepare for new tenant.

7. Make repairs to plumbing that include but are not limited to: leaky faucets, clogged drains, toilets, pipes, garbage disposals, dishwashers, sewer lines, and _____.

8. Work in addition to the responsibilities outlined above will be: _____
_____.

9. The consideration for these services and duties will be $_____ for _____ hours per month and/or _____.

___/___/___
Date   Owner

___/___/___
Date   Manager

___/___/___
Date   Manager

---

sible) as the screening of a prospective tenant. Here are some characteristics on-site managers should possess.

1. Should be able to handle minor repairs. They must know how to handle emergency situations such as water shut off, turning off boilers, electricity, and gas.
2. Should be people oriented. They must realize they will never be able to please all tenants all the time, but they must remember in stressful situations they are representing you and must act professionally. It is better for them to walk away from a situation and ask the tenant to call you than to start an insult match in the parking lot.
3. Must be trustworthy. If the property manager will be dealing with open accounts with local

merchants or collecting YOUR rents, protect yourself by having them bonded.
4. Must be enforcers of rules. Your policies must be spelled out in detail and followed through. Your rules are the law and only YOU can change the law—not the manager.
5. Must be capable of accepting criticism and learning from their mistakes and yours. If they make a mistake, it must only happen once and NEVER be repeated.

FORMS OF PAYMENT FOR ON-SITE MANAGERS

There are many different ways managers can be compensated but the bottom line is which method will keep them motivated the most and make them perform the best.

1. FLAT FEE PER UNIT - Call other complexes in the area and get a range of the "fee per unit" they are paying. Compare the range of services performed for this flat fee. Example: One complex manager is paid to screen tenants, show units, take repair calls, and cut the grass but not make repairs, for $10 a unit per month. Another manager will do all the above plus do minor repairs with plumbing and electrical at $14 a unit per month.

Your manager can do everything the other two can do plus do repairs to air-conditioners, dishwashers, garbage disposals, and refrigerators. His rate should be in the range of $20+ per unit per month. Whatever the going rate for the other make it slightly higher for your manager. He will feel he is being treated fairly and will give a better performance.

2. HOURLY WAGE - This approach can save you money or cost you dearly. Some type of control system must be set up to monitor the hours. Some weeks may have the limit reached by "padding" the time worked. In another case, will repairs that need fixing this week be postponed to the following week because the weekly time limit has been reached? As you can see, this is not a good approach.

INDEPENDENT CONTRACTOR AGREEMENT

I, _____, hereby acknowledge and agree that I am an independent contractor under IRS regulations and will be fully responsible for any damage, loss or injury the owner or any and all others may suffer or incur either directly or indirectly as a result of my work. I will be fully responsible for myself and all others associated with me for any damage, injury or loss of any kind whatsoever.

I further acknowledge that I am fully insured and my coverage includes workman's compensation and liability insurance. I have attached a copy of my Workman's Compensation and Certificate of Insurance.

Address of property where work will be performed:

_____

___/___/___
Date

_____
Contractor Signature

3. FIXED SALARY - Some managers want to know what they will be making each week or month, and it doesn't matter if they have to work a few hours or many hours. The bottom line is they need to know what will be coming in on a regular basis. Again, a control system is needed to monitor the tasks that need to be accomplished each week or month.

4. FEE PER OCCUPIED UNIT - This approach pays a flat fee per month only for units that are occupied. If the manager keeps units filled, he makes more money. This works best when you qualify and approve the prospective tenants. If the manager controls this, borderline qualifiers might be admitted just to boost his monthly unit fees.

5. PERCENTAGE OF GROSS RENTS - This technique is used most often with a professional management company, but can also be used with on-site managers. Again, the percentage will be based on the manager's job description and the size of the complex.

6. EXTRA COMPENSATION FOR A JOB WELL DONE - Your manager has performed above and beyond the call of duty for the year. Perhaps he has done an outstanding job in a particular circumstance. Maybe the exceptional job was keeping the vacancy factor under 3% when the year before it was 8%. Showing that you appreciate the extra effort will go a long way in keeping the manager loyal. The saying, "You take care of me and I'll take care of you," sure applies in this situation. The compensation could be tickets to a sporting event, a night out for dinner and a room at an exclusive hotel, pay for a month of child care, a cash bonus for Christmas presents, or whatever you feel is appropriate.

7. A PIECE OF THE PIE - It was mentioned earlier that giving a percentage interest to the individual managing your properties was well worth the investment, the same applies to on-site managers. A clause could be added to the management contract giving the on-site manager a percentage of the property equity if he stays faithful and in good standing for a certain number of years. Let him work the numbers and if the result is an amount he feels is substantial, he will stay loyal and work for the common good—yours and his for years to come.

There is no method to compensate on-site managers that is perfect. A combination of one or a few might be needed to meet everyone's needs. Discovering the goals and needs of the on-site managers will go a long way in deciding which approach is best for all concerned.

THE HORROR STORIES

Earlier I mentioned having a control system in place. Whether you use managers, management companies, or on-site managers, you need to stay in control. All three types can take money out of your pocket without you knowing it, if they are not monitored. Here are a few stories to give you a flavor of what it means to be taken advantage of when a control system is not in place:

Manager's Monthly Report

Month _____

Address	Rent Paid	Tenant's Name	Repairs

Comments to Owner: _____

___/___/___
Date   Manager's Signature

18

Repair / Service Record

Address of Property: _____

Hot Water Heater	Air Conditioner
Manufacturer: _____	Manufacturer: _____
Model #: _____	Model #: _____
Serial #: _____	Serial #: _____
Color: _____	Color: _____
Dimensions: _____	Dimensions: _____
Purchased on: ___/___/___	Purchased on: ___/___/___
Purchased from: _____	Purchased from: _____
Warranty good for _____ years.	Warranty good for _____ years.
	BTUs: _____ Filter size: _____

Repair / Service Record

Item	Date	Service Done By:	Work Completed	Costs

41

machine would bring in $50 a month and the other machine only $20.

These examples are petty compared to what can happen. One on-site manager would show an apartment to a husband, wife, two children, and a mother-in-law. They were told by the manager that he was permitted to place a maximum of four people in a two bedroom unit but if they would be willing to pay him $15 a month cash, he wouldn't tell the owner. The threat of eviction hung over their heads, encouraging them to pay each month. Since it was a cash transaction, it would be his word against theirs, and the owner would believe him. He did this with 10 different tenants before he was caught.

Another on-site manager was told not to charge tenants the $30 repair fee if the damage was caused by normal wear and tear. He conveniently forgot to inform new tenants of this rule when they moved in, and collected $30 from each one before doing any repairs.

Still another on-site manager was given the responsibility of writing the leases for new tenants. She told the owner the tenant could not move in until May 1 when they actually wanted to move in April 1. She allowed them to move in April 1, while the lease said May 1, and kept the first month's rent. She also encouraged friends with poor credit reports to apply and for a $100 fee would guarantee they would be accepted. Since the owner took her word about the credit reports, she was double dipping on this scam. When she was caught, over three years later, the owner estimated she had cost him over $20,000. He tried to prosecute, but she skipped bail and was never seen again. She had probably moved on to another part of the country and started working for another unsuspecting owner.

This next scam was a short lived one. The manager told the prospective tenant that the owner would only accept cash for the two months security deposit and the first month's rent. He called the owner and told him he would get money orders the next morning for the $2,000 collected and mail it to

A friend had an on-site manager who felt he was not being paid enough for the work that was required. He had a $50 limit at the local hardware store, to buy supplies as needed. He would buy $20 worth of light bulbs on each visit, and then when tenants' bulbs burned out, he would sell them replacements for half price. If the hardware bill came up short one month, he would buy something for himself and then keep it or sell it.

Another on-site manager stayed home from work one day to let the washer/dryer repair man in to replace a coin box that someone had vandalized. The on-site manager convinced the repair man to give him the new key to give to the owner. After the repair man left, a duplicate key was made and the original then given to the owner. For the next two years the owner could not figure out why one him. After a week with no money, the owner went to the post office and put a tracer on the letter. The post office called a week later to say all possible delivery routes had been traced and nothing was found. The owner told the on-site manager to use the back carbon copy to have the money orders replaced. When the on-site manager told the owner he had "forgotten" to tear off the customer copy before it was mailed, the owner fired him on the spot.

All these stories have one characteristic in common. In each case a manager betrayed the trust he was given. Having checks and balances in place could have gone a long way to preventing these incidents. The owner with the open $50 line of credit at the hardware store should have closed the account. If supplies were needed, the owner of the hardware store should have been instructed to wait for the owner's approval for each item the manager purchased. A better approach would be to have the manager call the owner with the needed supplies and then have the owner place the order with the hardware store.

In the cases involving extra people or friends moving in early, tenants being charged for repairs they should not have been, and money orders being mailed with receipts, a more active interest by the owner in the rental process would have nipped these problems in the bud.

Let the on-site manager process the initial phone call, show the unit and give out a rental application. From that point on it becomes the owner's job to run the credit check, do the background check, and call the applicant back to schedule a lease signing. The owner should probably visit the applicant's present home, discuss the rules and regulations governing tenancy, and finally, prepare a lease for signature. The manager can process the actual lease signing including the collection of deposits and first month's rent in the form of a money order or certified check made payable to the owner or business name.

No cash or personal or third party checks should be accepted, or any terms or conditions of the lease changed without the owner's written consent. With these precautions, the owner may not have to be present at the signing of the lease. All monies will end up in the right hands and everyone understands the lease. You should stress with the new tenant that if the on-site manager is not doing his job, your phone number is on the lease. Encourage the tenant to call. This shows the tenant a caring landlord, and also keeps the on-site manager on his toes because he never knows when a tenant will call with a complaint.

A landlord should visit his property every so often. Spend the day working with the manager by cutting the grass, planting bushes, making some repairs, or just talking to tenants. Close proximity to your rentals will foster a good relationship with both the manager and your tenants. As time goes on, these visits will become less work and more talking with tenants to keep them happy. Many times this will keep small fires from becoming major ones. Tenants are a wealth of information about other tenants and their habits. This information can make the lease renewal process much easier. Remember to keep the good apples and remove the bad ones before they spoil the others!

SIGN A MANAGEMENT CONTRACT

Avoid problems by signing a management contract so there are no misunderstandings about what is expected from your manager as well as what your obligations as owner are.

1. List a description of the property
2. Have a beginning and ending date for service and show how much notice each party must give to terminate the contract
3. Outline the On-Site Manager's Responsibilities —listed below are some examples:

Maintenance

- Maintain exterior of building: cut grass, shovel snow, trim bushes, rake leaves, paint, replace bulbs, keep gutter free of debris, pick up trash, and wash common windows
- Maintain interior (common areas) of building: vacuum carpets, sweep and mop floors (give number of times a week or month), change locks when keys are lost or stolen, replace hall bulbs, remove trash and litter wherever it is found, and wash common windows

BOND MANAGERS

Consider bonding any manager or "responsible tenant" who collects rent for you. Bonding is a guarantee by which the bonding company promises to cover any losses to the business. One, or more than one, employee can be bonded. Once the person is bonded, you are protected if they steal from you. The bond though, would not cover a person who accidentally damages or destroys a tenant's property.

Bonding is not an insurance policy, but is often handled by insurance agents. Once the bonding company covers the amount of the bond, it takes the person bonded to court to reclaim the loss.

Bonding on employees is called Fidelity Bonds. You can get an individual bond to cover just one employee or several employees or obtain a Position Schedule Bond which lists positions or employee titles rather than individual names. This way, if a new employee takes over they will automatically be covered. A third typed of bond is called a Blanket Bond. All employees are covered but no names or titles have to be listed.

Insurance agents who handle casualty insurance usually sell bonds. They are simple and cheap to obtain. Rates vary depending on the type of business and the number of employees. Most bonds are issued for $50–$150 a year. The size of the bond you should carry on your employee(s) will be determined by the amount of goods, money, or customers' property they could steal.

Bonding your managers, especially if they handle cash is great way to protect yourself from theft and embezzlement, which in almost all cases is done by a "trusted" employee.

COMMANDMENTS FOR HANDLING SERVICE REPAIRS

1. Do not enter a unit without authorization from the tenant or without the proper notice being given.
2. Knock and wait for the door to be opened. If no one answers, enter calling out the tenant's name.
3. Do repairs with a partner if possible, especially if the tenant is home and of the opposite sex.
4. Do not discuss landlord, management or other tenant situations.
5. Complete only work that is on work order.
6. Do not promise a date or time to do repairs not listed on the work order.
7. Do not make comments or observations about workmanship of other people's repairs, or a tenant's housekeeping abilities, or lack of, which caused the problem that is being repaired.
8. Do not move personal items unless absolutely necessary. Try to get permission first.
9. Do not enter rooms that are not part of the maintenance request.
10. Do not touch or operate tenant's belongings.
11. Do not make comments with sexual overtones. If a tenant makes sexual advances, make an excuse that you need to get a part. Don't come back.
12. Do not enter a property with children present unless an adult is home.

EMPLOYEE VS. INDEPENDENT CONTRACTOR - THE IRS'S "20 QUESTIONS"

When owning multi-family rentals there is often an on-site manager who handles maintenance calls and also does capital improvement work. Many times they are compensated with rent reductions for this work. If the on-site manager has an injury while performing one of these tasks and does not have a health insurance plan, he could file for insurance benefits from the state if he meets the guidelines of an employee and not an independent contractor.

Here is an abbreviated list taken from IRS form SS-8 that will determine if a person is an employee or an independent contractor.

1a) Describe the firm's business.
b) Describe the work done by the worker.
2a) If the work is done under a written agreement between the firm and the worker, attach a copy.
b) If the agreement is not in writing, describe the terms and conditions of the work arrangement.
c) If the actual working arrangement differs in any way from the agreement, explain the differences and why they occur.
3a) Is the worker given training by the firm? If yes: What kind? How often?
b) Attach representative copies of any written instructions or procedures.
c) Does the firm have the right to change the methods used by the worker or direct that person on how to do the work?
d) Does the operation of the firm's business require that the worker be supervised in his performance? Explain.
4a) The firm engages the worker to: A. Perform and complete a particular job only? B. Work for an indefinite time period?
b) Is the worker required to follow a routine or schedule established by the firm? If yes, what is the routine or schedule?
c) Does the worker report to the firm or its representative? If yes: How often? For what purpose? In what manner? (in person, in writing, by telephone, etc.) Attach copies of report forms used in reporting to the firm.
d) Does the worker furnish a time record to the firm? If yes, attach copies of the time records.
5a) State the kind and value of tools and equipment furnished by: The firm ... The worker ...
b) State the kind and value of supplies and materials furnished by: The firm ... The worker ...
c) What expenses are incurred by the worker in the performance or service of the firm?
d) Does the firm reimburse the worker for expenses? If yes, specify the reimbursed expenses.
6a) It is understood that worker will perform the services personally?

b) Does the worker have helpers? If yes: Are the helpers hired by: Firm? Worker? If hired by worker, is the firm's approval necessary? Who pays the helpers? Firm? Worker? Are FICA and FIT withheld from the helpers' wages? If yes: Who reports the helpers' income to the IRS? If the worker pays the helpers, does the firm repay the worker? What services do the helpers perform?

7. At what location are the services performed? Firms? Workers? Other? (Specify)

8a) Type of pay workers receive - Salary - Commission - Piecework - Hourly wage - Lump Sum - Other (Specify)

b) Does the firm guarantee a minimum amount of pay to the worker?

c) Does the firm allow the worker a drawing account or advances against pay? If yes, is the worker paid such advances on a regular basis? How does the worker repay such advances?

9a) Is the worker eligible for pension, bonuses, paid vacations, sick pay, etc? If yes specify.

b) Does the firm carry worker's compensation on the worker? Does the firm bond the worker?

c) Does the firm deduct either social security tax or Federal Income Taxes from the amount paid the worker?

d) How does the firm report the worker's income to the IRS? Form W-2 - Form 1099 - Does not report - Other?

10a) Approximately how many hours a day does the worker perform the service for the firm?

b) Does the worker perform similar services for others? If yes, on a daily basis? Does the firm have priority on his time?

c) Is the worker prohibited from competing with the firm either while on the job or during any later period?

11a) Can the firm discharge the worker at any time without incurring a liability. If no, explain.

b) Can the worker terminate the services at any time without incurring a liability? If no, explain.

12a) Does the worker perform service for the firm under: Firm's business name? Worker's business name? Other?

b) Does the worker advertise or maintain a business listing in the telephone directory, trade journal, etc? If yes, specify.

d) Does the worker have his/her own shop or office? If yes, where? How did the firm learn of the worker's services?

e) Does the firm represent the worker as an employee of the firm to its customers? If no, how?

13. Is a license required for the work? If yes, what kind of license? By whom is it issued? Who pays the license fee paid?

14. Does the worker have a financial investment in a business related to the services performed? If yes, specify?

15. Can the worker incur a loss in the performance of the service for the firm? If yes, how?

16a) Has any other government agency ruled on the status of the firm's workers? If yes, attach a copy.

b) Is the same being considered by any IRS office in connection with the worker's tax return or the firm's tax return?

17. Does the worker assemble or process a product at home or away from the firm's place of business? If yes: Who furnishes the materials used by the worker? Does the worker return the finished product to the firm?

18. Attach an explanation for any other reason why you believe the worker is an independent contractor or an employee.

CHAPTER 22

INSURANCE, FIRE SAFETY, AND SECURITY

Progress always involves risk. You can't steal second base and keep your foot on first.

— Frederick Wilcox

We are continually faced by great opportunities brilliantly disguised as insolvable problems.

Landlords who fail to consider these three very important areas are looking for lawsuits. This chapter will show the best types of insurance to carry, ways to prevent fires and ways to secure your property from crime.

INSURANCE

Before a mortgage company will release funds at settlement, buyers must provide a fire insurance policy. This is done not only to protect the mortgagee's interest, but it is also protection for the buyer. In addition to the fire insurance, he might also need flood, earthquake, loss of rent, liability, or crime insurance. If the property is in a flood zone or along an earthquake fault, this type of insurance is a must.

Loss of Rent Insurance is well worth the few extra dollars per month. This guarantees you will have rental income to make mortgage payments while the property is being rebuilt or repaired from a fire, natural disaster, etc. Liability insurance is needed for the personal injury accidents that can occur on your property. Tenants can sue you for their accident and, though you are not liable, many thousands of dollars can be spent on a defense. A minimum of one million dollars of liability insurance on each property is a necessity. The increased cost to take it from five hundred thousand to one million in coverage is about $50 a year.

Crime coverage is helpful if you are afraid the coin-operated laundry machines will be constantly vandalized, windows and doors to common halls will be smashed, or similar problems will occur.

Also consider buying mortgage premium insurance which pays off the mortgage upon your death. This type of policy is much better than a whole life policy. Your heirs will own a rental property free and clear. The rents will be a steady income that can be increased each year which will also increase the value of the property.

RENTERS INSURANCE

Reduce your odds of being sued by requiring tenants to carry personal property and liability insurance. The cost for a renter's insurance policy will run about $10 a month for $20,000 worth of personal content coverage and $200,000 in liability coverage. I realize that convincing some tenants, especially at the lower end of the economic scale, that this is a good idea may be difficult, but should be required for middle to upper end tenants.

Your odds of being sued can be reduced even further by *requiring the tenant to list you, the landlord, as an additional insured to their rental policy.* This means that if your tenant's guest falls and decides to sue both you and the tenant, the tenant's insurance company will be obligated to defend both parties. Your insurance company would not even know about the claim unless it went above the renter's liability limit.

That sounds better than you alone being sued because the tenant had no insurance or assets? Most insurance companies will not automatically add the landlord as an additional insured, but will do so *at no additional cost to the tenant* if asked. Another advantage of being listed as additional insured is you will receive notification if the tenant cancels and when it is time to renew.

Before signing the lease, require new tenants to show an *Insurance Certificate listing you as an additional insured.* The certificate will list the amount of coverage, terms, who is insured and length of the policy. Make sure your name is listed.

At time of renewal, raise your existing tenant's rent $10 a month more than projected and tell them by renewing, you will pay for a Renter's Insurance policy if they will list you as additional insured on the policy. When there is a tenant turnover, raise the rent $10 more than projected. After listing the rental amount in the ad say " includes Renter's Insurance."

Why would a tenant be willing to list you as additional insured? Explain it doesn't cost more to be added, and if for some reason they decide to drop the policy the only way you would know it was dropped was by being listed as an additional insured. If they have a dog it should be a must. Explain that there have been cases where dogs have attacked people and the landlord has been sued. I also stress that it protects them away from the apartment. If they injure a small child while pushing a cart in the supermarket they are covered.

This strategy has some built-in safe advantages. The tenant must buy the policy up front and you will give a $10 a month reduction in the rent. You will be paying for the policy with the tenant's money because the rent was raised $10 more than you would have gotten.

If raising the rent $10 a month is too much for your area, raise it $5 and pay the other $5 yourself. This is cheap compared to how your rates will increase if your tenant carries no insurance and you are sued.

Another overlooked advantage for requiring tenants to carry insurance is that some insurance companies allow the landlord to collect damages against the tenant's policy if the tenant causes damages to the premises during the term of the lease. In order to collect you must have a strong inspection sheet along with pictures to substantiate the condition on move in day.

INSURANCE RECORDS

Property Address	Insurance Co. Address	Policy Type / Policy Number	Type/Amount Coverage	Premium	Expiration Date
1.					
2.					
3.					
4.					
5.					
6.					
7.					
8.					
9.					
10.					
11.					
12.					
13.					
14.					
15.					

REDUCING THE RISK OF SLIP AND FALLS

Of course having tenants carry renter's insurance reduces your risk from slips and falls of the tenant or friend of the tenant. While prevention is the best protection, controlling what happens after the slip and fall injury can significantly help reduce the landlord's exposure.

1. Did the victim see the object that caused the slip and fall? Unless the victim is seriously injured ask them what it was that caused them to fall. If you discover the victim saw the object before the fall, try to get them to sign a document stating this fact. You are much less likely to be found liable for the accident even if the victim later changes the story.

2. What is the nature of the injury? Ask the victim what part of his body is hurt. If the right leg is injured, you may be able to prove inconsistencies if the victim sues you over injuries to both legs.

3. Did the victim comment on the accident? Talk to employees, fellow tenants, and anyone who might have been in

the vicinity of the accident to find out if the victim made any comments immediately after the accident. This type of third party testimony may be critical if things go to court.

4. How long was the object on the ground? The longer the object that caused the slip and fall was on the ground without the landlord removing it, the more likely the landlord is going to be found liable. On the other hand, the landlord might not be considered negligent if a tenant falls on a fresh puddle of oil left from a car that just pulled out of a parking space.

Get in the habit of taking pictures of the accident scene as soon as possible. Evidence could be melting, evaporating, blowing away, or being removed. Take wide angle shots of the whole area. These might become helpful if the item causing the fall is in clear view from a great distance away. This will help prove the victim was just not watching.

FIRE SAFETY
Fire Extinguishers
Fires are classified into three categories:
 A. Paper, rubbish, wood, cloth, and some plastics;
 B. Paint, grease, flammable liquids, and cooking oils;
 C. Electrical.

Written on a extinguisher, are numbers and letters which indicate the extinguisher's effectiveness on that class of fire. The higher the number, the more effective the extinguisher is in putting out that type of fire.

Provide each tenant with a two pound dry chemical 1A, 10B, C fire extinguisher. This size extinguisher is not going to put out a major blaze, but will put out small fires. It holds approximately ten seconds worth of chemicals so short bursts versus long bursts are recommended. The low cost is well worth the investment considering the damage a fire can cause.

Since most fires start in the kitchen, it's best to keep the fire extinguisher somewhere in the kitchen but not under the stove. You might not be able to get to it. Store the extinguisher in a pantry closet or in the bottom drawer of a cabinet that is away from the stove area, which can be the site of a fire.

Smoke Detectors
Most fatal fires occur at night while people are sleeping. Smoke detectors are considered to be the most effective, low cost fire alarm device available to consumers. Provide your tenants with them. Place one detector outside each sleeping area and another at the top of each stairway leading to an occupied area of the home. It would also be a good idea to mount a detector at the top of the basement steps.

Install the detectors approximately four inches away from a side wall and four to twelve inches from the ceiling. Remember to protect yourself by using the clause in the Additional Terms and Conditions that states that the smoke detectors were working when the lease was signed and it is the tenant's responsibility to replace the batteries. If a fire occurs and the battery was used in a Christmas toy, the tenant cannot plead that the landlord never replaced the old battery.

Smoke detectors that work from household current (hard wired) are acceptable, but be aware that if the current is broken, they will not work. If you use a hard wired system, back it up with a battery operated detector or buy a hard wired system that has a battery system as a back up.

Some insurance companies give discounts for having smoke detectors and fire extinguishers in your apartments. Ask your agent about these discounts.

Reasons To Install Carbon Monoxide Detectors

1. Carbon Monoxide (CO) cannot be detected by human senses. It is colorless, odorless, and tasteless.
2. Fire fatalities are often caused by Carbon Monoxide (CO) because the victims are overcome by the CO gas well before a smoke alarm goes off.
3. CO can cause death or permanent injury to oxygen-rich tissue such as the brain and the heart. It is a cumulative poison. Low levels of CO can cause irreversible learning and memory defects in fetuses.
4. Low levels of CO can impair judgment, impede faculties and greatly increase the risk of accidents and injuries to motorists and machine operators.
5. Early symptoms of carbon monoxide poisoning (dizziness, headaches, nausea, fatigue) are frequently misdiagnosed as flu or a virus.
6. Persons with cardiovascular impairment are very susceptible to carbon monoxide poisoning. Other high risk groups include children and pets. Effects of CO are inversely related to body mass. (The smaller the body, the faster and more damaging the impact of CO.) Persons suffering from anemia or respiratory ailments are also at extreme risks as are the elderly.
7. Heart attacks and other thoracic complaints have been correlated with high background CO in the atmosphere.
8. Half of all fatal poisonings in the U.S. are contributed to carbon monoxide.

9. Appliance malfunction and back drafting cause about 1,500 fatalities each year in the U.S. plus another 10,000 serious injuries (such as paralysis, blindness, permanent brain damage) as well as a larger number of long-term health problems. Chronic exposure to even moderately low levels of CO will lessen your life span. CO is a major component of cigarette smoke and a major cause of coronary artery disease.

10. Many CO poisonings occur because energy conservation measures may cause a vacuum effect in the home which causes back drafting.

11. Automobiles are a major source of CO. A faulty exhaust system can lead to CO poisoning.

12. Use of CO indicators will greatly decrease the number of deaths and injuries.

SECURITY

The easiest way to keep tenants happy is to provide the best possible security possible. Tenants want to come home from a hard day at work and feel safe entering their building and apartment and not feel as if they have to worry about being mugged or robbed on the front steps.

Security can come in many different forms. It could be an added dead bolt to each door or flood lights on the corners of the building. Burglars like to work in the dark. If every square foot of your property is lighted, they will probably move on to the house next door that is dark.

If one door is used for a number of apartments, a buzzer system to announce a visitor is useful. Common hallways or basements with sensor lights (that automatically go on with any type of movement) can add to the feeling of security. Additionally, you may want to place iron grill work on outside windows. If a key is lost or stolen, replace the lock and issue new keys immediately, particularly if the key is to a common door used by other tenants. Keep a spare lock and keys and rotate them when a key is lost or stolen.

Locks

Always change locks when changing tenants. The old tenant might have left the same number of keys he was given, but who knows how many sets he had made and had given to his friends.

I hope the following true stories will show you why we all need to take the time to change locks between tenants and learn from these landlords' mistakes. All of them lost property or suffered a major lawsuit because they didn't replace a $20 lock.

Case # 1. Tenant's belongings have been removed and landlord is doing a post inspection walk through with the tenant. As he writes a check for return of the security deposit, the tenant hands over two sets of keys. The landlord locks the door on the way out and goes home. The next morning he returns to change the locks and do some minor repairs and finds all the appliances missing - including the toilets. It seems the vacating tenants had not turned in all the keys and returned later that night to take a few additional items to improve their new apartment. The neighbors thought nothing odd about the tenant returning. They had been moving things out for the past two days.

Case # 2. Landlord changes locks between tenants and gives a key to his painting contractor. While the painter is working, the landlord brings around the good looking single female tenant who wants to measure for curtains. Three days after moving in, the tenant is raped by the painter who had made a spare key and let himself in the apartment. The painter, who the landlord had found in the yellow pages, had just gotten out of jail after serving time for another rape.

Case # 3. Landlord does not change locks after evicting the previous tenant and moves in a nice young family with elementary school age children. What the landlord didn't know was the previous tenant's brother had moved in and she had given him a key to the apartment. The brother was arrested just before the landlord did the eviction. After getting out of jail, he comes back to what he thinks is his sister's apartment. He noticed she had new furniture but being drunk decided to lay down on the sofa for a quick nap. Can you imagine the horror on the two latch key children's faces when they walked into their home to find a strange man sleeping on their sofa? They, fortunately, tiptoed to the neighbor, who called the police.

Case # 4. Locks are not changed after the tenant is evicted and the new tenants move in. One month after moving in the wife returns home from work to find her front door unlocked and everything has been removed from the living room. The police knew the old tenant had gambling problems and concluded he had given keys to friends so they could come over when he was not at home to watch his big screen TV set. The friends were owed money, so they rented a truck, unlocked the front door and exclaimed, "no wonder he hasn't paid us, look at all this new furniture." Guess who lost this lawsuit?

All of these scenarios could have been avoided with a simple change of locks.

If a tenant wants to change locks, he must give you the new key. Although, this does not give you license to enter his apartment at any time, in case of fire or a plumbing line break, you can protect your investment property promptly. I also stress with the tenants, that if one of these emergencies occurs and they have changed locks, I will have to break in, and any damage caused as a result of needing to enter forcibly will be their responsibility.

Change a Lock in 3 Seconds!

When a friend asked me if I could change a lock in three seconds, I started laughing. I told him it takes me more than three seconds to get the first screw loose and probably closer to three minutes to do just one lock - and that's if everything goes perfectly! If he could change a lock in three seconds, he was a magician and I wanted to learn the trick. He agreed to show me the next time we got together and guaranteed I could do the trick in three seconds after watching him do it just once. That was more than my curiosity could handle. I dropped everything and was at his front door five minutes later. Out came his master key which he inserted in the lock and after a quarter turn counter clockwise, out came the cylinder. He handed it to me and did the same steps with the dead bolt lock just above. Before I knew what was happening, two replacement cylinders came out of his pocket and were inserted in the empty cylinder holes. With a quarter turn clockwise, the new cylinders were in place. The locks had been changed in less time than it took you to read this!

I knew instantly that I needed this lock system. I have been a landlord for over two decades and can't remember when I have become more excited about a product. That's when he told me about Landlord's Lock Service who specializes in locks for landlords. The locks they sell are heavy duty Titan locks made by Kwikset and come with a 50 year mechanical warranty. The Titan lock features a pick resistant 6 pin cylinder that can be removed with a Master/Control key and are twice as resistant to forced entry than the normal lock on a tenant's door. Locks can be ordered with a bright brass finish or a satin chrome finish and come in either entry, single deadbolt or vestibule locks. Spare cylinders for quick and easy replacement can be order separately.

After looking at the price list, I realized they were selling this high grade lock set to a master key for less than what I was paying for a lower grade lock with no master key system. Since I have some townhouses that have a front and back door, I ordered three sets of two entry and two deadbolts for each townhouse. The locks came through with different keys for each tenant's unit and my master key worked them all! Each cylinder has a code sticker on it so if a tenant fails to return the keys, a quick call to

Landlord's Locksmith Service with the code number, and new keys are on the way to you. I also ordered a spare set of cylinders so when a tenant moves out, I just replace the four cylinders and use the old ones on the next unit that opens. Changing four cylinders can be done faster than it takes a prospective tenant to walk from his car to your front door.

Landlord's Lock Service can be reached at 800-847-8729. Say you heard about them from Don Beck and the master key set up charge will be waived.

Protect Yourself When Police Want Access

If two men approach you and flash police badges and say they want to search a tenant's property, what would you do? Most landlords would let them in. This could be a risky proposition. The men may be posing as police officers to get into the tenant's property illegally. The tenant could then sue you for illegal entry. Even if they are real police officers, the tenant could sue you if they did not have a warrant to search that unit. If you went with the officers to the property to unlock the door, you could be injured if shots are fired through the door.

There are four things you need to do when someone wants access to a unit.

1. Proof of Identify - ask for picture identification cards of the officers. They all carry them. You can buy authentic looking badges at any pawn shop so don't fall for just the badge. If they don't want to show you a picture ID or claim they don't have it with them, they are not real police.

As soon as possible call 911 and tell the operator that someone in your neighborhood is impersonating a police officer.

2. Get Proof of Warrant - In order to enter a unit the police will need either a search or arrest warrant to enter a tenant's apartment, except in limited situations. If you let them in without a warrant, you are now liable.

The warrant should identify the court and the judge who issued it, the date of issue, and the address of the unit the police need to access. If the police officers do not have the physical warrant with them, they should be able to give you the above information verbally. If they can not give this information, do not let them in. The correct tenant's name is not important. The warrant might just say John Doe.

If the officers can show a written warrant or give the required information verbally, the tenant will not have a recourse against you for letting them enter the unit. Most states have statues that all persons have a responsibility to assist police officers in carrying out their duties.

3. Fill Out Form - Police officers and people impersonating police officers can be very intimidating. This can cause you to forget vital information that you might need later on. Design a form for yourself or managers that will record: Names of officers, badge numbers, department name, department telephone number, warranty number, the court that issued the warranty, the warranty date, the person specified if any, and the purpose of the warrant for example search or arrest. Have the officers sign the form listing that the information you have gathered is complete and correct. They might also refuse to sign but it is worth a try.

4. When No Warrant Is Necessary - One of the few times police officers can enter a unit with a warrant is if they are in "hot pursuit" of a subject.

They can smash through the door to continue the pursuit if they feel the person they are after is in that unit. If they come to you at the manager's desk and ask for a key, then they are not in hot pursuit and need a warrant.

DEATH OF A TENANT

The longer you own rental property the higher chance that a tenant will die or a homicide will occur in your apartment. There are precautions you will need to take as the landlord.

If the tenant dies of natural causes, call the police and let them do their investigation. This might take a few hours or a few days but stay out of their way until you are given permission to begin repairs.

If death is caused because of a homicide, call the police and stay away from the area. If it is a multi-family building new ways to enter and exit the building might need to be established to keep people away from the area where the police are working. Your on-site presence or an on-site manager to direct this is important. The police will notify you when they have completed their work.

If there is loss of blood or other fluids, get a copy of the autopsy report to see if the person was infected with any contagious diseases. If so, take precautions when preparing the unit to be re-rented as well as the proper decontamination methods. Call your local public health department for guidelines.

Once relatives of the deceased learn of the death, they could be calling to get what they say mom promised them at her death. If the relative's name is not on the lease they should not be given access without written permission of the names on the lease.

While the family settles the estate and gets the house cleaned out, sign an agreement with the family, with your attorney's help to insure that you will be paid first from the estate proceeds. Otherwise,

you might be low in the pecking order of whatever remaining funds are available.

TEN SAFETY SHOWING TIPS

1. Use the buddy system. Go in pairs.
2. Carry a whistle, mace or shriek alarm.
3. Carry a portable phone. Call someone in the presence of the applicant, inform them where you are and them to call you back in a few minutes.
4. Always get a name and phone number when scheduling appointments. Use caller I.D.
5. As soon as you have finished showing the unit, move outside to continue the conversation.
6. Stay between an exit and the applicant. You can point the way, but allow the applicant to lead the way into each room.
7. While showing the unit, keep all blinds, drapes, and curtains open.
8. Dress conservatively and leave jewelry at home.
9. Never carry a case that has your name and address on it. If your keys are lost or stolen, this information could be used to burglarize your house.
10. Plan an escape route in advance.

CHECKLIST TO PROVE ABANDONMENT

A phone call comes in from a neighbor who lives a few doors away from one of your rentals. He says that a U-Haul truck was outside the unit last night and it looks like the tenant is gone for good. In fact he didn't even close the door when he left. After grabbing some locks from the garage, you drive to the property. The neighbor was correct. The door was open and most everything was gone except some clothes and miscellaneous items. In about an hour the locks had been changed and all items left in the house had been bagged and put out for trash pick up the next day. Two days later you receive a phone call from the tenant wanting to know what is going on. You reply. "What do you mean what is going on. You moved out and didn't even close the front door." The tenant responded with, "My wife and I just returned today from a week's vacation to find the door locked and all our belongings removed from the house. What's going on?" After I heard that story, I knew it was time to come up with ways to prove if the tenant was officially out or not.

Normally, an owner can not change locks unless he wins an eviction lawsuit against a tenant but in most states there is an exception to these "lockout" rules. If the tenant has "abandoned" the property, the landlord can change the locks without going through the eviction process. If the tenant returns and claims he had no intention of abandoning the property you better have some guidelines established that will show that you "reasonably" believed the property was abandoned before changing the locks.

The following checklist should only be used when residents are missing and behind in rent. If rent is paid, the apartment can't be considered abandoned even if the resident is missing.

The following suggestions will be helpful if taken to court. It will be your job to prove abandonment, not the tenant's. The best protection is a paper trail. Document everything. Verbal promises of tenants need to be put in writing and signed so memories do not fail in court.

1. Contact tenant at home or at work. Ask if they have moved out. If yes, make arrangements to pick up keys. If meeting face to face have them sign a release.

2. If home phone is no longer in service, record this message. If gives a forwarding number, do number 1.

3. Did they leave a forwarding address? If yes, this will be very helpful.

4. Talk to neighbors, fellow tenants - Did the tenant verbally tell more than one person they were moving? Did anyone see the move? List names, dates and phone numbers of anyone answering yes.

5. Call utility companies to check if service has been turned off. Get cut off date. Note if utilities are off when first entering apartment.

6. Call the school where the tenant's children attend and ask if they are still enrolled. If not, ask the date records were transferred.

Before entering the apartment, know what your lease and state law allows you to do. Take a neighbor, fellow tenant, police officer or friend (not a family member) as an impartial witness. Also take along a video camera and/or camera that will list date on picture. Before entering the apartment, start the video camera that prints the date and time on and keep it running until leaving. (If not documented, a tenant's 12 inch B&W TV can become a 52 inch color television that you stole!)

7. Note if there is a pet, is the pet food and water bowl gone.

8. Note if food is in cupboards and refrigerator and the condition of the food. Take pictures.

9. Note if bathroom medicine cabinet is empty. Take pictures.

10. Note if clothes have been removed. Clothes on floor doesn't mean abandonment. Take pictures.

11. Note if furniture and tenant supplied appliances have been removed. Furniture and appliances left behind and look in bad condition does not necessarily mean abandonment. Take pictures.

12. Note if garage, attic, or storage area has been cleaned out. Take pictures.

CHECKLIST TO PROVE ABANDONMENT

Rules in most states allow "lockout" exceptions for abandonment. The problem is knowing when the tenant has abandoned the property if no notice was given. The following suggestions will be helpful if taken to court. It will be your job to prove abandonment, not the tenants. The best protection is a paper trail. Document everything. Verbal promises of tenants need to be put in writing and signed so memories do not fail in court.

1. Contact tenant at home or at work. If you reach them, ask if they've moved out. If yes, list date, time, and person to whom you spoke. Make arrangements to pick up keys. If meeting face to face have them sign a release.

2. If home phone number of tenant is no longer in service, record this message or note time and day of call. If it gives a forwarding number, repeat number 1.

3. Is rent current? If not, note date rent was last paid. If current, assume the unit is still occupied. Don't do anything without a written release stating they have moved.

4. Information from the Post Office—Did they leave a forwarding address? This is better than mail piled at front door and a verbal from the mail carrier.

5. Information from employees, neighbors, fellow tenants: did the tenant verbally tell more than one person they were moving? Did anyone see the move? List names, dates, and phone numbers of anyone answering yes.

6. If tenant's car is not in the driveway or parking lot or in the usual area they park, note date and time. Check a few times, and during times a car would normally be there.

7. Call utility companies to check if service has been turned off. Get cut off date. Note if utilities are off when first entering apartment.

8. Call school where tenant's children attend and ask if they're still enrolled. If not, ask the date records were transferred.

Before entering the apartment know what your lease and state law allows you to do. If notice to enter is needed, give it before entering. Take a neighbor, fellow tenant, police officer, or friend (not a family member) as an impartial witness. Take along a video camera and/or camera that will list the date on the picture. Before entering the apartment, start the video camera with the date and time on and keep it running until leaving. (If not documented, a tenant's 12 inch black and white TV can become a 52 inch television that you stole!)

9. Note if tenant's pet, food, and water bowls are gone.

10. Note if food has been left in cupboards and refrigerator and the condition of the food. Take pictures.

11. Note if bathroom medicine cabinet is empty, or if toothbrushes, razors, shampoo, deodorant, etc. are still there. Take pictures.

12. Note if clothes have been removed. Clothes on the floor doesn't mean abandonment. Take pictures.

13. Note if furniture and tenant supplied appliances have been removed. Furniture and appliances that are left behind and that look in bad condition does not necessarily mean abandonment. Take pictures.

14. Note if garage, attic, or storage area has been cleaned out. Take pictures.

If many items on this list indicate abandonment, still be cautious. Before items left in the apartment are boxed or thrown out, note them with the movie camera and verbally explain the items. Check your state law for how long items must be held before they can be discarded or sold.

If there are many checked off on this list which could indicate abandonment, still be cautious. Before items left in the apartment are boxed or thrown out, note them on the movie camera and verbally explain the items. Check your state law for how long items must be held before they can be discarded or sold.

TENANT IN JAIL OR HOSPITAL

When a tenant is hospitalized or incarcerated personal property should not be released to anyone without a written authorization from the tenant, the police, or appropriate court. If the tenant will not be occupying the property for an extended period, you may ask the tenant if he wants to move out and have a friend or relative or other authorized person take charge of his personal property.

If no one is available the tenant may give written authorization to the landlord to move possessions to a location designated by the tenant the following steps should be taken.

1. Enter the property with an unrelated witness.
2. Take an inventory of all items - Pictures and movies are also a good idea.
3. Arrange and/or contract out pick-up and delivery to where tenant designates.
4. Mail a bill for expenses and a copy of inventory and pictures to tenant.

If the tenant continues to pay rent, tenancy is not terminated and abandonment procedures are not applicable. If the resident owes rent and refuses to move, a legal notice can be served in jail or the hospital by the sheriff or private process server.

CHAPTER 23

RECORD KEEPING

Your action, not your tenant's, is responsible for your success.

— Jeffrey Taylor

Diplomacy is the art of letting other people have your own way.

The last repair has been made and the last rent received for the month. But your desk is cluttered with other things that need attention. Two months of receipts are sitting in the shoe box and need to be filed. Mortgage checks must be sent and three "Notices to Change Terms of Tenancy" that should have been mailed yesterday are waiting for stamps. Welcome to the other side of property management.

Even when the phone is not ringing, it seems the desk is always calling. To be successful in landlording, it is imperative that you organize your record keeping. We are all in this business to make money and to pay less taxes. If the IRS decides to see why your refund checks have gotten larger in the last few years, you had better be ready to answer all their questions.

TENANT MOVE-IN CHECKLIST

From the moment a prospective tenant's application is received until the time the lease is signed, there will be information that needs to be recorded and kept for your files. The Tenant Move-In Checklist is a reminder to run credit checks, call employers and landlords, as well as visit the prospective tenant's home during the screening process. It also covers important steps after the prospective tenant has been approved, such as security deposit required to reserve the unit, signed inspection sheet, and providing your mailing address and phone number for emergencies.

TENANT LISTING

The Tenant Listing Sheet should have its own place on the top of the desk. It lists the name, address, phone number of each tenant, move in date, amount of security, and rent. It's easy to add

new tenants to the list and remove old ones. It is much more convenient to have all the phone numbers together on one sheet than having to find them in the phone book or go to a folder set up for the property.

BOOKKEEPING

Documenting what expenditures go with which property is very important. Keep two file folders for each property. One holds the insurance policy, title papers, loan records, copies of credit reports, mortgage papers, termite and heating contracts, and anything else that isn't in the safe deposit box. This file is kept in a separate drawer as this information does not need to be referred to as often as the second file. The second file contains the leases, building inspection sheets, letters to and from tenants, deposit slips, bank statements, and all receipts gathered during the year.

Separate file folders should be set up for each of the following forms that may be needed throughout the year:
- Rental Applications
- Late Charge Notices
- Three Day Notice to Pay or Vacate
- Notice to Change Terms of Tenancy
- Pet Policy
- Insurance Records
- Waterbed Agreement
- Insufficient Funds
- Blank leases

RENTAL INCOME AND EXPENSE RECORD

This sheet should be placed in the folder set up for individual buildings. This form is a valuable tool, especially at tax time. All the information needed for filling out your tax return is recorded here. The income section has space to list up to six tenants. It has a section to record monthly mortgage payments and annual payments for taxes and insurance. The bottom section is for expenses on the property.

The categories are set up to correspond with the categories on Schedule E of your tax return. At the end of the year the rents, mortgage interest, insurance, taxes, and expenses are totaled and transferred to your tax return. A new file is started every January 1, and the old ones are kept together in a safe place for your accountant. Keep these records for at least five years.

RENTAL INCOME

Another form that remains on top of the desk is the Rental Income Sheet. This sheet lists the address and unit number for each apartment and has columns for each month of the year. Each space is divided so the rent can be recorded in the larger area and the postmarked date on the envelope can be recorded in the smaller area. Make a copy of the first check the tenant sends and keep a copy of it on file. This check gives the bank, account number, and the number used when making a deposit. If a tenant's name is missed on the deposit slip, use this number to help identify to whom the check belongs.

After returning from the post office box, record the rent and postmark date on this sheet and then add the check to the deposit slip.

On the duplicate copy of the deposit slip, record the tenant's name. On the seventh of each month you can easily see who owes rent and start making phone calls. Don't be surprised to see a pattern develop, as the year progresses, as to the dates rents are postmarked. People who mail the rent on the first or second of each month (or earlier) will stay within these dates throughout the year. Tenants who pay on the fourth and fifth of each month will rarely mail their check on the first or second but will be more likely to mail on the fifth and try to sneak a few sixth and sevenths of the month past you. Don't let them, because if you let it happen once, it will happen again.

WORK ORDER

This form is very useful if a part-time or full-time maintenance person is working for you. When repairs are called in, a work order is immediately filled out and made available to the maintenance person when they return to the office. Analyzing work orders by building and/or by tenant, will show you things. Unusual patterns will prompt you to ask questions that may yield answers that in turn, will reduce unwarranted service calls. Furthermore, you may be able to save money in material purchases, by anticipating demand based on previous usage.

SERVICE REQUEST

This form is most often used in a large complex or a building with a maintenance person living on the premises. The tenants are given a half dozen of these forms

Tenant Listing

Tenant	Address	Phone	Lease Expires	Security Deposit	Rent	Moved In	Moved Out

when they sign the lease. They are encouraged to bring it to the on-site manager as repairs are needed. Stating the nature of the repair and whether the repair must be done when they are at home will save everyone time.

It is a good idea for the on-site manager to have the tenant sign the completion acknowledgment at the bottom of the sheet, as with the work order, to ensure the repair was completed. This will keep the on-site manager on his toes because the service requests will be reviewed weekly or monthly.

Encourage the tenant to make a copy of the request, or ask for one when submitting it, so they will have a copy as proof of the request date. Stress with tenants that if a major plumbing leak occurs, they are to forget a service request form and get on the phone immediately to report the problem.

PROFIT AND LOSS STATEMENT

This form can be used to give you a total accounting of individual properties. It is then compiled for a total profit and loss statement on all properties for the year. It can be very helpful to study previous statements so the overall picture of one year's cash flow can be compared to another.

ORGANIZE REGULAR MONTHLY BILLS

Most mortgage companies send a payment book each year, with coupons to be included with your payment. Other bills that do not include an envelope, but that must be paid each month, should also be organized.

Start by tearing the twelve payment coupons from the book and place them in 12 envelopes. Make sure to keep the envelopes in a monthly order. Lick the preprinted labels, place a stamp on the twelve envelopes, and put a rubber band around them. Each month after writing the check, pull out the top envelope, enclose the check, and it is ready to be mailed. Another approach is to organize all of January's bills into one pile with a rubber band around them and then do this for each month. Now each month the packet of envelopes is pulled out, checks inserted, and they're ready to be mailed.

The bills that do not have preprinted labels will need to be addressed on twelve separate envelopes. It takes time at the beginning of the year, to do both these jobs, but it's nothing that can't be done in a few free minutes. Try doing it while watching a football game or the news. You take the honor of placing the coupon in the envelope.

Rental Income and Expense Record

Repair / Service Record

Address of Property: _____

Hot Water Heater	**Air Conditioner**

Manufacturer: _____   Manufacturer: _____

Model #: _____   Model #: _____

Serial #: _____   Serial #: _____

Color: _____   Color: _____

Dimensions: _____   Dimensions: _____

Purchased on: ___/___/___   Purchased on: ___/___/___

Purchased from: _____   Purchased from: _____

Warranty good for _____ years.   Warranty good for _____ years.

BTUs: _____ Filter size: _____

Repair / Service Record

Item	Date	Service Done By:	Work Completed	Costs

2002

41

SERVICE REQUEST

Tenant's Name _____ Date ___/___/___

Address / Unit # _____

_____

Phone Numbers - Home: _____ Work: _____

Repair Needed: _____

_____

☐ I give permission for the repair person to enter my apartment.
☐ I do not give permission for the repair person to enter my apartment.
☐ Please call to schedule a time when I will be home.

Date Completed ___/___/___ By _____

Materials Used: _____   Cost of Materials $ _____.

Labor: _____   Cost of Labor $ _____.

Bill Tenant? YES ☐ NO ☐

REPAIR/SERVICE RECORD

The phone rings and it's your tenant calling to say he has no hot water. You remember replacing an element not too long ago but can't remember if it was the top or bottom element, if the heater is still under warranty, who did the repair, and how much it cost. Keeping a Repair/Service Record form in each property's folder will save hours, not only in trying to find the bill, but in discovering the make, model, and serial number to order the replacement part or a new heater.

Other appliances for which this information would be helpful are: Air Conditioner, Refrigerator, Dishwasher, Garbage Disposal, Oven/Stove, Washer, Dryer, Garbage Compactor, and the Furnace.

There are other items associated with the apartment where this type of information would also be useful: Carpets, Deck/Porch, Flooring, Paint, Roof, and Siding. It would be good to know, for example, the date carpets were installed and by whom, as well as where they were purchased, the type, color, type of pad, the length of the warranty, and the costs. A comparison can be made with another store or brand of carpet if needed in another unit.

NOTICE TO VACATING TENANT

After receiving the tenant's notice to vacate, mail him this form so that everyone understands what will be happening during this transition period. The tenant is informed that you will begin advertising and will need to show the unit, but only with 24 hours notice, and at times convenient to the tenant. A bonus is offered if the tenant recommends someone who qualifies and agrees to rent. The steps are listed in the lease as to what must be done to receive a full refund of the security deposit.

WORK ORDER

Address: _____ Date ___/___/___

Repair Requested:_____

_____

Repair Performed:_____

_____

Material Used: _____

_____

Time Required: _____ Date Completed ___/___/___ Repair Made By: _____

The repairs mentioned above have been satisfactorily completed.

_____   ___/___/___
Tenant's Signature   *Date*

Profit and Loss Statement

Property _____

Year _____

		Year's Totals
1		
2		
3	INCOME	
4	Rental	
5	Other	
6	TOTAL INCOME	
7		
8		
9		
10	EXPENSES	
11	Mortgage Principal	
12	Interest	
13	Taxes, Licenses	
14	Utilities	
15	Service, Repairs	
16	Insurance	
17	Management	
18	Payroll	
19	Merchandise, Supplies	
20	Miscellaneous Expenses	
21	Other	
22	TOTAL EXPENSES (GROSS)	
23	Less Mortgage Principal	
24	TOTAL	
25	Less Impounds	
26	TOTAL EXPENSES (NET)	
27	Plus Depreciation	
28	TOTAL EXPENSES (FOR TAXES)	
29		
30	TOTAL INCOME	
31	Less Total Expenses (Line 28)	
32		
33	**NET PROFIT OR (LOSS)**	

30

DISTRIBUTION OF SECURITY DEPOSIT

Each state has different laws regarding how soon the security deposit must be returned to the tenant. The average seems to be 30 days from the date of vacating. State laws also vary on when, or if, interest needs to be paid on the security deposit. Check with a local real estate attorney or the local Real Estate Investment Group in your area. See the beginning of Chapter 9 for a phone number to find out about a group in your area.

If damage is found beyond what is listed on the inspection sheet signed by the tenant when moving in, take pictures or record on a VCR camera. Label the back of each picture with the address of the property, what room the picture is taken, and the date. Even better, use a camera with the date included on the picture. If the tenant decides to question your expenses or the amount of damage you have listed, the pictures will be the ace in your hand in court.

Get bids to repair the damage and if you do the work yourself, keep all receipts. List these items under the Damage to Unit section of the Distribution of Security Deposit Form.

A lease that has been broken or other monetary issues that have not been satisfied will be listed under Damages From Breach of Agreement section. This would include such items as: late fees unpaid, advertising expenses to re-rent, bad check charges, unpaid utility bills, and unpaid repair bills.

Two other lines on the Distribution of Security Deposit Form cover "Past Rent Due" and "Rent Due Through Balance of Lease". Past Rent Due covers any prior rent owed up to the present date. The Rent Due Through Balance of Lease line covers rent that is owed to the expiration date.

This form should be mailed with copies of all receipts to justify deductions. Send it certified mail to validate the date it was mailed and that it was received within the allowable time limit.

If the tenant moves without leaving a forwarding address, send a certified letter to his last known address (your unit). State he has violated the terms and conditions of his lease and has forfeited his security deposit. If he wishes to discuss this further, you should be contacted. In most cases, the letter is returned to you because it was not picked up. This is your proof that an attempt was made to notify the tenant about his security deposit. Include the sealed letter in a file and hold in case the tenant tries later to lay claim to the security deposit.

DISTRIBUTION OF SECURITY DEPOSIT

Property Address _____ Date ___/___/___

To: _____

_____

_____

Dear _____,

Pursuant to the terms and conditions of your lease agreement, you are hereby advised that your security deposit will be disposed of as follows:

Total Security Deposit Paid	$ _____
Interest Due	$ _____
Less:	
Past Rent Due	$ _____
Damages to Unit	
_____	$ _____
_____	$ _____
_____	$ _____
Damages from breach of agreement	
_____	$ _____
_____	$ _____
_____	$ _____
Rent due through balance of lease	$ _____
NET REFUND DUE TENANT	$ _____
BALANCE OWED LANDLORD	$ _____

6

CHAPTER 24

TEN BIGGEST MISTAKES MADE BY LANDLORDS

As I travel around the country lecturing to real estate investor groups, I ask everyone to tell me what they feel is the biggest mistake they have made over the years as a landlord. It is amazing how often the same answers are mentioned. I decided to compile the data and share these common mistakes with you in the hope that it will keep you from making the same mistakes. All ten mistakes have one thing in common. They all have caused landlords to lose cash flow.

Recently I read a quote which said, "Learn from the mistakes of others because your cash flow won't last long enough to make them all yourself." I could not agree more. My only wish is that I had read this quote many years ago! I hope these responses will help you become a better landlord, and help you to learn from other people's mistakes so your cash flow does improve.

1. FAILING TO VERIFY INCOME/LEASE RECORDS AND LEASES BEFORE BUYING

A few times a year I receive a call from a fellow investor asking, after he has settled, what he can do with a Seller who had given bad or incomplete information about the property and tenants. My first question is to ask if he had a clause in the agreement to check leases, rental applications, rent roll, and expense records, within a certain number of days of signing the agreement? He admits he had not, which I find happens many times. Buyers take the realtor's or owner's word about the numbers or don't even ask.

Be sure you see all leases to verify if they are month-to-month with 30, 60, 90 days notice or a year-to-year lease. Find out the ending date of the lease. Knowing this helps to determine the sale price. If the leases come due in 9 months and are $50 under market, the price should reflect this. On the other hand, if the leases come due two months after purchase and each rental can be raised $50, there is room to negotiate to a higher price yet still maintain a strong cash flow.

Don't get caught taking the Seller's or Realtor's word about leases. Always ask to see them and check them thoroughly. A Seller told me his leases converted to month-to-month after the first year and since both tenants had been in for over a year, they were month-to-month with 60 days notice. I took his word and discovered after settlement, they renewed year-to-year and not month-to-month. One of the tenants had to be notified the day before settlement of an increase. The next day I wrote a $50 increase notice and went to introduce myself to my new tenant. After a few minutes of small talk I handed him the notice. Without even opening the envelope, he handed it back and said I should have given it to him yesterday—as of today his lease automatically renewed for another year. He was correct and I was stuck with $50 less per month for a whole year. All because I didn't ask to see the lease.

After that experience I always put in the agreement that I want to see all leases within 5 days of Seller's acceptance of the agreement. During one deal the Realtor presented the leases and I discovered the rents were $200 less than I was told. It seems the owner listed the property at the time he was going to raise the rents. He never told the Realtor he had "forgotten" to raise them. Needless to say they were both embarrassed and I was able to negotiate a price well below what it would have been with $200 more income. As soon as I bought it, I raised the rents $200 per month, which added about $20,000 to the value of the property. This instant equity and additional cash flow happened because I took the time to study the leases before settlement.

161

Buyers of investment properties must ask to see income and expense records for the property. Often this will be a Schedule E from the seller's tax return. Try to get a more detailed breakdown of this information for at least two years. You can learn a lot about a property and the management skills of the seller through this information.

Study the income flow sheet to see which tenants pay on time and which are always late. See if a tenant makes partial payments during the month and if the late fee is paid. These areas show potential problems after the sale.

Study the expense sheet for areas where the numbers look out of line. A $1,000 bill for advertising and a grass cutting for a duplex should send up red flags. Look for large ticket items such as new dishwasher, air conditioner, roof, etc., and make sure these items are part of the property.

Another paper to see before settlement and that you definitely must see at settlement is the rental application. If a tenant skips, the application is loaded with good sources to find him. You can run another credit check to find a new address. Call the employer to see if he is still working there and then follow him home after work. Use his driver's license number or car registration to track him through the state police. The emergency name and phone on the application can help locate a tenant—especially when they are told a substantial amount of money was left in the house (really the pennies and nickels found in the sofa)!

2. USING POOR TECHNIQUES FOR SCREENING PROSPECTIVE TENANTS

This was by far the number one answer given by fellow landlords as their biggest mistake. "If I had only done a more thorough screening before giving them the keys" was a common cry. It is my belief that 90% of management headaches can be solved by doing just this. The problem is that only 10% of Landlords do an adequate screening and that is why so many Landlords get burned and then want to sell. To be perfectly honest, some of my best purchases were deals with motivated sellers who had tenant problems and didn't want to, or know how to, solve their problem. I was able to purchase the property well under market value because of their motivation to sell and be rid of "those problem tenants." I quickly solved the problem by evicting the deadbeats and put in good tenants. This not only increased my cash flow but also the value of the building as mentioned earlier.

Screening a prospective tenant begins the minute you pick up the phone and say hello. Have a list of all the pertinent information about the property.

List the number of bedrooms and baths, the appliances, who pays what utilities and approximate cost if tenants are paying. Also list the amount of security deposit and when the unit will be available. Then start asking them questions. When are you available to move in; how many people will be living with you; do you have pets; where are you working and for how long; have you given notice to your current landlord? Find out their gross income per week and see if this meets your qualifying standards. If it doesn't, let them know they will need a co-signer who owns real estate. Explain there is a non-refundable application fee. This will cause the professional tenant looking for a place needing no credit checks to hang up and discourages all not seriously looking. During the conversation, write down the information the prospective tenant gives you in a notebook. You need to do this because after talking to five or more prospective tenants you will forget who had the dog, when they need the unit by and how many in their party. If they wish to schedule an appointment, get a phone number in case you run into an emergency and must cancel. If the appointment is more than 24 hours after your call, require them to call you to confirm the appointment, or you will not be there. This should help cut down on the number of no shows.

The prospective tenant shows for the appointment. Hopefully they have followed your instructions to bring everyone, including the pets who will be occupying the property. Check four things right away. First, were they on time? Good sign if they are. Second, what is the condition of the car? Since most tenants don't own real estate, many times the most money they have spent on any one purchase will be the car. If it looks like they could get $200 for it remind yourself you are probably looking at their net worth! Third, how are they dressed? I don't mean coat and tie, but not bare feet and a three day growth of beard. They should be coming as if they were on a job interview because in a way, that is what it is. I have something they want and looking like a slob or not showing up on time does not make a good first impression. Remember, you never get a second change to make a good first impression. Last but not least, look at their teeth. I have yet to have a good tenant that has bad teeth. Think about it. If they don't care about their own personal hygiene and looks what makes you think they will take care of your apartment?

Talk to them during the walk through but also be aware of the children's behavior. If they are running and screaming through the house while you give the tour it is obvious the parents do not have any control. If they behave this badly in front of their parents and a total stranger and in a strange house, guess what the behavior will be when they are around their own furniture and belongings. If they ask for a rental application, ask to see their driver's license first. Make sure they are who they say they are right up front.

When the application is returned, the screening process continues. Start by running a credit check and a judgment search. If they failed to pay another landlord there is a strong possibility you also will not get paid at some point during the lease. Call the previous landlord before calling the current landlord. The previous landlord has no reason to lie while the current landlord might have some good reasons not to be truthful. Call employers to verify employment and use the pay stub they returned with the application to determine if they financially qualify. Many times employers and current landlords will not give out information over the phone. They will ask you to mail or fax a letter with the tenants signature giving them permission to release the information to you. (These forms are part of the 49 Property Management forms found in my Home Study Course that will be explained at the end of this report.)

The last item in the screening process is to visit the prospective tenant at their home, unannounced, or with only 15 minutes notice. This is done so they will not have time to clean. Go on a day you don't have a cold and let your nose do the walking. Remember, what you see and what you smell is what will be in your apartment. Before or after the meeting, knock on the neighbor's door on either side of them. Introduce yourself and ask what type of neighbors they have been. Do they throw wild parties, lots of traffic at all hours of day or night (sign of drugs), dog barks outside all night, etc.

3. FAILING TO USE A LEASE OR USING A LEASE IMPROPERLY

In most states verbal leases are considered valid contracts for up to two years. Don't do it. Tenant's have too many rights with a lease and they have even more with no lease. The lease is the backbone of a landlord/tenant relationship. If all rules and regulations are spelled out so everyone knows exactly what they can and can not do, there is less chance of problems. If you are using a standard lease from a stationery store, talk to fellow landlords and ask to see their lease clauses. Some of the best clauses I am using now are ones I found in leases of landlords selling me their properties. One such clause said that tenants were required to carry Renter's Insurance and the landlord must be listed as additional insured. I called my insurance agent and learned that the landlord can be added to a renter's

policy at no additional charge. Now, if a friend of a tenant slips and falls and sues both of you, the tenant's insurance company covers both claims. There is a good chance if the claim is not too large, your insurance company will never know about it.

In some states, such as Pennsylvania and New Jersey, the state legislature has passed laws that all leases must be written using simple words and short sentences. No more Lessee, Lessor or terminate and vacate. This "Plain Language Lease" idea is a good one and more states in the future will also approve. I developed a Plain Language Lease for my tenants and had it approved by the State Attorney General's office. It has 52 of the most landlord-friendly lease clauses you will ever see. I developed this lease for my own tenants, and now over 12,000 landlords and tenants are using it. Many of them are attorneys who like the fact that it is also on a computer disk so they can customize it to fit each client's needs. More information about these clauses and how to purchase this lease will be given at the end of this report.

An inspection sheet should always be a part of your lease. Do a walk through with the new tenant and complete this form. Have the tenant sign and return it. This protects both parties. It protects the tenant from having a landlord claim damages that were in the house when they moved in and, at the same time, protects the landlord for damages not listed on the inspection sheet.

When filling out your lease paperwork do not list the tenants as Mr. and Mrs. John Smith. List them as John and Mary Smith because Mrs. Smith could really be Mary Jones. Do not list the number of occupants as four people. State it as TWO adults and TWO children. Spell out the number. It is harder to forge later on. Another mistake is not having everyone sign the lease who is over 18 years old or only getting one spouse's signature. Everyone not signing the lease could claim in court no responsibility because they did not sign the lease. They would claim it is an invalid contract with them. Another mistake is neglecting to list all things that could "walk" from the rental unit. Some examples are: wall to wall carpet, dining room chandelier, all appliances, air conditioners, smoke detectors, and fire extinguishers. It is also a good idea on the inspection sheet to list the make and model number of all appliances. No landlord wants to see his two year old 22 cubic foot frost free refrigerator replaced with a 20 year old 15 cubic foot ice box because the lease just said "refrigerator." Another landlord did not mention wall-to-wall carpet and when the tenant left, the carpet went with him. In both of these cases the landlords lost because of a poorly drafted lease, and no inspection sheet or pictures to prove what they said was true.

4. FAILING TO KNOW YOUR STATE'S LANDLORD/TENANT ACT

Playing any sport without knowing the rules of the game starts you off with a big disadvantage. Not knowing what you can and can not do with a tenant can be disastrous in lost rent and possible legal action. Every state has differences in its laws so it is very important to research your state's requirements before signing a lease. Here are a few examples of questions you should have answers for before writing and signing a lease with a tenant.

- What happens to the lease if the building burns down?
- What happens to the lease if the tenant dies?
- How much notice must landlord and tenant give each other to end the lease?
- How much security deposit can you collect when signing the lease?
- Must the security deposit be placed in an interest bearing account?
- When must interest be paid on the security deposit and how much?
- If more than one month of security deposit is collected are there requirements for returning a percentage or set amount at a later date?
- How soon after a tenant has moved must the security deposit be returned?
- If a tenant fails to give a written forwarding address after moving, are you allowed to keep the security deposit?
- How much notice must the tenant be given before filing for eviction?
- How must the eviction notice be served to the tenant?
- Where do you file the paperwork and do you need an attorney to do it?
- What steps are involved in filing for eviction?
- What is the cost to do an eviction from the beginning to the very end?
- Can a tenant appeal a judgment and if so how much time are they allowed?
- If your judgment is just monetary and they pay, can you still evict?
- If the tenant is physically removed but personal property remains, how long must you "hold" the property before it can be disposed of?
- How does your state define "Warranty of Habitability"?
- If you own the property in a corporation or trust, must you use an attorney to represent you at the hearings?

If you start by knowing these answers you have a strong beginning to your Property Management Division.

5. FAILING TO COLLECT ENOUGH SECURITY DEPOSIT

Always collect as much security deposit as your state will allow and see that it is more than one month's rent. A very high percentage of tenants that pay one month in security deposit don't pay the last month's rent when moving out which leaves nothing to cover any damages.

When thinking about charging one month or less than one month in security deposit consider the following. Think about the value of your property in comparison to how much of a "down payment," better known as security deposit, a prospective tenant gives you? It won't take long to realize that for approximately one percent of the total value of the property you are giving the tenant complete control the minute you hand them the keys. This is why screening prospective tenants is so important.

Let's pretend you walk into a car dealership and find the car of your dreams that has a price tag of $40,000. What do you think that car salesman will do when you tell him you would like to give him $400 as a down payment (1%), sign a contract to pay off the $36,500 balance over a set number of years, and leave with the car? It will take 5 minutes to get the guy off the floor from laughing at such a request.

Why do such a high percentage of tenants not pay the last month's rent? It is because they know it will take you at least a month, if not more, to have them legally evicted. While you wait for a court date, they not only have left with no forwarding address but have also left you with another month's worth of damage.

By charging two months in security, it forces the tenant to make some tough decisions. If he doesn't pay the next to last month's rent, you have time to get a judgment and evict before the end of the lease. If he pays the eleventh month and not the twelfth, he knows he is forfeiting one month of security. Since he doesn't want to do that he pays the last month's rent, and moves out very carefully to be sure no damage is done so he will get his full security deposit back. Whichever way you look at it, more security deposit is always better.

If a prospective tenant can't come up with an extra half or a full month in security what is he telling us? He doesn't have a savings account because he lives from paycheck to paycheck. But what if you get hurt and can't work, you ask? Well Mr. Landlord, you'll just have to wait until my unemployment check arrives and then I'll be glad to pay. What he is really saying? I'll pay you after I pay the phone, electric, doctor, cable, car payment, and water/sewer, etc. because they will shut me off before you can. He's right about that. When a prospective tenant can't come up with a month and a half or two months in security deposit, but qualifies, pro-rate any security deposit after collecting a minimum of one month. Divide the balance due over a few months, adding a clause stating the amount and dates of payment for the balance of the security deposit due.

If this arrangement is not acceptable ask them if they would be willing to put up some form of collateral. Consider writing a promissory note for a TV, stereo, motorcycle, car, baby grand piano, or other items of value.

The best form of collateral I have found though is a co-signer who owns real estate. As long as the co-signer is willing to sign the lease knowing any judgment against the tenant is a judgment against him, it helps me sleep better at night. One of the clauses in my "landlord friendly" lease gives me the right to go after all or any one individual whose name is on the lease for the money owed. So guess who I am going to go after, the tenants living in the apartment or Mom and Dad the co-signers, who own the real estate? I'll bet you guessed right! More information about my 52 landlord-friendly Plain Language Lease clauses at the end of this special report.

6. FAILING TO RAISE RENTS ENOUGH OR AT THE RIGHT TIME

Leases should come due when the most tenants are moving. In the northern states that is in the spring and summer months while in the south the winter months seem to be stronger. If your unit opens during an "off season" giving them a year lease leaves you in the same bad season next year. Negotiate a six month or eighteen month lease (with a higher rent.) This gets you out of the off season and if a vacancy does occur, there will be a better chance of finding a replacement.

If you allow a tenant to renew on a month-to-month basis, raise the rent approximately 5% over the year-to-year rate. If the tenant moves out during a slow season you will need the extra money for more ads to find a replacement.

Before placing an ad in the paper to fill a vacancy, you must determine the fair market rent in the area. Start by calling the landlord who placed an ad for a similar unit and pretend to be a prospective tenant. Find out such particulars as room sizes, what appliances are included, who pays utilities, any upgrades, etc. If the ad says the landlord has an open house on Saturday from 1–3 PM, go to it. Introduce yourself as

a fellow landlord and ask if you can take a tour. Exchange phone numbers so in case your unit rents first, you can give the names of qualified but rejected applicants you couldn't use to your new friend. Ask him to do the same for you. If you make this arrangement with enough landlords, many times you will have names of qualified people to call when a tenant moves or stops paying rent.

Another way to find market rent is to check supply and demand. Start the rent in the paper $25 higher than what you think is fair market rent. If the phone doesn't ring after 3 days, call the paper and lower it $5. Keep going down until the phone starts to ring. Supply and demand will also be a factor if your area is experiencing a slow market with many vacancies or a boom with few vacancies. In the slow market you can't be real aggressive with increasing rents, but if vacancies are low, get aggressive.

Should you keep rents at market level or just below market level? I believe there are two types of rent increases—it is either an economic increase or a nuisance increase. An economic increase is when the rent is $100 below market level and economically you need to get it up to market level. This type of increase usually occurs after purchasing a property where the landlord has not raised rents in years. A nuisance increase occurs when the rent is just at or slightly above the going rent in the area. It's a nuisance for the tenant to move to save $10 a month. They quickly determine that the savings do not justify having to rent the moving truck, round up friends to help with the move, buy the pizza and beverages for everyone, fill out change of address cards at the post office, send all friends the new address and phone number, notify the cable, phone, and utility companies, and the list goes on.

Here is another trick I use when raising rents. If you like this one you will find many more like it in my book "Down To Earth Landlording" under the "Rent" chapter. Send your rent increase notice regular mail about 15 days before the tenant has to tell you if they are staying or moving. Do not send it certified mail. Tenants don't like to pick up certified mail for the same reasons we don't like to pick it up. When was the last time you received good news from certified mail?

If they don't send the notice back with next month's rent, call them. If they say they never got it, send another notice that says "second notice" on the top of the page. In this notice raise the rent $5 more than the first notice. You will find 85% of the time the first notice mysteriously is found and mailed back in many strange conditions. Some look like they were crumbled up and then ironed smooth, others may have tomato juice stains in a corner, and other might have part of a store list on the bottom. The great part about this plan is if they really did not receive the first notice, they will never know you just increased your cash flow $60 a year!

7. USING POOR RENT COLLECTION TECHNIQUES AND LATE FEE ENFORCEMENT

Too many landlords find themselves in the rent subsidy business. This happens when tenants' stories about why they can't pay the rent are believed and the eviction process is not started because "the check is in the mail." The best way to make sure you don't fall for the stories is to have a lease that spells out exactly what will happen and on what dates no matter what the excuse. My lease clause spells out when rent is due, when it is late, when I will send a Notice to Pay or Vacate letter, when I will go to court, and how much will be added to the rent for my time to take them to court. (This clause alone could save you the cost of my lease and Home Study Course the first time you use it!)

Do not get in the habit of going to the tenant to collect rent. It is his responsibility to pay you, not your responsibility to go get it from him. If the tenant pays at your office during business hours, give him a receipt in duplicate. This supplies both you and the tenant with a record of the transaction. The duplicate copy will also make the tenant think twice before changing any numbers on their copy to make it look as if rent has been paid in full. Do not collect rent at home or let tenants know where you live. Use an unlisted phone number or have the phone book list your number but without the address. Have rent payments mailed to a post office box with the postmark date being the date the rent has been received.

If you let tenants get away with not paying late fees, rents will come in anytime of the month because there is no penalty for not paying on time. I enjoy charging and collecting late fees because of the additional cash flow it generates with very little work. One year my occupancy was 102%. I did it with little turnover and collected lots of late fees.

As I lecture around the country I hear many different ways landlords collect late fees. Some examples are: a flat dollar amount each day until paid ($5 a day) , a percentage of rent (5%), a flat fee if it is one day late or twenty days late ($25-$50), rent credits if paid on time (show rent to include late fee-tenant gets that amount of credit if paid on time). I like the rent credit or a two tier late fee. Rent is due on first, and late on the sixth. For rent postmarked between the sixth and tenth the late fee is $30. If postmarked after the tenth the late fee jumps to $50. Adjust these numbers to your rental market. These could be too high if your rents are in the $200-$400 range but too low if renting for $900 or more.

Train your tenants to automatically include the late fee if mailing after the due date. If rent is received or postmarked after the due date and no late fee has been included, immediately send a "Late Charge Notice."

Another form you need is an "Insufficient Funds Notice" for when a tenant bounces a check. Charge the tenant whatever your bank charges for an insufficient fund fee. All of the forms mentioned plus many more are found in my Property Management Forms which are found in the Home Study Course and can be purchased copy ready and on computer disk for easy customization.

One final tip. It is not illegal to deposit cash into another person's account. If a tenant's rent check bounces and you don't think it will clear because they are moving, find out how much money is in the account. Once you know how much needs to be deposited, pay the difference in cash to their account to make the check clear. How do you find out how much money is in their account? It's covered in detail in my "Down To Earth Landlording" Home Study Course. Here is one more technique that would pay for the whole course the first time you use it!

8. FAILING TO HAVE A CONTROL SYSTEM IN PLACE FOR MANAGERS

A control system for managers is a checks and balance system to make sure property managers, contractors, and on-site managers are not stealing you blind. I devote a complete chapter in my book on this topic but let me give just a few examples of things you need to do to protect yourself.

Insist that all contractors give a written bid and include a certificate of insurance. Before paying a contractor, call the tenant to make sure the repair was completed properly and they are satisfied with the work. If the repair is to the roof, sidewalk, driveway, etc. don't pay until it rains to make sure that whatever was the problem the first time is not still happening.

If planning on hiring a property manager to handle your rentals there are some dos and don'ts you need to know. Always sign a contract and make sure it states their job description and when you need to be contacted. Do you want them to call and review an applicant before accepting? Do you want to see a copy of the application and credit report to make the final decision and also to make sure they really did run a credit report? Who will prepare the lease for the tenant to sign? Do you not want to be called if repairs are under a certain amount? If over a certain amount, do you want three bids before they call for your approval? Who keeps late fee charges collected? Who takes the tenant's phone calls and how are repairs scheduled? Does the management company add a percentage to the repair bill to "cover their costs?" Is the property manager going to inspect the job before calling in a plumber or is the plumber called to replace a five cent washer in the faucet and you are billed $50.05 — $50 for the house call and $.05 for the washer?

On-site managers need to be trained to your system of management. They need to know what to say and what not to say to prospective tenants. If they say something discriminatory it might as well come out of your mouth. Do not let them collect rent unless bonded. Do not let them run credit checks and write the leases. More examples are outlined in the Home Study course, plus a sample copy of a management contract.

9. FAILING TO FILE FOR EVICTION SOON ENOUGH

As mentioned earlier, don't fall for the excuses. Be sympathetic but firm. You understand and are sorry but the owners are pressuring you to collect the rent. Always be a partner or a manager and not the owner. If they know you are the owner they also know the "buck stops here." You are the one who needs to make the not so pleasant decision and they want it now! Make the owners or partners the bad guys who are telling you to do these terrible things. When a tenant calls and says the rent will be just one day late could you wave the late fee, as an owner you must say yes or no right on the spot. If they think you manage the property for a group of investors (your spouse and kids) or are a limited partner, the tenant is now told you will get back to them with an answer.

If it looks like the tenant is not going to pay and wait out the court process, consider paying the tenant to move. Keep the time frame to move less than a week and stress that if no damage is done they will receive a full refund of their security deposit plus some additional cash to cover moving costs. The unit will be left in better condition, the stress of court is avoided and it can be re-rented sooner to make up the money paid.

When tenants start causing problems, do not threaten, remove doors, change locks, or turn off utilities. There are other legal ways to have them leave and many avoid the court eviction process. The example above of paying them to move is a good one.

Another method explained in detail in the Home Study Course deals with the Internal Revenue Service. This technique will definitely get tenants attention. I collect over $1,000 a year in rent that I would normally have lost. I am now collecting it because of this one technique.

Here is one more example. Have a tenant you suspect of doing drugs? Contact your local or state police and see if they have any rookie drug sniffing dogs that need a workout. Offer to use your building as a training site. Notify the tenants of what you are doing and let them know you will try to give 24 hour notice but you can't promise. The tenant I suspected with the drugs moved out two days after getting the letter with no forwarding address. His security deposit was used for repairs and two weeks later I had a new tenant. If you liked these examples, they are only the tip of the iceberg of examples I share with you in the Home Study Course.

10. FAILING TO RUN REAL ESTATE INVESTMENTS AS A BUSINESS

Landlording is a unique business. Tenants use our product (housing) and pay us for this privilege. Our business does not require a store front and fourteen hour days to work it. If we get sick or take a vacation our customers (tenants) still make payments. If something breaks we can fix it ourselves or pay someone else to fix it. Our tenants pay off our mortgages for us while we save more than we spend each month. I can not think of another investment that allows us to control 100% of the asset with only 10 to 30 cents on the dollar as collateral, finds someone else to pay off the money you borrowed, plus if the asset goes up in value, you get to keep the profit. If that is not enough, the government gives us tax advantages via depreciation when many times the property is going up, not down in value. If anyone finds another investment that gives as many benefits as investment real estate, call me.

Something tells me I won't get many calls.

CHAPTER 25

A FINAL WORD

Every era has its promise and dangers. Every era produces its millionaires and its pau-pers. In the final analysis, it is you and what is inside you that will dictate if you fail or accomplish your goals.

— Steve Osborne

97% of Americans do not have written goals. That's like going through life driving without your hands on the wheel.

— Brian Tracy

MAKE THEM ACCOUNTABLE

The following speech was written by Jane Garvey and Nick Sidoti and was delivered by Nick Sidoti at a meeting of investors with New York State Assemblymen and a New York State Senator. It addresses the subject of Property Rights and Tenant Accountability. It was also presented at the Michigan and Ohio State Real Estate Investor Conventions. It says so much about what we need to do as landlords.

Every day more and more landlords across this country are losing more of their rights as property owners and being treated more and more like crimi-nals. We are up against a bureaucratic system of bleeding heart liberals who make laws on the local, county, state and federal levels.

We are facing:

- *Outrageous property taxes*
- *Eviction laws which encourage and foster theft of services*
- *Lead paint laws which give tenants and their lawyers the ability to actually reach into our pockets and steal our hard earned money.*
- *Laws that tell us who we have to rent to, what we can ask them, what we can't ask them, how much we can charge, and what kind of agree-ment we can make with them.*

We are facing:

- *Laws which force us to pay for water and utilities that tenants use, and, the worst of all,*
- *Those laws in which government forces property owners to allow inspectors to enter their property*

to do an inspection. This is nothing more than an illegal search, an invasion of privacy, and a violation of our Constitutional Rights.

Who are we?

We are honest, conscientious, and hardworking citizens who invest our hard-earned money in our cities. Many real estate investors purchase and rehab properties that have been repossessed by the city for delinquent taxes. We put these properties back on the tax roles, taking them from being city liabilities to assets.

We provide one of the most basic human needs, housing. We are responsible people who are tax payers, not tax takers. We pay city taxes, county taxes, school taxes, state income taxes, and federal income taxes. We are the backbone of this country.

We are also voters. Yes, you will find our names on the prime voters list, along with our mothers', fathers', sisters', brothers', aunts', uncles', sons', daughters', nieces', nephews', neighbors', and grand-children. Let's get it straight. We are not second class citizens, and we refuse to be treated as such.

We do not:

- *spray graffiti on our buildings or go out and look for drug dealers to rent our apartments*
- *Break our own windows and doors and sell drugs on the corner*
- *Blast music all day and night and steal our own plumbing*
- *Beat, shoot, and stab our neighbors and destroy our own buildings*

- *Throw garbage on the street and loiter on the corners in gangs.*
- *Tear up our own apartments and call the building inspector*
- *And it's not our children on the street corners wearing Raiders jackets and baggy pants, terrorizing senior citizens*

Real Estate investors have a vested interest in our cities. We are on the same side as the conscientious owner occupant and the responsible tenant. We have more to lose than any owner occupant who only owns one house. We own a number of houses and we have more at risk.

We are victims of a system that allows tenants to rob us; a system that is driving us into bankruptcy and turning our cities in to living hell holes. If something is not done you will soon see cities of good neighborhoods turn into cities of no neighbors.

We have been hearing over and over the buzzword of the nineties - CHANGE. As real estate investors we have seen change. Good neighborhoods becoming bad neighborhoods and bad neighborhoods becoming worse. Change is what we have left in our pockets after we pay our mortgages, taxes, insurance and utilities. Change, and sometimes not enough change is left to repair our properties. Do we want change? Of course we do. Here is how we spell change.

Accountability is what we want. There are many laws that hold property owners legally, financially and criminally liable for their behavior, and occasionally for that of their tenants. There are no laws governing the actions and behavior of tenants. We must unite to change current laws and to have new laws written that make tenants equally accountable for their behavior. We must also challenge any laws which violate our constitutional rights as property owners.

My question is: What are you doing, and what are you going to do to protect our rights as a property owner and citizen?

GET INVOLVED POLITICALLY OR LOSE YOUR RIGHTS AS A LANDLORD

Tenants usually don't vote, and landlords usually live outside the community where they own real estate. This fact alone make landlords politically vulnerable. Government takes advantage of us whenever they can. They want to inspect our rental units to make sure our tenant housing is safe but don't inspect the homeowners next door to see that their property is safe. If the neighbor's house burns down, would they have a case against the governing body that requires inspections of tenant occupied units but not owner-occupied houses? I think equal protection under the law says we should all be protected by the same laws and standards. If inspections are required, than inspect everyone's home for violations. Don't pick on just the rental market housing.

In one township that I own property, I'm charged $30 per apartment for cleaning the streets and cutting the grass in the community parks. This fee is assessed because the state won't allow them to raise taxes any higher. This fact inspired them to think about how to raise the needed funds and do it without losing lots of votes. You guessed it. Pick on the landlords.

This same Borough charges an amusement tax. This means that anyone who has a coin operated machine on the premises must pay an amusement tax. This can be a soda, candy, cigarette machine, washer, dryers, pool tables, etc.. If the machine has a slot for change you must pay this tax for the privilege of doing business in this town. It doesn't matter that the coin boxes are to the six washers and dryers that are located on my private property, that I pay for the water and gas to run these machines.

I let tenants know of this situation by raising the cost of a wash by .25 cents and placing the name of the councilman that sponsored the bill above the machines. I encouraged them to register to vote and then vote this person off council.

CHOOSE TO CONTROL YOUR FINANCIAL DESTINY

Now you have a strong foundation to be a successful landlord. Your success though, will be determined by how well you apply the techniques you have learned. If you allow a tenant to break the rules you have established, it shows the tenant he is in control, not you. The longer these bad habits are allowed to continue, the more stress, aggravation, and loss of rental income you will have. The choice is yours. You must choose to get yourself under control or be prepared to allow your tenants to control you with their non-acceptable behavior.

Never again blame tenants for your poor management. Never again blame tenants because your cash flow is poor. Never again allow the behavior of a single tenant to cause you to have a terrible day. Instead, change your behavior and begin taking steps today to correct any problems and take control. If you don't see eye to eye with a tenant, remove him and find a replacement who will follow your guidelines.

The average landlord who constantly complains about his tenants is really telling the world he does not know how to be in control of his business. Your life goals and dreams are within your reach. Make the decision to take control of your life and become financially independent through investment real estate.

Once a week give yourself this pep talk: I CHOOSE to control my financial destiny. I CHOOSE to be a strong enforcer of my rules and not allow my tenants to form bad habits. I CHOOSE to find tenants who will work with me and not against me. I CHOOSE to be a landlord because I enjoy the many benefits it brings when done correctly. I CHOOSE to take action when necessary to make sure I stay in control. My Real Estate success will happen because of what I CHOOSE TO DO and not because of what my tenants do or do not do. Every morning promise to look at yourself in the mirror and say …

I GIVE MYSELF PERMISSION TO SUCCEED.

GLOSSARY

ABANDONMENT - The act of a renter (lessee) permanently moving out of his rented property without the consent of the owner (lessor) before the lease expires.

ABSENTEE OWNER - An owner (landlord) who does not dwell or live in his property held in absentee ownership.

ACTUAL EVICTION - The act of putting a renter (lessee) out of rented property as a result of a court order.

AFFIDAVIT OF SERVICE - A sworn statement that an eviction notice has been served properly.

AGENT - A person who enters into a legal, fiduciary, and confidential arrangement with a second party and is authorized to act for that party.

ALLOIDAL SYSTEM - This type of ownership is the distinguishing feature of real property ownership in the United States. Private ownership of land is free and absolute, subject only to governmental and voluntary private restrictions.

APARTMENT - A suite or set of rooms used for a dwelling.

ATTACHMENT - the taking of another person's property, by court order, to hold it available to be sold for payment of that person's debt.

AUTOMATIC RENEWAL CLAUSE - A lease provision that automatically ensures renewal of the lease unless either the tenant or the landlord notifies the other party of a desire to terminate the agreement.

BASE-UNIT-RATE APPROACH - A method of establishing rental rates in which a typical unit within a specific sub-market is defined and becomes the standard against which all similar units may be measured.

BILATERAL CONTRACT - A contract between two people, each of whom promises to perform a definite commitment.

BREACH - Breaking a law, or violating a condition or term requirement of a contract.

CASH FLOW - The amount of money available after all payments have been made for operating expenses and mortgage principal and interest.

CERTIFIED PROPERTY MANAGER - The professional designation conferred by the Institute of Real Estate Management on individuals who distinguish themselves in the areas of education, experience, and ethics.

CERTIFICATE OF OCCUPANCY - Regulated by local municipalities and must be secured before being allowed to occupy a new residence.

COMMON AREA - Space that is used by tenants and visitors, such as lobbies, corridors, and stairways; in a condominium, the property in which a unit owner has a divided interest, such as parking lots, sidewalks, playground, etc.

COMPLAINT - The legal written document that begins a civil lawsuit. It gives the person who is charged with wrongdoing (the defendant) all the important facts that will be part of the case against him/her.

CONDITION - Term of an agreement. A restricting or modifying factor.

CONDOMINIUM Λ form of ownership that combines absolute ownership of an apartment-like unit and joint ownership of areas used in common with others.

CONDOMINIUM UNIT - A three-dimensional space of air located within the walls, floor, and ceiling of the condominium structure.

CONFESSION OF JUDGMENT - The landlord may ask the tenant to sign a lease with a confession of judgment clause. If a tenant signs a lease with this clause, the tenant agrees to let the landlord get a court order against the tenant without giving the tenant notice and a chance for a hearing to present the tenant's side of the story. The court order should say that the tenant owes the landlord money, or that the tenant must move out of the house or apartment. This procedure may not be enforceable in the courts.

CONSTRUCTIVE EVICTION - The inability of a renter (lessee) to occupy his rented property because of building conditions that make his move dangerous or impractical.

CONTRACT - A binding agreement between two or more legally competent people.

COOPERATIVE - A corporation that owns real estate, usually a multi-family dwelling, including the building and land on which it is built; individual shareholders do not own their units but have the right to live in them.

CORPORATION - A form of business organization created by statute law and which is considered legally as a separate entity.

CORRECTIVE MAINTENANCE - Ongoing repairs that must be made to a building and its equipment.

COST APPROACH - A method of estimating a property's value by determining the value of the land plus the cost of reproducing improvements.

COUNTER CLAIM - If one person (plaintiff) brings a suit against another (the defendant), and the person being sued has some claim or charge to make against the first, that charge or claim against the person bringing the suit is called a counterclaim.

COVENANT OF FITNESS OF THE PREMISES - An assurance that the premises are fit for habitation.

COVENANT OF QUIET ENJOYMENT - A warrant by the landlord that the tenant will have the premises free from interference by the landlord or anyone claiming better right to the premises than the landlord.

COVENANT TO DELIVER POSSESSION - The landlord promises to deliver the right of possession to the tenant at the time the lease is scheduled to start.

DEBTOR - One who owes a debt; he/she who may be compelled to pay a claim or demand; anyone liable on a claim, whether due or to become due.

DEFENDANT -The person being sued.

DEFERRED MAINTENANCE - Ordinary maintenance that is not performed and negatively affects a property's use and value.

DEMISED PREMISES - Property transferred by a lease or will.

DISTRAINT - The name for the procedure when the landlord levies on the tenant's furniture or other belongings and sells them as payment for rent the landlord claims the tenant owes. This procedure has been held unconstitutional and no landlord should do it. The only proper procedure to collect back rent is to obtain a judgment and execute on it.

ECONOMIC RENT INCREASE - An increase in rent determined by market shortage and general consumer income level.

EJECTMENT - An action for the recovery and possession of real estate and damages and costs from one who has occupied it illegally.

ESCALATION CLAUSE - A provision in a lease which guarantees automatic rent adjustments for increased operating expenses.

ESTOPPEL - A doctrine that prevents a person from denying the consequences of facts or actions that lead another person to rely on them and suffer loss.

EVICTION - The recovery of property from the possession of another by legal process.

EVICTION NOTICE - A written notice to a tenant to pay the rent immediately or leave the leased premises within a specified time.

EXCULPATORY CLAUSES - A lease clause by which the landlord attempts to excuse himself or herself from liability for negligence in maintaining the leasehold premises.

EXECUTION - The legal way to enforce a judgment. If it is a "judgment for possession," the Sheriff or Constable, after giving warning, may forcibly remove the tenant, the tenant's furniture and belongings, putting the furniture in storage at the tenant's expense. If it is a "judgment for money," the plaintiff (person bringing the lawsuit) may, twenty days after the judgment is entered, file the judgment with the County Court House or District Justice Court for levy through a Constable. The plaintiff then files a paper called a "writ of execution," which is a paper directing the Sheriff or Constable to levy on and schedule a Sheriff's or Constables sale of the tenant's belongings. The Sheriff or Constable can sell any goods which are not exempt and use the money to pay the plaintiff the amount of the judgment plus costs.

EXEMPTION - Those belongings of the debtor that are free from "execution." Pennsylvania law says that no one can take all of another person's belongings away from him/her by "execution" on a judgment for money. The "defendant" or debtor, can keep $300 worth of his/her belongings plus his/her personal clothing, a sewing machine, and personal papers. The "defendant" or debtor, can decide which belongings he/she will claim which total $300. Tenants may waive this right under any written leases.

FEE SIMPLE - Most land in the United States is held in fee simple title. It is a freehold estate and possesses the most extensive rights known to the law.

FIXTURE - Personal property permanently attached to real estate so that it becomes a part of the real estate.

FORGERY - Signing or altering a written document with intent to deceive. Illegally counterfeiting or imitating documents or signatures to deceive.

FREEHOLD ESTATE - An interest in real property to last for an uncertain period of time. Most freehold estates may pass their interest along to their heirs.

GENERAL PARTNER - The participant in a limited partnership who manages the real estate operation and is liable for all debts.

GROSS LEASE - A lease of property under which the landlord pays all the maintenance charges including repairs, taxes, insurance, and operating costs.

GROUND LEASE - A specialized type of net lease in which the lessor leases a piece of vacant land to the lessee, usually with the stipulation that the lessee at his or her own expense will construct a building thereon.

HOLDOVER TENANCY - A tenancy in which the renter (lessee) continues to occupy the leased premises after the lease expires and the landlord continues to accept rent. See Tenancy at Sufferance.

IMPLIED WARRANT OF HABITABILITY - a warranty imposed by law on the landlord by which he or she warrants that a residential property is safe and sanitary and fit for living at the time the tenant enters and during the period of tenancy.

INCOME APPROACH - A method of estimating a property's value by capitalizing the flow of income that can be expected from the property during its remaining useful life.

INDEX ESCALATION CLAUSE - A provision ensuring rent adjustments in an amount equal to the annual change in a specified index, usually the Consumer Price Index.

JUDGMENT FOR POSSESSION - The ruling of a court, a court order, that a person in a suit is entitled to possession of certain property, i.e., to have the right to be in the property. In a landlord-tenant suit, either the landlord or the tenant may be awarded the judgment of possession.

JUDGMENT FOR MONEY - A ruling of a court, a court order, that a person in a suit owes the other person a certain amount of money. In landlord-tenant cases, these judgments are most often for back rent, damages, or return of a security deposit.

LANDLORD - One who owns property and leases it to a tenant (lessee).

LEASE - An oral or written contract between the landlord and tenant setting forth the terms and conditions for the possession of the property for a specified time, and in exchange for fixed payments.

LEASEHOLD ESTATE - The legal right of a renter (lessee) to occupy and use rented property during the period covered by his lease.

LESSEE - The tenant (renter) in a lease.

LESSOR - The landlord in a lease.

LIMITED PARTNER - A participant in a limited partnership whose liability is limited to the amount invested and who does not have a voice in the management of the partnership.

LIMITED PARTNERSHIP - A business arrangement which allows certain partners to invest, take no part in the management, and assume limited liability.

MAINTENANCE - The upkeep of property or equipment.

MARKET APPROACH - A method of estimating a property's value by comparing it with similar properties that have been sold recently.

MORTGAGE - A conditional pledge of real property to a creditor as security against a debt.

NET LEASE - An agreement in which the tenant pays the rent and also certain operating expenses connected with the leased premises.

NET-NET LEASE - An agreement in which the tenant pays all maintenance and operating expenses plus taxes.

NET-NET-NET (TRIPLE NET) LEASE -An agreement in which the tenant pays maintenance and operating expenses, property taxes, and insurance.

NONCONTROLLABLE EXPENSES - Items such as real estate taxes, insurance, and labor union wages over which the management has no control.

NUISANCE RENT INCREASE - The rent raise a tenant will pay to avoid the expense, discomfort, and inconvenience of moving.

OCCUPANCY - Possession and use of property as owner or renter.

PERCENTAGE LEASE - A lease for commercial property that usually provides for a regular monthly rent plus a percentage of gross sales exceeding a certain amount.

PERCENTAGE OF GROSS FEE - A property manger's regular compensation based on a given percentage of monthly gross collections.

PERIODIC TENANCY - An estate from period to period, continuing from period to period until terminated by proper notice from one of the parties.

PERSONAL PROPERTY - Property that is not real property; generally characterized as having substance and being movable.

PLAINTIFF - The person bringing the lawsuit, the person who is suing the defendant.

POSSESSION - Control or occupancy of property without regard to ownership.

PREVENTATIVE MAINTENANCE - A program of regular inspection and care that allows potential problems to be prevented or at least detected and solved before major repairs are needed.

PROPERTY - Legal rights that a person possesses with respect to a thing; rights that have economic value.

PROPERTY ANALYSIS - A complete description of a piece of real estate, including its accommodations, architectural design, and physical condition.

PROPERTY MANAGEMENT - A service profession in which someone other than the owner supervises a property's operation, according to the owner's objectives.

PROPERTY MANAGER - A professional who administers real estate according to the owner's objectives.

REAL ESTATE - The land and the improvements upon it. A part of the earth's surface extending down to the middle of the earth and upward into space including everything permanently attached to it.

REAL PROPERTY - Land, buildings, and other improvements permanently affixed to land.

RECISION - A cancellation of a contract that results in the parties being restored to the position they were in before the contract was made.

RENT - A certain sum agreed to by tenant (lessee) and his landlord (lessor), and paid by the lessee to the lessor in the form of regular payments for the use of the landlord's property.

RENT CONTROL - Government regulation imposed on rents to prevent them from being increased beyond governmentally imposed limitations.

RENTER - One who rents. Lessee. Tenant.

RESIDENT MANAGER - The person responsible for general administration and maintenance of a property and supervising its personnel and resources.

SECTION 8 HOUSING - The federal government's principal medium for housing assistance, authorized by the Housing and Community Development Act of 1974, which provides for new construction and rehabilitation.

SECURITY DEPOSIT - Money deposited by the tenant, usually at the inception of the lease, over and above the advance payment of rent to cover possible damages and ensure faithful performance of the lease by the tenant.

SUBLETTING - If a tenant rents the house or apartment to another tenant, the contract or agreement between the first tenant and the second tenant is called a sublease. The first tenant still has responsibility under the original lease, unless the landlord agrees to accept the second tenant as a substitute for the first. If the landlord does not agree, the first tenant is still responsible to the landlord for any unpaid rent or damages to the property. If problems develop, the first tenant can sue the second tenant to recover the back rent and damages.

TENANCY - Legally contracted temporary possession or occupancy of property that belongs to another.

TENANCY AT SUFFERANCE - The tenancy of the lessee who continues to occupy the premises improperly after his lease rights have expired. See Holdover Tenancy.

TENANCY AT WILL - a tenancy which gives the lessee the right of possession until terminated by notice or death of the landlord.

TENANT - One who holds or possesses real estate by any kind of leased right.

TERM LEASE - The period of time which the tenant is entitled to be in the house or apartment under the lease. If there is an oral lease, the term is usually one month; the rent is usually paid month-to-month, usually in advance.

The PROPERTY MANAGEMENT FORMS

Being prepared to solve tenant problems and having the necessary forms on hand will save hours of time and money. A description of each form is listed alphabetically below.

1. **ACCEPTANCE LETTER** - Get a copy of the lease, plus the additional terms and conditions, in the tenant's hands before signing the lease. This letter explains what has been paid and what is due when signing.
2. **ADVERTISING REPORT** - Track how well your ads work on a weekly basis. See which ad draws the most phone calls for the least money.
3. **CHECKLIST TO PROVE ABANDONMENT** - How do you know if a tenant moved out in the middle of the night or was robbed while on vacation? Do not throw anything out until you can answer yes to most of these questions on the checklist.
4. **CO-SIGNER AGREEMENT** - The applicant looks good from a credit check standpoint but they are just under your qualifying standards for income. Suggest they ask a relative who owns real estate to co-sign with them.
5. **DENIAL OF REQUEST FOR TENANCY** - Check off the appropriate reason for the denial and put it in the mail.
6. **DISTRIBUTION OF SECURITY DEPOSIT** - Your tenant has vacated the property and now his security deposit must be returned. This form will help you to make sure nothing is missed.
7. **EMPLOYMENT VERIFICATION** - The tenant signs this form which gives you permission to contact his employer.
8. **FIVE DAY NOTICE TO PAY OR VACATE** - Mail immediately after the grace period has expired. If the tenant does not call or send the rent, file for eviction as soon as the five days have expired.
9. **HAPPY THANKSGIVING** - Show your tenants in November how much you appreciate their on-time payments each month for the year. This wil show your "Thanks" by "giving" them a Thanksgiving Turkey.
10. **IMPORTANT NUMBERS AND HELPFUL HINTS** - When new tenants move in they are often not from the area. This form will list phone numbers they will need as well as helpful hints for finding shut off valves, main circuit breaker box, etc.
11. **INDEPENDENT CONTRACTOR AGREEMENT** - Before repair work is started, have the contractor doing the work sign this agreement. It states you will not be held liable for any damage, injury, or loss and that the contractor carries workman's compensation and liability insurance.
12. **INSPECTION CHECKLIST** - Who needs the aggravation of a tenant taking you to court, claiming the damage that a security deposit was subtracted from to cover was there when they moved in? This form will protect both parties from claiming that something was broken or damaged before or after move-in.
13. **INSTALLMENT PROMISSORY NOTE** - When a tenant does not pay the rent on time have him sign this form. It is his written promise to pay the specified amount in installment payments with interest.
14. **INSURANCE RECORDS** - Keeping all insurance policies for each property on one sheet with the name of the carrier, the amount, and type of coverage will help at the end of each year when reviewing and updating your policies.
15. **LANDLORD VERIFICATION** - The tenant signs this form which gives you permission to contact present and previous landlords.

16. **LEASE CANCELLATION AGREEMENT** - When the tenant calls to ask if the lease can be broken with six months still remaining, turn a negative situation to a win-win situation for both of you with this form.

17. **MANAGEMENT CONTRACT (ON-SITE)** - Don't leave anything to chance. Spell out the exact responsibilities so there will be no questions later.

18. **MANAGERS' MONTHLY REPORT** - If you are an absentee owner, this form will keep tabs on your manager and your property.

19. **NOTICE OF DEBT FORGIVENESS** - The tenant has moved. Going after his belongings won't cover the money that is owed, so forgive the debt and report it as income to IRS. If they are on public assistance this might raise their income enough so they won't qualify for any more free handouts.

20. **NOTICE OF INSUFFICIENT FUNDS** - The bank will charge you when a tenant's check bounces and this could causes some of your checks to bounce. Tenants don't bounce many more checks after paying this fee plus the bounced check fee charged by their bank.

21. **NOTICE OF LATE FEE CHARGE** - Rent arrives late but the late fee is not included. Use this form to let the tenant know you expect it to be paid.

22. **NOTICE OF LATE RENT** - Send this notice the day after rent is past due reminding the tenant that they owe the late fee. If no money arrives shortly, further action to collect the rent will be started that could hurt their credit rating for a long time.

23. **NOTICE OF LEASE TERMINATION** - This is used after the tenant has been given the Notice to Perform or Quit form and they have not performed what was asked.

24. **NOTICE TO CHANGE TERMS OF TENANCY** - Knowing how and when to raise rents is the key. Use this valuable form at least once a year and watch your net worth increase with your cash flow.

25. **NOTICE TO PERFORM OR QUIT** - Use this one first before sending the Lease Termination form. This form gives the tenant so many days to correct any provisions of the lease he is violating such as getting a pet, playing music too loud, or storing three junker cars in the back yard. This form gives notice that the agreement has been broken and the tenant can be evicted because of it.

26. **NOTICE TO VACATING TENANT** - Explain what happens now that the tenant has given notice to move: when will showings be scheduled, bonus money if he recommends the person who rents, etc.

27. **PET AGREEMENT** - Put the responsibility and liability where it belongs, on the pet owner.

28. **PET VIOLATION** - When the pet does appear this form will place the tenant on notice and state the consequences if not removed.

29. **PHONE SCREENING** - Spells out what to say to prospective tenants and in what order to qualify the tenants over the phone. This saves time in not having to show to someone who doesn't fit your qualifying standards.

30. **PROFIT AND LOSS STATEMENT** - Tally the income and expense numbers on this sheet to see how your net worth increased for the year.

31. **PROMISE TO PAY OR VACATE** - If the tenant signs this form there is a good chance you will have your money in 72 hours. If they don't, give them the Five Day Notice to Pay or Vacate because the odds of being paid are not good. Research local laws as to the exact amount of days allowed and whether this form can be used at all.

32. **PROMISSORY NOTE** - When a tenant has not paid rent on time, have him sign this form. It is a written promise to pay the specified amount at a fixed time or on demand.

33. **PROSPECTIVE TENANT CHECKLIST** - Check off the questions that apply to each applicant. The one with the most points will probably be the one you want anyway.

34. **RENT INCREASE SCHEDULE** - This form lists the tenant's name, address, when the lease expires, when the rent increase notice needs to be mailed, their current rent, your projected rent, and what they accepted after the Rent Increase Notice is returned.

35. **RENTAL APPLICATION** - What good is a no money down deal or a great cash flow property if the tenants don't pay the rent? This application gives you the information needed to do the proper screening so only the best have the privilege of renting from you.

36. **RENTAL INCOME** - This form never makes it to a drawer. It stays on top of the desk so as rents come in they are recorded right away. It allows you to list 18 tenants on one sheet and will provide not only room for the rent each month, but the date it was received or postmarked. Total down for the monthly building rent and across for each tenant's annual rent received.

37. **RENTAL DEPOSIT TO HOLD UNIT** - The tenant is approved and places a deposit to hold the unit until move in date. A week before the move in date, they call to cancel and ask for their deposit back. With this form they will not.

38. **RENTAL INCOME AND EXPENSE** - This form belongs in a folder labeled for each property. Use it to compile all the information needed to be placed on your income tax return. Rents can be copied directly from the Rental Income form. The expense columns are labeled to match the categories found on IRS Schedule E. There are also columns for taxes, insurance, license fees, and principal/ interest payments for the year.

39. **RENTAL STANDARDS FOR TENANT SELECTION** - Be prepared if the Fair Housing Council in your area comes knocking. Use this criteria to show that all prospective tenants were screened based on the same guidelines.

40-45 **REPAIR SERVICE RECORD** - Have you memorized the make, model, serial number, date purchased, warranty period, and when repairs were made to the furnace, garbage disposal, garbage compactor, refrigerator, washer, dryer, hot water heater, air conditioner, stove/oven? If not, this information will now be at your fingertips.

46. **REQUEST FOR PAYMENT OF JUDGMENT** - Send this notice after receiving a judgment against the tenant. It gives the tenant a specific date to pay and what will happen if they do not pay. If not paid by the due date, send the Notice of Debt Forgiveness letter.

47. **SERVICE REQUEST** - This form is completed by the tenants and turned into the manager to schedule needed repairs. It also sets up the paper trail for the control system.

48. **TENANT LISTING** - Keep in a handy place because it will get a lot of use. Lists the names, addresses, phone numbers, security deposit, present rent, and move in/out dates of each tenant.

49. **TENANT MOVE-IN CHECKLIST** - Good reminder list so items are not skipped that could haunt you later.

50. **TENANT MOVE-OUT CHARGES** - Give to the tenant when signing the lease so there is not doubt what things will cost if not left in the same condition they were found.

51. **WATERBED AGREEMENT** - Use this one for the same reason as the Pet Agreement. Put responsibility for damage where it belongs - on the tenant. The key feature with this form is having the tenant make you the beneficiary of the insurance policy.

52. **WORK ORDER** - Once you're into a larger number of units per building this form can be helpful for organizing needed repairs while providing a paper trail to keep track of on-site managers.

WITH
DONALD BECK'S

DOWN TO EARTH LANDLORDING HOME STUDY COURSE

LEARN HOW YOU TOO CAN BECOME A PART TIME LANDLORD WITH A FULL TIME INCOME

Don has been a Landlord for more than two decades. He quit a tenured teaching position after only five years of investing to manage his 80 + rental units which he had acquired during that time. That is more than one unit a month, every month, for five years! Thousands of students from around the country have benefited from his tried and proven "Down to Earth Landlording" techniques. His concern for attention to detail has earned him the respect of tenants and property owners alike.

"IGNORANCE IS FREE BUT THE UPKEEP IS TREMENDOUS"

This Down To Earth Landlording Home Study Course will jump start you into doing the small things that many times makes the difference between success and failure. Many of the examples will not take extra time to do - it's just doing it right the first time.

DON'S HOME STUDY COURSE INCLUDES THE FOLLOWING MUST HAVE MATERIALS

* BOOK - "DOWN TO EARTH LANDLORDING"

This book took Don three years of research, 22 years of hands-on experience and one year to produce. It has been geared to the small time investor who wants the hands on, nuts and bolts, walk me through it so I can understand approach. Don's 12 years of public teaching helps with detailed descriptions from how to screen prospective tenants, through the easiest and cheapest way to evict a bad tenant.

"EFFICIENCY IS DOING THINGS RIGHT.
EFFECTIVENESS IS DOING THE RIGHT THINGS EFFICIENTLY."

* 50 COPY READY PROPERTY MANAGEMENT FORMS

Managing with forms helps to keep you organized and leaves the all-important paper trail. These forms have been developed to save you from hours of writing and give you peace of mind knowing everything is correctly worded. They are professionally type set with borders for that official look. All forms are displayed in Don's "Down To Earth Landlording" book. He describes the use of each form and under what circumstances it should be used.

One of Don's students served the "Notice to Pay or Vacate" form to one of his tenants three days after purchasing Don's course. The letter states that the Landlord was going to start eviction proceedings within three days if she did not pay. She thought it meant she would be thrown out after three days and moved out the next evening. He had just saved one and a half months in the court process and more than paid for the whole "Down To Earth Landlording" Home Study Course by using just one form.

"YOUR ACTION—NOT YOUR TENANT'S—IS RESPONSIBLE FOR YOUR SUCCESS"

* COMPUTER DISK OF PROPERTY MANAGEMENT FORMS

The CD (or 3½ inch floppy disk) is set up for IBM and Macintosh users. There are several versions of the forms on this disk: plain text (ASCII) files (with the .TXT extension), and Microsoft Word files (with the .DOC extension). The unique feature of the computer disk is that it allows you to customize to your specific needs. Change the wording to meet your local guidelines for rentals and you're ready to go. Load it in, type the name of the tenant in the blanks, and while it is printing, put the stamp and address on the envelope.

* CRUISE CONTROL LANDLORDING

This tape series is the backbone of the Home Study Course. Don recorded 8 tapes (each one hour) that will train you to become an effective Landlord by gaining control of your tenants. Don's philosophy of Landlording is "What good is a no money down deal if the tenant doesn't pay the rent." All Landlords must learn to be "firm but fair." It can be done and Don will show you how in this tape series. The tape topics are:

Tape 1 - Prepare to Manage Before Owning	Tape 5 - Rental Application
Tape 2 - Prepare to Manage Before Renting	Tape 6 - Lease Add. Terms
Tape 3 - Filling Vacancies	Tape 7 - Collecting Rents
Tape 4 - Screening Techniques	Tape 8 - Increasing Cash Flow

* PLAIN LANGUAGE LEASE DESIGNED FOR LANDLORDS
(COPY READY)

This lease has been designed by a landlord for landlords and has received excellent reviews by attorneys who also own investment real estate. Landlords need to protect themselves from the less than honorable Tenant. This can be accomplished with a strong lease that is Landlord friendly. Three pages of additional lease clauses are also included to help customize your lease to a specific property.

* A LEASE DESIGNED FOR LANDLORDS - COMPUTER DISK

If you have a computer this is an absolute must. The computer disk allows you to customize your lease. Remove the clauses you don't need and substitute some from the additional clauses. Type in all the blanks and just change the tenant's name and rental amount and you're done.

The lease is on a 3 1/2" disk for Macintosh or Windows under the same formats outlined under the Property Management Forms Computer Disk section. If you have a problem getting the disk up and running, a phone call to Don's computer expert will take care of any problems quickly and easily.

* THREE SPECIAL REPORTS

SHORT BUT SENSATIONAL SURVIVAL TIPS

This special report covers over 170 tips which can save you thousands of dollars by simply applying the advice. Some examples are: Change locks between tenants. You have no idea how many keys they made for friends. Install same type faucets and toilets so when a repair is needed, the odds of having a spare part handy at 9 PM on a Sunday night greatly increases. If a prospective tenant is borderline qualifying, require a co-signer who owns real estate. This way if they fall behind in rent, you can lien the property.

DO'S AND DON'TS WHEN SCREENING TENANTS

One of the most critical parts of our business is the screening of prospective tenants. Many thousands of dollars can be lost if this step is skipped or not done completely. This report will show the do's and don'ts in this screening process. You need to find the most qualified prospect who will then be given the privilege of renting from you.

TEN BIGGEST MISTAKES MADE BY LANDLORDS

This report was over two years in the making. Over 1500 landlords were asked to name the biggest mistake they made as a landlord. I took these responses and categorized them. It did not take long to see that they fell into ten different categories. Learn from this report what 1500 fellow landlords say was their biggest mistake. Learn from them and save years of making them yourself.

YES, I WOULD LIKE TO LEARN HOW TO MAKE LANDLORDING AS STRESS-LESS AS POSSIBLE

Don's goal in producing this Home Study Course is to share his knowledge and techniques with Landlords who see the many advantages of owning investment properties and who want to make Landlording as stress-less as possible. Landlords have a tendency to burn out because of the stress of managing tenants. It does not have to be that way. In fact, Don is buying more property and spending less time managing today than he did when he owned half the number of units. He has accomplished this because his tenants know and understand his rules (his lease makes sure of that) and they know the consequences if they are broken.

"LEARN FROM THE MISTAKES OF OTHERS. YOUR CASH FLOW WON'T LAST LONG ENOUGH TO MAKE THEM ALL YOURSELF"

A recent survey asked Landlords the one management mistake that cost them the most money. The number one answer was not doing a thorough screening of prospective tenants. Don could not agree more. He does an intensive screening of all prospective tenants to make sure he selects the best qualified tenant who will have the privilege of renting one of his apartments. You too can have the best tenant for the highest rent while cutting down on management headaches. Follow Don's easy to use techniques.

Don't let tenants drive you away from the best investment opportunity of today. This Home Study Course will show you how to bring your existing tenants under control, set up a screening program for new tenants that will sort out the good from the bad, and show you how to remove problem tenants quickly and legally.

ABOUT THE AUTHOR

With an undergraduate degree in Elementary Education from Eastern College and a Masters Degree in Media from West Chester University, **DONALD BECK** started his professional career as an elementary school teacher. In 1984, after teaching for twelve years, and with his first child due in six months, he gave up his tenured teaching position to devote his full attention to the 80 rental units he and his wife owned and managed.

After the birth of their daughter, his wife went back to work full time and Don took on the role of "Mr. Mom." He quickly learned that "Mr. Mom" was a full time job and was thankful that his strong management techniques allowed him to put the investment properties on "cruise control."

Today, Don is a Real Estate Broker in suburban Philadelphia where he continues to managing his ever growing investment portfolio.

He was President of the Diversified Investor Group, a Non-Profit Real Estate Educational Corporation, of Real Estate Investors and Landlords from 1990–1999.

He lectures extensively on a multitude of real estate topics in the Philadelphia area and also travels the country speaking to real estate organizations on property management issues.

His e-mail is: <**mgmtexpert@aol.com**>

ABOUT THE EDITOR/MARKETER

PAUL BAUER — Paul is a Past President of the National Real Estate Investors Association and is a major promoter for national speakers. His company, Capital Marketing Solutions, helps speakers develop and enhance their real estate products and services as well as design creative marketing strategies.

ABOUT THE BOOK DESIGNERS

MICHAEL HÖHNE and **ANGELA WERNER** are a freelance graphic design team who specialize in book design. With over twenty years of experience in computers and printing, they are now indulging their life-long love of books by creating them.

By combining the efficiency of the computer with a strong sense of design, they package the author's work in a high quality presentation, free of the usual clumsiness found in amateur desktop publishing ventures.

Based in the wooded hills of upper Bucks County, Pennsylvania, Michael Höhne Design works without distraction in the quiet of the country while staying in touch with associates through electronic data transfer and package express services.

Michael and Angela are currently hard at work on their next design projects, but you can reach them at <**michael@heyneon.com**> and <**angela@heyneon.com**>

This book
was set in the Adobe types:
Utopia, Futura, Lithos, and Courier.
It was designed by
Michael Höhne.
www.heyneon.com